T0184535

# Big Data Integration

# Synthesis Lectures on Data Management

Editor
**Z. Meral Özsoyoğlu**, *Case Western Reserve University*

Founding Editor
**M. Tamer Özsu**, *University of Waterloo*

**Synthesis Lectures on Data Management** is edited by Meral Özsoyoğlu of Case Western Reserve University. The series publishes 80- to 150-page publications on topics pertaining to data management. Topics include query languages, database system architectures, transaction management, data warehousing, XML and databases, data stream systems, wide-scale data distribution, multimedia data management, data mining, and related subjects.

© Springer Nature Switzerland AG 2022

Reprint of original edition © Morgan & Claypool 2015

All rights reserved. No part of this publication may be reproduced, stored in a retrieval system, or transmitted in any form or by any means—electronic, mechanical, photocopy, recording, or any other except for brief quotations in printed reviews—without the prior permission of the publisher.

Big Data Integration

Xin Luna Dong, Divesh Srivastava

ISBN: 978-3-031-00725-5      paperback
ISBN: 978-3-031-01853-4      ebook

DOI: 10.1007/978-3-031-01853-4

A Publication in the Springer series
*SYNTHESIS LECTURES ON DATA MANAGEMENT*
Series ISSN: 2153-5418 print   2153-5426 ebook

Lecture #40
Series Editor: M. Tamer Özsu, *University of Waterloo*

First Edition
10 9 8 7 6 5 4 3 2 1

# Big Data Integration

Xin Luna Dong
Google Inc.

Divesh Srivastava
AT&T Labs-Research

*SYNTHESIS LECTURES ON DATA MANAGEMENT #40*

## ABSTRACT

The big data era is upon us: data are being generated, analyzed, and used at an unprecedented scale, and data-driven decision making is sweeping through all aspects of society. Since the value of data explodes when it can be linked and fused with other data, addressing the *big data integration* (BDI) challenge is critical to realizing the promise of big data.

BDI differs from traditional data integration along the dimensions of *volume*, *velocity*, *variety*, and *veracity*. First, not only can data sources contain a huge volume of data, but also the number of data sources is now in the millions. Second, because of the rate at which newly collected data are made available, many of the data sources are very dynamic, and the number of data sources is also rapidly exploding. Third, data sources are extremely heterogeneous in their structure and content, exhibiting considerable variety even for substantially similar entities. Fourth, the data sources are of widely differing qualities, with significant differences in the coverage, accuracy and timeliness of data provided.

This book explores the progress that has been made by the data integration community on the topics of schema alignment, record linkage and data fusion in addressing these novel challenges faced by big data integration. Each of these topics is covered in a systematic way: first starting with a quick tour of the topic in the context of traditional data integration, followed by a detailed, example-driven exposition of recent innovative techniques that have been proposed to address the BDI challenges of volume, velocity, variety, and veracity. Finally, it presents emerging topics and opportunities that are specific to BDI, identifying promising directions for the data integration community.

## KEYWORDS

big data integration, data fusion, record linkage, schema alignment, variety, velocity, veracity, volume

*To Jianzhong Dong, Xiaoqin Gong, Jun Zhang, Franklin Zhang,*
*and Sonya Zhang*


*To Swayam Prakash Srivastava, Maya Srivastava,*
*and Jaya Mathangi Satagopan*

# Contents

# List of Figures

# List of Tables

# Preface

Big data integration is the confluence of two significant bodies of work: one quite old—data integration—and the other relatively new—big data.

As long as there have been data sets that people have sought to link and fuse to enhance value, data integration has been around. Even before computer scientists started investigating this area, statisticians had already made much progress, given their pressing need to correlate and analyze census data sets collected over time. Data integration is challenging for many reasons, not the least being our ability to represent and misrepresent information about real-world entities in very diverse ways. To effectively address these challenges, considerable progress has been made over the last few decades by the data integration community on the foundational topics of schema alignment, record linkage, and data fusion, especially for well-structured data.

Recent years have seen a dramatic growth in our ability to capture each event and every interaction in the world as digital data. Concomitant with this ability has been our desire to analyze and extract value from this data, ushering in the era of big data. This era has seen an enormous increase in the amount and heterogeneity of data, as well as in the number of data sources, many of which are very dynamic, while being of widely differing qualities. Since the value of data explodes when it can be linked and fused with other data, data integration is critical to realizing the promise of big data of enabling valuable, data-driven decisions to alter all aspects of society.

Data integration for big data is what has come to be known as big data integration. This book explores the progress that has been made by the data integration community in addressing the novel challenges faced by big data integration. It is intended as a starting point for researchers, practitioners and students who would like to learn more about big data integration. We have attempted to cover a diversity of topics and research efforts in this area, fully well realizing that it is impossible to be comprehensive in such a dynamic area. We hope that many of our readers will be inspired by this book to make their own contributions to this important area, to help further the promise of big data.

## ACKNOWLEDGMENTS

Several people provided valuable support during the preparation of this book. We warmly thank Tamer Özsu for inviting us to write this book, Diane Cerra for managing the entire publication process, and Paul Anagnostopoulos for producing the book. Without their gentle reminders, periodic nudging, and prompt copyediting, this book may have taken much longer to complete.

Much of this book's material evolved from the tutorials and talks that we presented at ICDE 2013, VLDB 2013, COMAD 2013, University of Zurich (Switzerland), the Ph.D. School of ADC 2014 and BDA 2014. We thank our many colleagues for their constructive feedback during and subsequent to these presentations.

We would also like to acknowledge our many collaborators who have influenced our thoughts and our understanding of this research area over the years.

Finally, we would like to thank our family members, whose constant encouragement and loving support made it all worthwhile.

Xin Luna Dong and Divesh Srivastava
December 2014

# CHAPTER 1

# Motivation: Challenges and Opportunities for BDI

The big data era is the inevitable consequence of *datafication*: our ability to transform each event and every interaction in the world into digital data, and our concomitant desire to analyze and extract value from this data. Big data comes with a lot of promise, enabling us to make valuable, data-driven decisions to alter all aspects of society.

Big data is being generated and used today in a variety of domains, including data-driven science, telecommunications, social media, large-scale e-commerce, medical records and e-health, and so on. Since the value of data explodes when it can be linked and fused with other data, addressing the *big data integration* (BDI) challenge is critical to realizing the promise of big data in these and other domains.

As one prominent example, recent efforts in mining the web and extracting entities, relationships, and ontologies to build general purpose knowledge bases such as Freebase [Bollacker et al. 2008], the Google knowledge graph [Dong et al. 2014a], ProBase [Wu et al. 2012], and Yago [Weikum and Theobald 2010] show promise of using integrated big data to improve applications such as web search and web-scale data analysis.

As a second important example, the flood of geo-referenced data available in recent years, such as geo-tagged web objects (e.g., photos, videos, tweets), online check-ins (e.g., Foursquare), WiFi logs, GPS traces of vehicles (e.g., taxi cabs), and roadside sensor networks has given momentum for using such integrated big data to characterize large-scale human mobility [Becker et al. 2013], and influence areas like public health, traffic engineering, and urban planning.

In this chapter, we first describe the problem of data integration and the components of traditional data integration in Section 1.1. We then discuss the specific challenges that arise in BDI in Section 1.2, where we first identify the dimensions along which BDI differs from traditional data integration, then present a number of recent case studies that empirically study the nature of data sources in BDI. BDI also offers opportunities that do not exist in traditional data integration, and we highlight some of these opportunities in Section 1.3. Finally, we present an outline of the rest of the book in Section 1.4.

## 1.1    TRADITIONAL DATA INTEGRATION

Data integration has the goal of providing *unified access to data* residing in multiple, autonomous data sources. While this goal is easy to state, achieving this goal has proven notoriously hard, even for a small number of sources that provide structured data—the scenario of traditional data integration [Doan et al. 2012].

To understand some of the challenging issues in data integration, consider an illustrative example from the Flights domain, for the common tasks of tracking flight departures and arrivals, examining flight schedules, and booking flights.

### 1.1.1    THE FLIGHTS EXAMPLE: DATA SOURCES

We have a few different kinds of sources, including two airline sources Airline1 and Airline2 (e.g., United Airlines, American Airlines, Delta, etc.), each providing flight data about a different airline, an airport source Airport3, providing information about flights departing from and arriving at a particular airport (e.g., EWR, SFO), a comparison shopping travel source Airfare4 (e.g., Kayak, Orbitz, etc.), providing fares in different fare classes to compare alternate flights, and an informational source Airinfo5 (e.g., a Wikipedia table), providing data about airports and airlines.

Sample data for the various source tables is shown in Tables 1.1–1.8, using short attribute names for brevity. The mapping between the short and full attribute names is provided in Table 1.9 for ease of understanding. Records in different tables that are highlighted using the same color are related to each other, and the various tables should be understood as follows.

**Source** Airline1

Source Airline1 provides the tables Airline1.Schedule(<u>Flight Id</u>, Flight Number, Start Date, End Date, Departure Time, Departure Airport, Arrival Time, Arrival Airport) and Airline1.Flight(<u>Flight Id</u>, <u>Departure Date</u>, Departure Time, Departure Gate, Arrival Date, Arrival Time, Arrival Gate, Plane Id). The underlined attributes form a key for the corresponding table, and Flight Id is used as a join key between these two tables.

Table Airline1.Schedule shows flight schedules in Table 1.1. For example, record $r_{11}$ in table Airline1.Schedule states that Airline1's flight *49* is scheduled to fly regularly from *EWR* to *SFO*, departing at *18:05*, and arriving at *21:10*, between *2013-10-01* and *2014-03-31*. Record $r_{12}$ in the same table shows that the same flight *49* has different scheduled departure and arrival times between *2014-04-01* and *2014-09-30*. Records $r_{13}$ and $r_{14}$ in the same table show the schedules for two different segments of the same flight *55*, the first from *ORD* to *BOS*, and the second from *BOS* to *EWR*, between *2013-10-01* and *2014-09-30*.

Table Airline1.Flight shows the actual departure and arrival information in Table 1.2, for the flights whose schedules are shown in Airline1.Schedule. For example, record $r_{21}$ in table Airline1.Flight

TABLE 1.1: Sample data for Airline1.Schedule

|  | FI | FN | SD | ED | DT | DA | AT | AA |
|---|---|---|---|---|---|---|---|---|
| $r_{11}$ | 123 | 49 | 2013-10-01 | 2014-03-31 | 18:05 | EWR | 21:10 | SFO |
| $r_{12}$ | 234 | 49 | 2014-04-01 | 2014-09-30 | 18:20 | EWR | 21:25 | SFO |
| $r_{13}$ | 345 | 55 | 2013-10-01 | 2014-09-30 | 18:30 | ORD | 21:30 | BOS |
| $r_{14}$ | 346 | 55 | 2013-10-01 | 2014-09-30 | 22:30 | BOS | 23:30 | EWR |

TABLE 1.2: Sample data for Airline1.Flight

|  | FI | DD | DT | DG | AD | AT | AG | PI |
|---|---|---|---|---|---|---|---|---|
| $r_{21}$ | 123 | 2013-12-21 | 18:45 | C98 | 2013-12-21 | 21:30 | 81 | 4013 |
| $r_{22}$ | 123 | 2013-12-28 | 21:30 | C101 | 2013-12-29 | 00:30 | 81 | 3008 |
| $r_{23}$ | 345 | 2013-12-29 | 18:30 | B6 | 2013-12-29 | 21:45 | C18 | 4013 |
| $r_{24}$ | 346 | 2013-12-29 | 22:35 | C18 | 2013-12-29 | 23:35 | C101 | 4013 |

records information about a specific flight, corresponding to the regularly scheduled flight $r_{11}$ (the Flight Id *123* specifies the join key), using a plane with id *4013*, actually departing on *2013-12-21* at *18:45* (40 minutes later than the scheduled departure time of *18:05*) from gate *C98*, and actually arriving on *2013-12-21* at *21:30* (20 minutes later than the scheduled arrival time of *21:10*) at gate *81*. Both $r_{11}$ and $r_{21}$ use yellow highlighting to visually depict their relationship. Record $r_{22}$ in the same table records information about a flight on a different date, also corresponding to the regularly scheduled flight $r_{11}$, with a considerably longer delay in departure and arrival times. Records $r_{23}$ and $r_{24}$ record information about flights on *2013-12-29*, corresponding to regularly scheduled flights $r_{13}$ and $r_{14}$, respectively.

### Source Airline2

Source Airline2 provides similar data to source Airline1, but using the table Airline2.Flight(<u>Flight Number</u>, <u>Departure Airport</u>, <u>Scheduled Departure Date</u>, Scheduled Departure Time, Actual Departure Time, Arrival Airport, Scheduled Arrival Date, Scheduled Arrival Time, Actual Arrival Time).

Each record in table Airline2.Flight, shown in Table 1.3, contains both the schedule and the actual flight details. For example, record $r_{31}$ records information about Airline2's flight *53*, departing from *SFO*, scheduled to depart on *2013-12-21* at *15:30*, with a 30 minute delay in the actual departure time, arriving at *EWR*, scheduled to arrive on *2013-12-21* at *23:35*, with a 40 minute

TABLE 1.3:  Sample data for Airline2.Flight

|  | FN | DA | SDD | SDT | ADT | AA | SAD | SAT | AAT |
|---|---|---|---|---|---|---|---|---|---|
| $r_{31}$ | 53 | SFO | 2013-12-21 | 15:30 | 16:00 | EWR | 2013-12-21 | 23:35 | 00:15 (+1d) |
| $r_{32}$ | 53 | SFO | 2013-12-22 | 15:30 | 16:15 | EWR | 2013-12-22 | 23:35 | 00:30 |
| $r_{33}$ | 53 | SFO | 2014-06-28 | 16:00 | 16:05 | EWR | 2014-06-29 | 00:05 | 23:57 (-1d) |
| $r_{34}$ | 53 | SFO | 2014-07-06 | 16:00 | 16:00 | EWR | 2014-07-07 | 00:05 | 00:09 |
| $r_{35}$ | 49 | SFO | 2013-12-21 | 12:00 | 12:35 | EWR | 2013-12-21 | 20:05 | 20:45 |
| $r_{36}$ | 77 | LAX | 2013-12-22 | 09:15 | 09:15 | SFO | 2013-12-22 | 11:00 | 10:59 |

TABLE 1.4:  Sample data for Airport3.Departures

|  | AL | FN | S | A | GT | TT | T | G | R |
|---|---|---|---|---|---|---|---|---|---|
| $r_{41}$ | A1 | 49 | 2013-12-21 | 2013-12-21 | 18:45 | 18:53 | C | 98 | 2 |
| $r_{42}$ | A1 | 49 | 2013-12-28 | 2013-12-28 | 21:29 | 21:38 | C | 101 | 2 |

delay in the actual arrival time; its arrival on *2013-12-22* (the day after its scheduled arrival) is indicated by the *(+1d)* associated with the actual arrival time. Note that this table contains a record $r_{35}$ for Airline2's flight *49*, which is different from Airline1's flight *49*, illustrating that different airlines can use the same flight number for their respective flights.

Unlike source Airline1, source Airline2 does not publish the departure gate, arrival gate, and the plane identifier used for the specific flight, illustrating the diversity between the schemas used by these sources.

Source Airport3

Source Airport3 provides tables Airport3.Departures(Air Line, Flight Number, Scheduled, Actual, Gate Time, Takeoff Time, Terminal, Gate, Runway) and Airport3.Arrivals(Air Line, Flight Number, Scheduled, Actual, Gate Time, Landing Time, Terminal, Gate, Runway).

Table Airport3.Departures, shown in Table 1.4, publishes information only about flight departures from *EWR*. For example, record $r_{41}$ in table Airport3.Departures states that Airline1's flight *49*, scheduled to depart on *2013-12-21*, departed on *2013-12-21* from terminal *C* and gate *98* at *18:45* and took off at *18:53* from runway *2*. There is no information in this table about the arrival airport, arrival date, and arrival time of this flight. Note that $r_{41}$ corresponds to records $r_{11}$ and $r_{21}$, depicted by the consistent use of the yellow highlight.

TABLE 1.5: Sample data for Airport3.Arrivals

|  | AL | FN | S | A | GT | LT | T | G | R |
|---|---|---|---|---|---|---|---|---|---|
| $r_{51}$ | A2 | 53 | 2013-12-21 | 2013-12-22 | 00:21 | 00:15 | B | 53 | 2 |
| $r_{52}$ | A2 | 53 | 2013-12-22 | 2013-12-23 | 00:40 | 00:30 | B | 53 | 2 |
| $r_{53}$ | A1 | 55 | 2013-12-29 | 2013-12-29 | 23:35 | 23:31 | C | 101 | 1 |
| $r_{54}$ | A2 | 49 | 2013-12-21 | 2013-12-21 | 20:50 | 20:45 | B | 55 | 2 |

Table Airport3.Arrivals, shown in Table 1.5, publishes information only about flight arrivals into *EWR*. For example, record $r_{51}$ in table Airport3.Arrivals states that Airline2's flight *53*, scheduled to arrive on *2013-12-21*, arrived on *2013-12-22*, landing on runway *2* at *00:15*, reaching gate *53* of terminal *B* at *00:21*. There is no information in this table about the departure airport, departure date, and departure time of this flight. Note that $r_{51}$ corresponds to record $r_{31}$, both of which are highlighted in lavender.

Unlike sources Airline1 and Airline2, source Airport3 distinguishes between the time at which the flight left/reached the gate and the time at which the flight took off from/landed at the airport runway.

## Source Airfare4

Travel source Airfare4 publishes comparison shopping data for multiple airlines, including schedules in Airfare4.Flight(<u>Flight Id</u>, Flight Number, Departure Airport, Departure Date, Departure Time, Arrival Airport, Arrival Time) and fares in Airfare4.Fares(<u>Flight Id</u>, <u>Fare Class</u>, Fare). Flight Id is used as a join key between these two tables.

For example, record $r_{61}$ in Airfare4.Flight, shown in Table 1.6, states that Airline1's flight *A1–49* was scheduled to depart from Newark Liberty airport on *2013-12-21* at *18:05*, and arrive at the San Francisco airport on the same date at *21:10*. Note that $r_{61}$ corresponds to records $r_{11}$, $r_{21}$, and $r_{41}$, indicated by the yellow highlight shared by all records.

The records in table Airfare4.Fares, shown in Table 1.7, gives the fares for various fare classes of this flight. For example, record $r_{71}$ shows that fare class *A* of this flight has a fare of $5799.00; the flight identifier *456* is the join key.

## Source Airinfo5

Informational source Airinfo5 publishes data about airports and airline in Airinfo5.AirportCodes(<u>Airport Code</u>, Airport Name) and Airinfo5.AirlineCodes(<u>Air Line Code</u>, Air Line Name), respectively.

TABLE 1.6:  Sample data for Airfare4.Flight

|  | FI | FN | DA | DD | DT | AA | AT |
|---|---|---|---|---|---|---|---|
| $r_{61}$ | 456 | A1-49 | Newark Liberty | 2013-12-21 | 18:05 | San Francisco | 21:10 |
| $r_{62}$ | 457 | A1-49 | Newark Liberty | 2014-04-05 | 18:05 | San Francisco | 21:10 |
| $r_{63}$ | 458 | A1-49 | Newark Liberty | 2014-04-12 | 18:05 | San Francisco | 21:10 |
| $r_{64}$ | 460 | A2-53 | San Francisco | 2013-12-22 | 15:30 | Newark Liberty | 23:35 |
| $r_{65}$ | 461 | A2-53 | San Francisco | 2014-06-28 | 15:30 | Newark Liberty | 23:35 |
| $r_{66}$ | 462 | A2-53 | San Francisco | 2014-07-06 | 16:00 | Newark Liberty | 00:05 (+1d) |

TABLE 1.7:  Sample data for Airfare4.Fares

|  | FI | FC | F |
|---|---|---|---|
| $r_{71}$ | 456 | A | $5799.00 |
| $r_{72}$ | 456 | K | $999.00 |
| $r_{73}$ | 456 | Y | $599.00 |

TABLE 1.8:  Sample data for Airinfo5.AirportCodes, Airinfo5.AirlineCodes

|  | Airinfo5.AirportCodes | |  | Airinfo5.AirlineCodes | |
|---|---|---|---|---|---|
|  | AC | AN |  | ALC | ALN |
| $r_{81}$ | EWR | Newark Liberty, NJ, US | $r_{91}$ | A1 | Airline1 |
| $r_{82}$ | SFO | San Francisco, CA, US | $r_{92}$ | A2 | Airline2 |

For example, record $r_{81}$ in Airinfo5.AirportCodes, shown in Table 1.8, states that the name of the airport with code *EWR* is *Newark Liberty, NJ, US*. Similary, record $r_{91}$ in Airinfo5.AirlineCodes, also shown in Table 1.8, states that the name of the airline with code *A1* is *Airline1*.

## 1.1.2   THE **FLIGHTS** EXAMPLE: DATA INTEGRATION
While each of the five sources is useful in isolation, the value of this data is considerably enhanced when the different sources are integrated.

TABLE 1.9:  Abbreviated attribute names

| Short Name | Full Name | Short Name | Full Name |
|---|---|---|---|
| A | Actual | AA | Arrival Airport |
| AAT | Actual Arrival Time | AC | Airport Code |
| AD | Arrival Date | ADT | Actual Departure Time |
| AG | Arrival Gate | AL | Air Line |
| ALC | Air Line Code | ALN | Air Line Name |
| AN | Airport Name | AT | Arrival Time |
| DA | Departure Airport | DD | Departure Date |
| DG | Departure Gate | DT | Departure Time |
| ED | End Date | F | Fare |
| FC | Fare Class | FI | Flight Id |
| FN | Flight Number | G | Gate |
| GT | Gate Time | LT | Landing Time |
| PI | Plane Id | R | Runway |
| S | Scheduled | SAD | Scheduled Arrival Date |
| SAT | Scheduled Arrival Time | SD | Start Date |
| SDD | Scheduled Departure Date | SDT | Scheduled Departure Time |
| T | Terminal | TT | Takeoff Time |

### Integrating Sources

First, each airline source (e.g., Airline1, Airline2) benefits by linking with the airport source Airport3 since the airport source provides much more detailed information about the actual flight departures and arrivals, such as gate time, takeoff and landing times, and runways used; this can help the airlines better understand the reasons for flight delays. Second, airport source Airport3 benefits by linking with the airline sources (e.g., Airline1, Airline2) since the airline sources provide more detailed information about the flight schedules and overall flight plans (especially for multi-hop flights such as Airline1's flight 55); this can help the airport better understand flight patterns. Third, the comparison shopping travel source Airfare4 benefits by linking with the airline and airport sources to provide additional information such as historical on-time departure/arrival statistics; this can be very useful to customers as they make flight bookings. This linkage makes critical use of the informational source Airinfo5, as we shall see later. Finally, customers benefit when the various sources are integrated since they do not need to go to multiple sources to obtain all the information they need.

For example, the query *"for each airline flight number, compute the average delays between scheduled and actual departure times, and between actual gate departure and takeoff times, over the past one month"* can be easily answered over the integrated database, but not using any single source.

However, integrating multiple, autonomous data sources can be quite difficult, often requiring considerable manual effort to understand the semantics of the data in each source to resolve ambiguities. Consider, again, our illustrative Flights example.

## Semantic Ambiguity

In order to *align* the various source tables correctly, one needs to understand that (i) the same conceptual information may be modeled quite differently in different sources, and (ii) different conceptual information may be modeled similarly in different sources.

For example, source Airline1 models schedules in table Airline1.Schedule within date ranges (specified by Start Date and End Date), using attributes Departure Time and Arrival Time for time information. However, source Airline2 models schedules along with actual flight information in the table Airline2.Flight, using different records for different actual flights, and differently named attributes Scheduled Departure Date, Scheduled Departure Time, Scheduled Arrival Date, and Scheduled Arrival Time.

As another example, source Airport3 models both actual gate departure/arrival times (Gate Time in Airport3.Departures and Airport3.Arrivals) and actual takeoff/landing times (Takeoff Time in Airport3.Departures, Landing Time in Airport3.Arrivals). However, each of Airline1 and Airline2 models only one kind of departure and arrival times; in particular, a careful examination of the data shows that source Airline1 models gate times (Departure Time and Arrival Time in Airline1.Schedule and Airline1.Flight) and Airline2 models takeoff and landing times (Scheduled Departure Time, Actual Departure Time, Scheduled Arrival Time, Actual Arrival Time in Airline2.Flight).

To illustrate that different conceptual information may be modeled similarly, note that Departure Date is used by source Airline1 to model actual departure date (in Airline1.Flight), but is used to model scheduled departure date by source Airfare4 (in Airfare4.Flight).

## Instance Representation Ambiguity

In order to *link* the same data instance from multiple sources, one needs to take into account that instances may be represented differently, reflecting the autonomous nature of the sources.

For example, flight numbers are represented in sources Airline1 and Airline2 using digits (e.g., *49* in $r_{11}$, *53* in $r_{31}$), while they are represented in source Airfare4 using alphanumerics (e.g., *A1-49* in $r_{61}$). Similarly, the departure and arrival airports are represented in sources Airline1 and Airline2 using 3-letter codes (e.g., *EWR, SFO, LAX*), but as a descriptive string in Airfare4.Flight (e.g., *Newark Liberty, San Francisco*). Since flights are uniquely identified by the combination of attributes (Airline, Flight Number, Departure Airport, Departure Date), one would not be able to link the data in Airfare4.Flight with the corresponding data in Airline1, Airline2, and Airport3 without additional tables mapping airline codes to airline descriptive names, and airport codes to airport descriptive names, such as Airinfo5.AirlineCodes and Airinfo5.AirportCodes in Table 1.8. Even with such tables, one might need approximate string matching techniques [Hadjieleftheriou and Srivastava 2011] to match *Newark Liberty* in Airfare4.Flight with *Newark Liberty, NJ, US* in Airinfo5.AirportCodes.

## Data Inconsistency

In order to *fuse* the data from multiple sources, one needs to resolve the instance-level ambiguities and inconsistencies between the sources.

For example, there is an inconsistency between records $r_{32}$ in Airline2.Flight and $r_{52}$ in Airport3.Arrivals (both of which are highlighted in blue to indicate that they refer to the same flight). Record $r_{32}$ states that the Scheduled Arrival Date and Actual Arrival Time of Airline2's flight *53* are *2013-12-22* and *00:30*, respectively, implying that the actual arrival date is the same as the scheduled arrival date (unlike record $r_{31}$, where the Actual Arrival Time included *(+1d)* to indicate that the actual arrival date was the day after the scheduled arrival date). However, $r_{52}$ states this flight arrived on *2013-12-23* at *00:30*. This inconsistency would need to be resolved in the integrated data.

As another example, record $r_{62}$ in Airfare4.Flight states that Airline1's flight *49* on *2014-04-05* is scheduled to depart and arrive at *18:05* and *21:10*, respectively. While the departure date is consistent with record $r_{12}$ in Airline1.Schedule (both $r_{12}$ and $r_{62}$ are highlighted in green to indicate their relationship), the scheduled departure and arrival times are not, possibly because $r_{62}$ incorrectly used the (out-of-date) times from $r_{11}$ in Airline1.Schedule. Similary, record $r_{65}$ in Airfare4.Flight states that Airline2's flight *53* on *2014-06-28* is scheduled to depart and arrive at *15:30* and *23:35*, respectively. While the departure date is consistent with record $r_{33}$ in Airline2.Flight (both $r_{33}$ and $r_{65}$ are highlighted in greenish yellow to indicate their relationship), the scheduled departure and arrival times are not, possibly because $r_{65}$ incorrectly used the out-of-date times from $r_{32}$ in Airline2.Flight. Again, these inconsistencies need to be resolved in the integrated data.

### 1.1.3    DATA INTEGRATION: ARCHITECTURE & THREE MAJOR STEPS

Traditional data integration addresses these challenges of semantic ambiguity, instance representation ambiguity, and data inconsistency by using a pipelined architecture, which consists of three major steps, depicted in Figure 1.1.

FIGURE 1.1:  Traditional data integration: architecture.

The first major step in traditional data integration is that of *schema alignment*, which addresses the challenge of semantic ambiguity and aims to understand which attributes have the same meaning and which ones do not. More formally, we have the following definition.

**Definition 1.1** (Schema Alignment)    Consider a set of source schemas in the same domain, where different schemas may describe the domain in different ways. *Schema alignment* generates three outcomes.

1. A *mediated schema* that provides a unified view of the disparate sources and captures the salient aspects of the domain being considered.

2. An *attribute matching* that matches attributes in each source schema to the corresponding attributes in the mediated schema.

3. A *schema mapping* between each source schema and the mediated schema to specify the semantic relationships between the contents of the source and that of the mediated data.

The result schema mappings are used to reformulate a user query into a set of queries on the underlying data sources for query answering.

This step is non-trivial for many reasons. Different sources can describe the same domain using very different schemas, as illustrated in our Flights example. They may use different attribute names even when they have the same meaning (e.g., Arrival Date in Airline1.Flight, Actual Arrival Date in Airline2.Flight, and Actual in Airport3.Arrivals). Also, sources may apply different meanings for attributes with the same name (e.g., Actual in Airport3.Departures refers to the actual departure date, while Actual in Airport3.Arrivals refers to the actual arrival date).

The second major step in traditional data integration is that of *record linkage*, which addresses the challenge of instance representation ambiguity, and aims to understand which records represent the same entity and which ones do not. More formally, we have the following definition.

**Definition 1.2** (Record Linkage)    Consider a set of data sources, each providing a set of records over a set of attributes. *Record linkage* computes a partitioning of the set of records, such that each partition identifies the records that refer to a distinct entity.

Even when schema alignment has been performed, this step is still challenging for many reasons. Different sources can describe the same entity in different ways. For example, records $r_{11}$ in Airline1.Schedule and $r_{21}$ in Airline1.Flight should be linked to record $r_{41}$ in Airport3.Departures; however, $r_{11}$ and $r_{21}$ do not explicitly mention the name of the airline, while $r_{41}$ does not explicitly mention the departure airport, both of which are needed to uniquely identify a flight. Further, different sources may use different ways of representing the same information (e.g., the alternate ways of representing airports as discussed earlier). Finally, comparing every pair of records to determine whether or not they refer to the same entity can be infeasible in the presence of billions of records.

The third major step in traditional data integration is that of *data fusion*, which addresses the challenge of data quality, and aims to understand which value to use in the integrated data when the sources provide conflicting values. More formally, we have the following definition.

**Definition 1.3** (Data Fusion)    Consider a set of data items, and a set of data sources each of which provides values for a subset of the data items. *Data fusion* decides the true value(s) for each data item.

Such conflicts can arise for a variety of reasons including mis-typing, incorrect calculations (e.g., the conflict in actual arrival dates between records $r_{32}$ and $r_{52}$), out-of-date information (e.g., the conflict in scheduled departure and arrival times between records $r_{12}$ and $r_{62}$), and so on.

We will describe approaches used for each of these steps in subsequent chapters, and move on to highlighting the challenges and opportunities that arise when moving from traditional data integration to big data integration.

## 1.2    BDI: CHALLENGES

To appreciate the challenges that arise in big data integration, we present five recent case studies that empirically examined various characteristics of data sources on the web that would be integrated in BDI efforts, and the dimensions along which these characteristics are naturally classified.

> When you can measure what you are speaking about, and express it in numbers, you know something about it. —Lord Kelvin

### 1.2.1    THE "V" DIMENSIONS

Big data integration differs from traditional data integration along many dimensions, paralleling the dimensions along which big data is characterized as differing from traditional databases.

#### Volume

In the big data era, not only can data sources contain a huge volume of data, but also the number of data sources has grown to be in the millions; even for a single domain, the number of sources has grown to be in the tens to hundreds of thousands.

There are many scenarios where a single data source can contain a huge volume of data, ranging from social media and telecommunications networks to finance.

To illustrate a scenario with a large number of sources in a single domain, consider again our Flights example. Suppose we would like to extend it to all airlines and all airports in the world to support flexible, international travel itineraries. With hundreds of airlines worldwide, and over

40,000 airports around the world,[1] the number of data sources that would need to be integrated would easily be in the tens of thousands.

More generally, the case studies we present in Sections 1.2.2, 1.2.3, and 1.2.5 quantify the number of web sources with structured data, and demonstrate that these numbers are much higher than the number of data sources that have been considered in traditional data integration.

### Velocity

As a direct consequence of the rate at which data are being collected and continuously made available, many of the data sources are quite dynamic, and the number of data sources is also rapidly exploding.

To illustrate the scenario with dynamic data sources, in our (extended) Flights example, there are tens of thousands of data sources that provide information changing over time. Some of this information changes at the granularity of minutes and hours, such as the estimated departure and arrival times of flights, and the current locations of flights. Other information changes more slowly at the granularity of months, weeks, and days, such as the changes in scheduled departure and arrival times of flights. Providing an integrated view of such dynamically changing data across all these sources is beyond that ability of traditional methods for data integration.

To illustrate the growth rate in the number of data sources, the case study we present in Section 1.2.2 illustrates the explosion in the number of deep web sources within a few years. Undoubtedly, these numbers are likely to be even higher today.

### Variety

Data sources from different domains are naturally diverse since they refer to different types of entities and relationships, which often need to be integrated to support complex applications. Further, data sources even in the same domain are quite heterogeneous both at the schema level regarding how they structure their data and at the instance level regarding how they describe the same real-world entity, exhibiting considerable variety even for substantially similar entities. Finally, the domains, source schemas, and entity representations evolve over time, adding to the diversity and heterogeneity that need to be handled in big data integration.

Consider again our Flights example. Suppose we would like to extend it to other forms of transportation (e.g., flights, ships, trains, buses, taxis) to support complex, international travel itineraries. The variety of data sources (e.g., transportation companies, airports, bus terminals) that would need to be integrated would be much higher. In addition to the number of airlines and airports

---

1. https://www.cia.gov/library/publications/the-world-factbook/fields/2053.html (accessed on October 1, 2014).

worldwide, there are close to a thousand active seaports and inland ports in the world;[2] there are over a thousand operating bus companies in the world;[3] and about as many operating train companies in the world.[4]

The case studies we present in Sections 1.2.2, 1.2.4, and 1.2.5 quantify the considerable variety that exist in practice in web sources.

### Veracity

Data sources are of widely differing qualities, with significant differences in the coverage, accuracy, and timeliness of data provided.

Our Flights example illustrates specific quality issues that can arise in practice. These quality issues only get exacerbated with an increasing number and diversity of data sources, due to copying between the sources and different types of correlations between the sources in practice.

The case studies we present in Sections 1.2.3, 1.2.4, and 1.2.6 illustrate the significant coverage and quality issues that exist in data sources on the web, even for the same domain. This provides some context for the observation that "one in three business leaders do not trust the information they use to make decisions."[5]

## 1.2.2    CASE STUDY: QUANTITY OF DEEP WEB DATA

The deep web consists of a large number of data sources where data are stored in databases and obtained (or surfaced) by querying web forms. He et al. [2007] and Madhavan et al. [2007] experimentally study the *volume*, *velocity*, and domain-level *variety* of data sources available on the deep web.

### Main Questions

These two studies focus on two main questions related to the "V" dimensions presented in Section 1.2.1.

- What is the scale of the deep web?

    For example, how many query interfaces to databases exist on the web? How many web databases are accessible through such query interfaces? How many web sources provide query interfaces to databases? How have these deep web numbers changed over time?

---

2. http://www.ask.com/answers/99725161/how-many-sea-ports-in-world (accessed on October 1, 2014).

3. http://en.wikipedia.org/wiki/List_of_bus_operating_companies (accessed on October 1, 2014).

4. http://en.wikipedia.org/wiki/List_of_railway_companies (accessed on October 1, 2014).

5. http://www-01.ibm.com/software/data/bigdata/ (accessed on October 1, 2014).

- What is the distribution of domains in web databases?

  For example, is the deep web driven and dominated by e-commerce, such as product search? Or is there considerable domain-level variety among web databases? How does this domain-level variety compare to that on the surface web?

## Study Methodology

In the absence of a comprehensive index to deep web sources, both studies use sampling to quantify answers to these questions.

He et al. [2007] take an IP sampling approach to collect server samples, by randomly sampling 1 million IP addresses in 2004, using the Wget HTTP client to download HTML pages, then *manually* identifying and analyzing web databases in this sample to extrapolate their estimates of the deep web to the estimated 2.2 billion valid IP addresses. This study distinguishes between deep web sources, web databases (a deep web source can contain multiple web databases), and query interfaces (a web database could be accessed by multiple query interfaces), and uses the following methodology.

1. The web sources are crawled to a depth of three hops from the root page. All the HTML query interfaces on the retrieved pages are identified.

   Query interfaces (within a source) that refer to the same database are identified by manually choosing a few random objects that can be accessed through one interface and checking to see if each of them can be accessed through the other interfaces.

2. The domain distribution of the identified web databases is determined by manually categorizing the identified web databases, using the top-level categories of the http://yahoo.com directory (accessed on October 1, 2014) as the taxonomy.

Madhavan et al. [2007] instead use a random sample of 25 million web pages from the Google index from 2006, then identify deep web query interfaces on these pages in a *rule-driven manner*, and finally extrapolate their estimates to the 1 billion+ pages in the Google index. Using the terminology of He et al., this study mainly examines the number of query interfaces on the deep web, not the number of distinct deep web databases. For this task, they use the following methodology.

1. Since many HTML forms are present on multiple web pages, they compute a signature for each form by combining the host present in the action of the form with the names of the visible inputs in the form. This is used as a lower bound for the number of distinct HTML forms.

2. From this number, they prune away non-query forms (such as password entry) and site search boxes, and only count the number of forms that have at least one text input field, and between two and ten total inputs.

## Main Results

We categorize the main results of these studies according to the investigated "V" dimensions.

**Volume, Velocity.** The 2004 study by He et al. [2007] estimates a total of 307,000 deep web sources, 450,000 web databases, and 1,258,000 distinct query interfaces to deep web content. This is based on extrapolation from a total of 126 deep web sources, containing 190 web databases and 406 query interfaces identified in their random IP sample. This number of identified sources, databases, and query interfaces enables much of their analysis to be accomplished by manually inspecting the identified query interfaces.

The subsequent 2006 study by Madhavan et al. [2007] estimates a total of more than 10 million distinct query interfaces to deep web content. This is based on extrapolating from a total of 647,000 distinct query interfaces in their random sample of web pages. Working with this much larger number of query interfaces requires the use of automated approaches to differentiate query interfaces to the deep web from non-query forms. This increase in the number of query interfaces identified by Madhavan et al. over the number identified by He et al. is partly a reflection of the *velocity* at which the number of deep web sources increased between the different time periods studied.

**Variety.** The study by He et al. [2007] shows that deep web databases have considerable domain-level *variety*, where 51% of the 190 identified web databases in their sample are in non e-commerce domain categories, such as health, society & culture, education, arts & humanities, science, and so on. Only 49% of the 190 identified web databases are in e-commerce domain categories. Table 1.10 shows the distribution of domain categories identified by He et al., illustrating the domain-level variety of the data in BDI. This domain-level variety of web databases is in sharp contrast to the surface web, where an earlier study identified that e-commerce web sites dominate with an 83% share.

The study by Madhavan et al. [2007] also confirms that the semantic content of deep web sources varies widely, and is distributed under most directory categories.

## 1.2.3    CASE STUDY: EXTRACTED DOMAIN-SPECIFIC DATA

The documents that constitute the surface web contain a significant amount of structured data, which can be obtained using web-scale information extraction techniques. Dalvi et al. [2012] experimentally study the *volume* and coverage properties of such structured data (i.e., entities and their attributes) in several domains (e.g., restaurants, hotels).

TABLE 1.10: Domain category distribution of web databases [He et al. 2007]

| Domain Category | E-commerce | Percentage |
|---|---|---|
| Business & Economy | Yes | 24% |
| Computers & Internet | Yes | 16% |
| News & Media | Yes | 6% |
| Entertainment | Yes | 1% |
| Recreation & Sports | Yes | 2% |
| Health | No | 4% |
| Government | No | 2% |
| Regional | No | 4% |
| Society & Culture | No | 9% |
| Education | No | 16% |
| Arts & Humanities | No | 4% |
| Science | No | 2% |
| Reference | No | 8% |
| Others | No | 2% |

## Main Questions

Their study focuses on two main questions related to the "V" dimensions presented in Section 1.2.1.

- How many sources are needed to build a complete database for a given domain, even restricted to well-specified attributes?

    For example, is it the case that well-established head aggregators (such as http://yelp.com for restaurants) contain most of the information, or does one need to go to the long tail of web sources to build a reasonably complete database (e.g., with 95% coverage)? Is there a substantial need to construct a comprehensive database, for example, as measured by the demand for tail entities?

- How easy is it to discover the data sources and entities in a given domain?

    For example, can one start with a few data sources or seed entities and iteratively discover most (e.g., 99%) of the data? How critical are the head aggregators to this process of discovery of data sources?

## Study Methodology

One way to answer the questions is to actually perform web-scale information extraction in a variety of domains, and compute the desired quantities of interest; this is an extremely challenging task, for which good solutions are currently being investigated. Instead, the approach that Dalvi et al. [2012] take is to study domains with the following three properties.

1. One has access to a comprehensive structured database of entities in that domain.

2. The entities can be uniquely identified by the value of some key attributes available on the web pages.

3. One has access to (nearly) all the web pages containing the key attributes of the entities.

Dalvi et al. identify nine such domains: books, restaurants, automotive, banks, libraries, schools, hotels & lodging, retail & shopping, and home & garden. Books are identified using the value of ISBN, while entities in the other domains are identified using phone numbers and/or home page URLs. For each domain, they look for the identifying attributes of the entities on each web page in the Yahoo! web cache, group web pages by hosts into sources, and aggregate the entities found on all the web pages of each data source.

They model the problem of ease of discovery of data sources and entities using a bi-partite graph of entities and sources, with an edge $(E, S)$ indicating that an entity $E$ is found in source $S$. Graph properties like connectivity of the bi-partite graph can help understand the robustness of iterative information extraction algorithms with respect to the choice of the seed entities or data sources for bootstrapping. Similarly, the diameter can indicate how many iterations are needed for convergence. In this way, they don't need to do actual information extraction, and only study the distribution of information about entities already in their database. While this methodology has its limitations, it provides a good first study on this topic.

## Main Results

We categorize the main results of this study according to the investigated "V" dimensions.

**Volume.**   First, they find that all the domains they study have thousands to tens of thousands of web sources (see Figure 1.2 for phone numbers in the restaurant domain). These numbers are much higher than the number of data sources that are considered in traditional data integration.

Second, they show that tail sources contain a significant amount of information, even for domains like restaurants with well-established aggregator sources. For example, http://yelp .com is shown to contain fewer than 70% of the restaurant phone numbers and fewer than

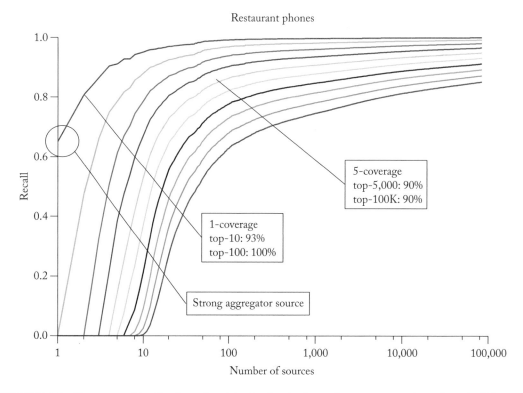

FIGURE 1.2:  K-coverage (the fraction of entities in the database that are present in at least $k$ different sources) for phone numbers in the restaurant domain [Dalvi et al. 2012].

40% of the home pages of restaurants. With the top 10 sources (ordered by decreasing number of entities found on the sources), one can extract around 93% of all restaurant phone numbers, and with the top 100 sources one can extract close to 100% of all restaurant phone numbers, as seen in Figure 1.2. However, for a less available attribute such as home page URL, the situation is quite different: one needs at least 10,000 sources to cover 95% of all restaurant home page URLs.

Third, they investigate the redundancy of available information using $k$-coverage (the fraction of entities in the database that are present in at least $k$ different sources) to enable a higher confidence in the extracted information. For example, they show that one needs 5000 sources to get 5-coverage of 90% of the restaurant phone numbers (while 10 sources is sufficient to get 1-coverage of 93% of these phone numbers), as seen in Figure 1.2.

Fourth, they demonstrate (using user-generated restaurant reviews) that there is significant value in extracting information from the sources in the long tail. In particular, while both

| Domain | Graph Attr | Avg. no. sites per entity | Diameter | No. conn. comp. | Percent entities in largest comp. |
|---|---|---|---|---|---|
| Books | ISBN | 8 | 8 | 439 | 99.96 |
| Automotive | phone | 13 | 6 | 9 | 99.99 |
| Banks | phone | 22 | 6 | 15 | 99.99 |
| Home | phone | 13 | 8 | 4507 | 99.76 |
| Hotels | phone | 56 | 6 | 11 | 99.99 |
| Libraries | phone | 47 | 6 | 3 | 99.99 |
| Restaurants | phone | 32 | 6 | 52 | 99.99 |
| Retail | phone | 19 | 7 | 628 | 99.93 |
| Schools | phone | 37 | 6 | 48 | 99.97 |
| Automotive | homepage | 115 | 6 | 10 | 98.52 |
| Banks | homepage | 68 | 8 | 30 | 99.57 |
| Home | homepage | 20 | 8 | 5496 | 97.87 |
| Hotels | homepage | 56 | 8 | 24 | 99.90 |
| Libraries | homepage | 251 | 6 | 4 | 99.86 |
| Restaurants | homepage | 46 | 6 | 146 | 99.82 |
| Retail | homepage | 45 | 7 | 1260 | 99.20 |
| Schools | homepage | 74 | 6 | 122 | 99.57 |
| | | High data redundancy | Low diameter | | Highly connected data |

FIGURE 1.3: Connectivity (between entities and sources) for the nine domains studied by Dalvi et al. [2012].

the demand for and the availability of review information reduces towards the tail, information availability reduces at a faster rate, suggesting that tail extraction can be valuable in spite of the lower demand.

Fifth, as seen in Figure 1.3, they observe that there is a significant amount of data redundancy (tens to hundreds of sources per entity on average), and the data within a domain is well connected. This redundancy and well connectedness is critical for discovery of sources and entities in BDI. In particular, for almost all the (domain, attribute) pairs, over 99% of the entities are present in the largest connected component of the bi-partite graph, establishing that even a randomly chosen small seed set of entities is sufficient to reach most of the entities in the domain. Further, a small diameter (around 6–8) implies that iterative approaches would converge fairly rapidly. Finally, they show that the graphs remain well connected (with over 90% entities) even after the top 10 aggregator sources are removed, demonstrating that the connectivity does not depend only on the head aggregator sources.

### 1.2.4   CASE STUDY: QUALITY OF DEEP WEB DATA

While the studies by He et al. [2007] and Madhavan et al. [2007] shed light on the *volume*, *velocity*, and domain-level *variety* of deep web data, they do not investigate the quality of data present in these sources. To overcome this limitation, Li et al. [2012] experimentally study the *veracity* of deep web data.

## Main Questions

This study focuses on two main questions related to the "V" dimensions presented in Section 1.2.1.

- What is the quality of deep web data?

  For example, are there a lot of redundant data among deep web sources? Are the data consistent across sources in a domain? Is the quality of data better in some domains than others?

- What is the quality of the deep web sources?

  For example, are the sources highly accurate? Are correct data provided by the majority of the sources? Is there an authoritative source that can be trusted while all the other sources are ignored, in case of inconsistency across sources? Do sources share data with or copy from other sources?

## Study Methodology

One way to answer these questions is to actually perform big data integration across all the deep web sources in each of multiple domains; this is an extremely challenging task that has not yet been solved. Instead, the approach that Li et al. [2012] take is to study a few domains with the following properties.

1. The deep web sources in these domains are frequently used, and believed to be clean since incorrect values can have an adverse effect on people's lives.

2. The entities in these domains are consistently and uniquely identified across sources by the value of some key attributes, making it easy to link information across deep web sources.

3. Focusing on a moderate number of popularly used sources is sufficient to understand the quality of data experienced by users in these domains.

The study by Li et al. [2012] identifies two such domains: Stock and Flight. Stocks are consistently and uniquely identified by stock symbols (e.g., *T* for *AT&T Inc.*, and *GOOG* for *Google, Inc.*) across sources, and flight numbers (e.g., *UA 48*) and departure/arrival airport codes (e.g., *EWR* and *SFO*) are typically used to identify flights on a given day across sources. They identify a moderately large number of popular deep web sources in each of the domains by: (i) using domain-specific search terms on popular search engines and manually identifying deep web sources from the top 200 returned results; (ii) focusing on those sources that use the GET method (i.e., the form data are encoded in the URL itself), and don't use Javascript. This results in 55 sources (including popular financial aggregators such as Yahoo! Finance, Google Finance, and MSN Money, official stock exchange sources such as NASDAQ, and financial news sources such as Bloomberg and MarketWatch) in the Stock domain and 38 sources (including 3 airline sources, 8 airport hub sources, and 27 third-party sources such as Orbitz, Travelocity, etc.) in the Flight domain.

In the Stock domain, they pick 1000 stock symbols from the Dow Jones, NASDAQ, and Russell 3000, and query each stock symbol on each of the 55 sources every week day in July 2011. The queries are issued one hour after the stock market closes each day. Extracted attributes are manually matched across sources to identify globally distinct attributes; of these, 16 popular attributes whose values should be fairly stable after the stock market closes (such as daily closing price) are analyzed in detail. A gold standard is generated for 200 stock symbols by taking the majority voting results from 5 popular financial sources.

In the Flight domain, they focus on 1200 flights departing from or arriving at the hub airports of the three airlines, United, Continental, and American, and query for each flight at least one hour after the scheduled arrival time every day in December 2011. Extracted attributes are manually matched across sources to identify globally distinct attributes; of these, six popular attributes are analyzed in detail. A gold standard is generated for 100 flights by taking the data provided by the corresponding airline source.

## Main Results

We categorize the main results of this study according to the "V" dimensions presented in Section 1.2.1, as in the previous study.

Although the primary focus of this study is *veracity*, the results of this study also cast some light on the schema-level *variety* of deep web sources.

**Variety.** Li et al. [2012] identify considerable schema-level *variety* among the deep web sources examined. For example, the 55 sources in the Stock domain provide different numbers of attributes, ranging from 3–71, for a total of 333 attributes. After manually matching these attributes across sources, they identify a total of 153 globally distinct attributes, many of which are computed using other attributes (e.g., 52 week high and low prices). The distribution of the number of providers for these attributes is highly skewed, with only 13.7% of the attributes (a total of 21) provided by at least one third of the sources, and over 86% attributes provided by fewer than 25% of the sources. The Flight domain does not exhibit as much schema-level variety, with the 38 sources providing 43 attributes, which are manually matched to obtain 15 globally distinct attributes.

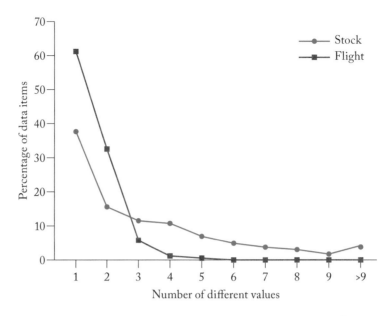

FIGURE 1.4: Consistency of data items in the Stock and Flight domains [Li et al. 2012].

**Veracity.**   The quality of data is not as high as expected, given that the data in the domains studied are expected to be quite clean. In particular, the data in these domains exhibit significant levels of inconsistency. In the Stock domain, for example, the number of different values (even after allowing for some value tolerance) for a data item ranges from 1–13, with an average of 3.7; further, inconsistent values are provided by different sources for over 60% of the data items. Value inconsistency is much lower in the Flight domain, where the number of different values (after allowing for value tolerance) for a data item ranges from 1–5, with an average of 1.45; further, inconsistent values are provided by different sources for fewer than 40% of the data items. There are different reasons for the observed inconsistencies, including semantic ambiguity, out-of-date data, and errors. Figure 1.4 illustrates the distribution of number of values for data items for both domains. Li et al. show that these inconsistencies cannot be effectively addressed by using *naive voting*, which often has an even lower accuracy than the highest accuracy from a single source.

Similarly, they observe that the accuracy of deep web sources can vary a lot. In the Stock domain, the average source accuracy is just 0.86, and only 35% of the sources have an accuracy above 0.9. While most of the authoritative sources have an accuracy above 0.9, their coverages are all below 0.9, implying that one cannot rely on a single authoritative source and ignore all other sources. In the Flight domain, the average source accuracy is even lower, just 0.8, and

29% of sources have an accuracy below 0.7. Authoritative sources in this domain again have accuracies above 0.9, but their coverages are all below 0.9.

Finally, Li et al. [2012] observe copying between deep web sources in each domain. In some cases, the copying is claimed explicitly, while in other cases it is detected by observing embedded interfaces or query redirection. Interestingly, the accuracy of the original sources that are copied is not always high, ranging from 0.75–0.92 for Stock, and from 0.53–0.93 for Flight.

### 1.2.5    CASE STUDY: SURFACE WEB STRUCTURED DATA

The static HTML pages on the surface web obviously contain a vast volume of unstructured data, but also include a huge volume of structured data in the form of HTML tables, such as the table in Figure 1.5. Cafarella et al. [2008b] and Lautert et al. [2013] experimentally study the *volume* and structural *variety* of such tables on the web.

This work is motivated by the fact that the surface web is typically modeled as a hyperlinked collection of unstructured documents, which tends to ignore the relational data contained in web documents. For example, most wikipedia pages contain high-quality relational data that provide

| Rank ⬍ | Airline ⬍ | country ⬍ | revenue ($B) ⬍ | profit ($B) ⬍ | assets ($B) ⬍ | market cap. ($B) ⬍ |
|---|---|---|---|---|---|---|
| 1 | Deutsche Lufthansa | | 39.7 | 1.3 | 37.5 | 9.7 |
| 2 | American Airlines [1] | | 38.7 | -1.3 | 32.9 | 3.9 |
| 3 | United Continental Holdings | | 37.2 | -0.7 | 37.6 | 10.3 |
| 4 | Delta Air Lines | | 36.7 | 1 | 44.6 | 13.6 |
| 5 | Air France-KLM | | 33.8 | -1.6 | 34.7 | 3.1 |
| 6 | International Airlines Group | | 23.9 | -1.2 | 25.6 | 7.6 |
| 7 | All Nippon Airways | | 17.1 | 0.3 | 23.5 | 7.8 |
| 8 | Southwest Airlines | | 17.1 | 0.4 | 18.6 | 9 |
| 9 | Qantas Airways | | 16.1 | -0.3 | 21.7 | 4.1 |
| 10 | China Southern Airlines | | 15.7 | 0.4 | 22.9 | 5.8 |

FIGURE 1.5:  High-quality table on the web.

valuable information on just about every topic. By explicitly recognizing relational tables on the surface web, which are accessible to crawlers, web search engines can return such tables as well in response to user keyword queries.

## Main Questions

These studies focus on two main questions related to the "V" dimensions presented in Section 1.2.1.

- How many high-quality relational tables are present on the surface web? How does one distinguish them from other uses of HTML tables (for example, form layout)?

- How heterogeneous are these tables?

  For example, what is the distribution of table sizes, in terms of number of rows and columns? How many of these tables have a richer structure (for example, nested tables, cross-tabs) than conventional relational tables?

## Study Methodology

Cafarella et al. [2008b] start from a multi-billion page english language portion of the Google crawl, and use an HTML parser to obtain all occurrences of the HTML `table` tag. Only a small fraction of the identified tables are high-quality relational tables, and they use the following methodology to distinguish them from non-relational uses of the HTML tag.

1. They use parsers to eliminate obviously non-relational tables, including extremely small tables (fewer than two rows or two columns), those that are embedded in HTML forms (which are used for visual layout of user input fields), and calendars.

2. They use a sample of the remaining tables, and human labeling to estimate the total fraction of high-quality relational tables.

3. They train a classifier to distinguish between relational tables and other uses of the HTML `table` tag, such as page layout and property sheets, using a variety of table-level features. They subsequently collect distributional statistics using the output of the classifer.

Lautert et al. [2013] observe that even high-quality tables on the web are structurally heterogeneous, with horizontal, vertical, and matrix structures, some having cells that span multiple rows or columns, some with multiple values in individual cells, and so on. They use the following methodology to quantify the structural heterogeneity of tables on the web.

1. They extract all HTML tables from a collection of crawled sources starting from wikipedia, e-commerce, news, and university sources, visiting a total of 174,927 HTML pages, and extracting 342,795 unique HTML tables.

TABLE 1.11: Row statistics on high-quality relational tables on the web [Cafarella et al. 2008b]

| Number of Rows | Percent of Tables |
|---|---|
| 2-9 | 64.07 |
| 10–19 | 15.83 |
| 20–29 | 7.61 |
| 30+ | 12.49 |

2. They develop a supervised *neural network* classifer to classify tables into different categories, using a list of 25 layout, HTML, and lexical features. The training set uses 4,000 web tables.

## Main Results

We categorize the main results of these studies according to the investigated "V" dimensions.

**Volume.**   First, Cafarella et al. [2008b] extract approximately 14.1 billion raw HTML tables from the crawl. Of these, 89.4% (or 12.5 billion) are eliminated as obviously non-relational (almost all of which are extremely small tables) using their parsers. Of the remaining tables, human judgement is used on a sample to determine about 10.4% (or 1.1% of raw HTML tables) as high-quality relational tables. This results in an estimate of 154 million high-quality relational tables on the web.

First, Cafarella et al. [2008b] train a classifier using features such as numbers of rows and columns, number of rows with mostly nulls, number of columns with non-string data, average and standard deviation of string lengths in cells, and so on, to identify high-quality relational tables with a high recall of 0.81, even though the precision is lower at 0.41. Using the results of the classifier, they identify distributional statistics on numbers of rows and columns of high-quality relational tables. More than 93% of these tables have between two and nine columns; there are very few high-quality tables with a very large number of attributes. In contrast, there is a greater diversity in the number of rows among high-quality tables, as shown in Table 1.11.

**Variety.**   Lautert et al. [2013] determine that there is considerable structural variety even among the high-quality tables on the web. Only 17.8% of the high-quality tables on the web are akin to traditional RDBMS tables (each cell contains a single value, and does not span more than one row or column). The two biggest reasons for tables on the web differing from RDBMS tables are: (i) 74.9% of the tables have cells with multiple values (of the same type or of different types) and (ii) 12.9% of the tables have cells that span multiple rows or columns.

### 1.2.6    CASE STUDY: EXTRACTED KNOWLEDGE TRIPLES

Our final case study is about domain-independent structured data represented as ⟨subject, predicate, object⟩ knowledge triples, obtained using web-scale information extraction techniques. In our Flight example, the triples ⟨*Airline1_49*, *departs_from*, *EWR*⟩ and ⟨*Airline1_49*, *arrives_at*, *SFO*⟩ represent that the Departure Airport and Arrival Airport of Airline1's flight *49* are *EWR* and *SFO*, respectively. Dong et al. [2014b] experimentally study the *volume* and *veracity* of such knowledge triples obtained by crawling a large set of web pages and extracting triples from them.

This work is motivated by the task of automatically constructing large-scale knowledge bases by using multiple extractors to extract (possibly conflicting) values from each data source for each data item, then resolving various ambiguities present in the extracted triples to construct a high quality knowledge base.

#### Main Questions

This study focuses on two main questions related to the "V" dimensions presented in Section 1.2.1.

- What are the number and distributional properties of knowledge triples that can be extracted from web pages?

  For example, how many triples can be extracted from DOM trees found in web pages vs. using natural language processing techniques on unstructured text?

- What is the quality of the extracted triples, and the accuracy of the extractors that are used for this purpose?

#### Study Methodology

Dong et al. [2014b] crawl over 1 billion web pages, to extract knowledge triples from four types of web content, using the following methodology.

1. They extract knowledge triples from: (i) text documents, by examining phrases and sentences; (ii) DOM trees, which can be found on surface web pages (e.g., web lists), as well as in deep web sources; (iii) web tables, which contain high quality relational information, where rows represent subjects, columns represent predicates, and the corresponding cells contain the objects of the triples; and (iv) web annotations, manually created by webmasters using standard web ontologies such as http://schema.org.

2. They limit attention to extracting triples whose subjects and predicates exist in the manually curated *Freebase* knowledge base [Bollacker et al. 2008].

3. The quality of the extracted knowledge is also evaluated against the Freebase knowledge base as a gold standard. Specifically, if an extracted triple ⟨$s$, $p$, $o$⟩ occurs in Freebase, it is considered to be true; if ⟨$s$, $p$, $o$⟩ does not occur in Freebase, but ⟨$s$, $p$, $o'$⟩ does, then the extracted triple ⟨$s$, $p$, $o$⟩ is considered to be false; otherwise it is not included in the gold standard.

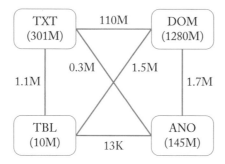

FIGURE 1.6: Contributions and overlaps between different types of web contents [Dong et al. 2014b].

## Main Results

We categorize the main results of this study according to the investigated "V" dimensions.

**Volume.** First, Dong et al. [2014b] extract 1.6 billion distinct triples, with about 80% of the triples from DOM trees, followed by about 19% from text documents, with little overlap between the triples extracted from the different types of web content, as shown in Figure 1.6.

Second, these extracted triples are associated with 43 million subjects and 4.5 thousand predicates (with 337 million (subject, predicate) pairs) from Freebase. Most distributions (such as #triples per subject) are highly skewed, with a long tail; for example, there are over 1 million triples for each of the top 5 entities, whereas for 56% entities they extract no more than 10 triples each.

**Veracity.** Among the 1.6 billion triples, 40% (or 650 million) have gold standard labels, of which 200 million are considered as true. Thus, the overall accuracy of extracted triples is only about 30%. Most of the errors are due to errors in the extractions, but a small percentage are due to wrong information provided by the sources.

The study also shows a high variance in the accuracy of the extractors.

## 1.3   BDI: OPPORTUNITIES

BDI does not only come with difficult challenges, characterized along the "V" dimensions, as we discussed in Section 1.2. There are also interesting opportunities enabled by BDI and the infrastructures used for managing and analyzing big data, to effectively address these challenges. We focus on three such opportunities.

### 1.3.1   DATA REDUNDANCY

The data obtained from different sources often overlap, resulting in a *high data redundancy* across the large number of sources that need to be integrated.

This is evident in our motivating Flights example, where information such as Departure Airport, Scheduled Departure Time, Arrival Airport, and Scheduled Arrival Time about Airline1's flight *49* can be obtained from each of the sources Airline1, Airport3 and Airfare4.

The case studies presented in Sections 1.2.3 and 1.2.4 illustrate the redundancy that exists in many domains. Specifically, the study by Dalvi et al. [2012] mentions that the average number of sources per entity is quite large in all the domains studied, with 56 sources per hotel phone number and 251 sources per library home page as particularly notable, as shown in Figure 1.3. Further, this high average value is not just due to extreme skew; for example, over 80% of restaurant phone numbers are present in at least 10 distinct sources, as shown by the 10-coverage plot in Figure 1.2. Similarly, the study by Li et al. [2012] identifies 16 popular attributes in the Stock domain and 6 popular attributes in the Flight domain that are provided by at least one third of the sources analyzed in each of these domains.

One key advantage of this data redundancy is to effectively address the *veracity* challenge in BDI, as we discuss in detail in Chapter 4. Intuitively, if there are only a few sources that provide overlapping information, and the sources provide conflicting values for a particular data item, it is difficult to identify the true value with high confidence. But with a large number of sources, as is the case in BDI, one can use sophisticated data fusion techniques to discover the truth.

A second advantage of data redundancy is to begin to address the *variety* challenge in BDI, and identify attribute matchings between the source schemas, which are critical for schema alignment. Intuitively, if there is significant data redundancy in a domain, and the bi-partite graph of entities and sources is well connected (as in the domains studied by Dalvi et al. [2012]), one can start with a small seed set of known entities, and use search engine technology to discover most of the entities in that domain. When these entities have different schemas associated with them in the different sources, one can naturally identify attribute matchings between the schemas used by the different sources.

A third advantage of data redundancy is the ability to discover relevant sources for BDI in a domain, when sources are not all known *a priori*. The key intuition again is to take advantage of a well-connected bi-partite graph of entities and sources, start with a small seed set of known entities, and use search engine technology to iteratively discover new sources and new entities, in an alternating manner.

## 1.3.2    LONG DATA

A significant source of big data in practice is *long data*, that is, data collected about evolving entities over time.

In our motivating Flights example, the schedules of airlines evolve over time, as illustrated in the table Airline1.Schedule. In practice, airline and airport sources typically provide estimated flight departure and arrival times, which can vary considerably over short time periods; airplane maintenance and repair logs provide insight about airplane quality over time, and so on.

While the case studies that we presented earlier in this chapter do not specifically deal with long data, some of the techniques that we will describe in subsequent chapters, especially for record linkage (Chapter 3) and data fusion (Chapter 4), take considerable advantage of the presence of long data.

Intuitively, entities in the real world evolve, which result in their attribute values changing over time. The information provided by data sources that contain such entities is not always fresh, and out-of-date values are common, as illustrated in the table Airfare4.Flight. Record linkage and data fusion in such scenarios are challenging, but can take advantage of the fact that evolution of entities is typically a gradual and relatively smooth process: (i) even when some attributes of a flight (e.g., Scheduled Departure Time) evolve, other attributes (e.g., Departure Airport) do not necessarily change; and (ii) even when entities evolve over short time periods, changes in attribute values are usually not erratic (e.g., the changes to estimated arrival time of a flight as reported by the airline).

### 1.3.3    BIG DATA PLATFORMS

The management and analysis of big data has benefited considerably from significant advances in recent years from scalable big data platforms on clusters of commodity hardware (e.g., Hadoop), and distributed programming models (e.g., MapReduce).

Big data integration can be extremely resource intensive, with each of the tasks of schema alignment, record linkage, and data fusion requiring significant computational resources. While much work remains to be done to take full advantage of the big data platforms available, recent work in this area has brought hope that these tasks can in fact be effectively parallelized. We present a few such techniques, especially for record linkage and data fusion, in subsequent chapters.

## 1.4    OUTLINE OF BOOK

The rest of the book is structured as follows. In the next three chapters, we focus on each of the main tasks of data integration. Chapter 2 focuses on *schema alignment*, Chapter 3 focuses on *record linkage*, and Chapter 4 focuses on *data fusion*. Each of these chapters is organized similarly: we start with a quick tour of the task in the context of traditional data integration, before describing how the various BDI challenges of volume, velocity, variety, and veracity have been addressed in the recent literature. In Chapter 5, we outline emerging topics that are specific to BDI and identify promising directions of future work in this area. Finally, Chapter 6 summarizes and concludes the book.

CHAPTER 2

# Schema Alignment

The first component of data integration is *schema alignment*. As we showed in Section 1.2.3, there can be thousands to millions of data sources in the same domain, but they often describe the domain using different schemas. As an illustration, in the motivating example in Section 1.1, the four sources describe the flight domain using very different schemas: they contain different numbers of tables and different numbers of attributes; they may use different attribute names for the same attribute (e.g., Scheduled Arrival Date in Airline2.Flight vs. Scheduled in Airport3.Arrivals); they may apply different semantics for attributes with the same name (e.g., Arrival Time may mean landing time in one source and arrival-at-gate time in another source). To integrate data from different sources, the first step is to align the schemas and understand which attributes have the same semantics and which ones do not.

When data integration started, the goal was often to integrate tens to hundreds of data sources created independently in an organization. Semi-automatic tools such as Clio [Fagin et al. 2009] were created to simplify schema alignment. Section 2.1 briefly overviews traditional solutions.

The big data environment makes the problem significantly harder. Instead of integrating data within an organization, the goal is often to integrate structured data from the web, either in the form of deep web data, or in the form of web tables or web lists. As a result, the number of data sources available for integration explodes from hundreds of sources to millions of sources; and the schemas of the data are constantly changing. Such *volume* and *velocity* of big data also increase the *variety* of data remarkably, calling for new techniques and infrastructures to resolve the schema heterogeneity.

Section 2.2 describes how *dataspace systems* extend the traditional data integration infrastructure to address the *variety* and *velocity* challenges of big data. Dataspaces follow a *pay-as-you-go* principle: they provide best-effort services such as simple keyword search at the beginning, and gradually evolve schema alignment and improve search quality over time.

Section 2.3 describes new techniques for schema alignment, which make it possible to address both the *volume* and the *variety* challenges in integrating structured data on the web. This includes surfacing deep web data by crawling and indexing, and searching and integrating data from web tables and web lists.

FIGURE 2.1:  Traditional schema alignment: three steps.

## 2.1    TRADITIONAL SCHEMA ALIGNMENT: A QUICK TOUR

The traditional approach for schema alignment contains three steps: creating a mediated schema, attribute matching, and schema mapping, depicted in Figure 2.1.

### 2.1.1   MEDIATED SCHEMA

First, a mediated schema is created to provide a unified and virtual view of the disparate sources and capture the salient aspects of the domain being considered. Often times the mediated schema is created manually. For the motivating example, one possible mediated schema is shown as follows.

| Mediated schema Mediate for the motivating example |
| --- |
| Flight(Airline (AL), Flight ID (FI), Flight Number (FN), Flight date (FD), Departure Airport (DA), Departure Gate (DG), Departure Terminal (DTE), Scheduled Departure Time (SDT), Actual Departure Time (ADT), Arrival Airport (AA), Arrival Gate (AG), Arrival Terminal (ATE) Scheduled Arrival Time (SAT), Actual Arrival Time (AAT)) |
| Fare(Flight ID (FI), Fare Class (FC), Fare (F)) |
| Airport(Airport Code (AC), Airport Name (AN), Airport City (ACI), Airport State (AST), Airport Country (ACO)) |

The mediated schema Mediate contains three tables: Flight for flight information; Fare for fare information; and Airport for airport information. As a unified view, the mediated schema often contains more information than each schema. For example, it contains information for flight fares and airports, which do not exist in Airline1, Airline2, and Airport3; on the other hand, it contains the actual departure and arrival times and other information that do not exist in Airfare4. Also note that the mediated schema may not contain every piece of information from every source. For example, Airport3 provides information about runway but that is not included in the mediated schema as it is deemed as rarely queried by users.

### 2.1.2   ATTRIBUTE MATCHING

Next, attributes in each source schema are matched to the corresponding attributes in the mediated schema. In many cases the attribute correspondence is one-to-one; however, sometimes one attribute

FIGURE 2.2: Attribute matching from Airline1.Flight to Mediate.Flight.

in the mediated schema may correspond to the combination of several attributes in the source schema, and vice versa. For example, the combination of ACI, AST, ACO in Mediate.Airport corresponds to AN in Airinfo5.AirportCodes. Figure 2.2 gives an example of schema matching from Airline1.Flight to Mediate.Flight.

There have been many techniques proposed for attribute matching, exploring similarity of attribute names, types, values, and the neighborhood relationships between attributes. Comprehensive surveys are by Rahm and Bernstein [2001] and Bellahsene et al. [2011].

### 2.1.3    SCHEMA MAPPING

According to the correspondences of attribute matching, a *schema mapping* is built between each source schema and the mediated schema. Such mappings specify the semantic relationships between the contents of different data sources and would be used to reformulate a user query on the mediated schema into a set of queries on the underlying data sources.

There are three types of schema mappings: *global-as-view (GAV)*, *local-as-view (LAV)*, and *global-local-as-view (GLAV)*. Global-as-view specifies how to obtain data in the mediated schema by querying the data in source schemas; in other words, the mediated data can be considered as a database *view* of the source data. Local-as-view specifies the source data as a view of the mediated data; this approach makes it easy to add a new data source with a new schema. Finally, global-local-as-view specifies both the mediated data and the local data as views of data of a virtual schema.

As an example, the following table gives the GAV mapping and the LAV mapping between the mediated schema and Airline1. The mappings are given in Datalog. The GAV mapping states that one can obtain attribute values in Mediate.Flight by joining Airline1.Schedule and Airline1.Flight on Flight ID (FI). The LAV mapping states that one can obtain values in Airline1.Schedule and Airline1.Flight by projecting on Mediate.Flight for all database tuples with *Airline1* as the value for Airline (AL).

| Mappings between mediated schema Mediate and source schema Airline1 |
|---|

GAV    Mediate.Flight('*Airline1*', *fi, fn, fd, da*, gate(*dg*), terminal(*dg*), *sdt, adt, aa,*
          gate(*ag*), terminal(*ag*), *sat, aat*)
       :- Airline1.Schedule(*fi, fn, sd, ed, sdt, da, sat, aa*), Airline1.Flight(*fi, fd, adt,*
          *dg, ad, aat, ag, pi*)

LAV    Airline1.Schedule(*fi, fn,* —, —, *sdt, da, sat, aa*)
          :- Mediate.Flight('*Airline1*', *fi, fn, fd, da, dg, dt, sdt, adt, aa, ag, at, sat, aat*)

       Airline1.Flight(*fi, fd, adt,* CAT(*dg, dt*), —, *aat,* CAT(*ag, at*), —)
          :- Mediate.Flight('*Airline1*', *fi, fn, fd, da, dg, dt, sdt, adt, aa, ag, at, sat, aat*)

Tools have been developed for semi-automatically building schema mappings according to attribute matching results [Fagin et al. 2009]. A user query on the mediated schema will be reformulated to queries on the source schemas according to schema mappings [Halevy 2001].

### 2.1.4    QUERY ANSWERING

Figure 2.3 depicts query answering in a traditional data integration system.

Users query the underlying data in a data-integration system by formulating queries over the mediated schema. As an example, a user can query information about all flights departing from *EWR*, arriving at *SFO*, and having a fare below $1000 as follows.

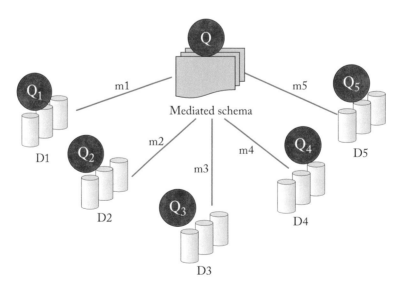

FIGURE 2.3: Query answering in a traditional data-integration system.

```
SELECT DISTINCT Flight.*
FROM Flight, Fare
WHERE Flight.DA='EWR' AND Flight.AA='SFO'
    AND Flight.FI = Fare.FI AND Fare.F < 1000
```

The user query is reformulated according to schema mappings between the mediated schema and each source schema. For the example query, it cannot be answered on Airline1, Airline2, and Airport3 since they lack information on flight fares; however, it can be answered on Airfare4, together with Airinfo5, using the following reformulated query.

```
SELECT DISTINCT Fl.FI, Fl.FN, Fl.DD, A1.AC, . . .
FROM Airfare4.Flight AS Fl, Airfare4.Fares AS Fa,
    Airinfo5.AirportCodes AS A1, Airinfo5.AirportCodes AS A2
WHERE A1.AC='EWR' AND A2.AC='SFO'
    AND A1.AN CONTAINS Fl.DA AND A2.AN CONTAINS Fl.AA
    AND Fl.FI = Fa.FI AND Fa.F < 1000
```

Finally, the query processor answers the queries on the source data, and returns a union of the answers to the users.

## 2.2    ADDRESSING THE VARIETY AND VELOCITY CHALLENGES

A data integration system heavily relies on the schema mappings between the data sources and the mediated schema for query reformulation. However, it is well known that creating and maintaining such mappings is non-trivial and requires significant resources, upfront effort, and technical expertise. Schema mapping tools have been built to help generate schema mappings; however, domain experts still need to get involved in refining the automatically generated mappings. As a result, schema alignment is one of the major bottlenecks in building a data integration system. In the big data context, where there can be a huge number of data sources and the schemas of the data can keep changing, having perfect schema mappings and keeping them up-to-date with the constantly evolving source schemas is infeasible.

Franklin et al. [2005] propose a *dataspace support platform* that addresses the *variety* and *velocity* of data by *pay-as-you-go* data management: provide some services from the outset and evolve the schema mappings between the different sources on an as-needed basis. Given a query, such a platform generates *best-effort* or approximate answers from data sources where perfect schema mappings do not exist. When it discovers a large number of sophisticated queries or data mining tasks over certain sources, it will guide the users to make additional efforts to integrate those sources more precisely.

This section describes some key techniques for dataspace systems. Section 2.2.1 describes how to provide best-effort querying by building probabilistic mediated schemas and probabilistic schema mappings. Section 2.2.2 describes how to solicit user feedback for confirming candidate mappings in a pay-as-you-go manner.

## 2.2.1    PROBABILISTIC SCHEMA ALIGNMENT

To provide best-effort services on dataspaces, uncertainty needs to be handled at various levels. First, when the number of data sources is large, there will be uncertainty about how to model the domain; thus, there is uncertainty on the creation of the mediated schema. Second, attributes can have ambiguous meanings, some attributes can overlap in their meanings and the meanings can evolve over time; thus, there is uncertainty on attribute matching. Third, the scale of the data and the constant evolution of source schemas prevent generating and maintaining precise mappings; thus, there is uncertainty on schema mapping.

Such uncertainties can be addressed in two ways. First, a probabilistic mediated schema can be built to capture the uncertainty on how to model the domain. Each possible mediated schema in the probabilistic mediated schema represents one way of clustering the source attributes, where attributes in the same cluster are considered as having the same semantics [Das Sarma et al. 2008].

Second, a probabilistic schema mapping can be built between each source schema and each possible mediated schema in the probabilistic mediated schema. A probabilistic schema mapping contains a set of attribute matchings, each describing one possible matching between source attributes and the attribute clusters in a mediated schema [Dong et al. 2009c].

This section focuses on a setting in which each of the sources is a single relational table. As a result, the schema mapping can be easily inferred from the attribute matching. We next describe each component in detail and describe query answering in this new architecture at the end.

### Probabilistic Mediated Schema

The mediated schema is the set of schema terms (e.g., relational table, attribute names) on which queries are posed. It describes the aspects of the domain that are important for the integration application. Consider automatically inferring a mediated schema from a set of data sources each with a single relational table. In this context, the mediated schema can be thought of as a "clustering" of source attributes, where similar attributes are grouped into the same cluster to form a *mediated attribute*. Note that whereas in a traditional mediated schema an attribute has a name, naming of an attribute is not necessary in such a mediated schema. Users can use any source attribute in their queries and the source attribute will be replaced everywhere with the mediated attribute whose corresponding cluster contains that source attribute. In practice, the most frequent source attribute can be used to represent a mediated attribute when exposing the mediated schema to users.

The quality of query answers critically depends on the quality of this clustering. However, because of the heterogeneity of the data sources being integrated, typically the semantics of the source attributes and in turn the clustering is uncertain, illustrated using the next example.

**Example 2.1**    Consider the following two source schemas both describing flights.

S1(Flight Number (FN), Departure Gate Time (DGT), Takeoff Time (TT),

Landing Time (LT), Arrival Gate Time (AGT))

S2(Flight Number (FN), Departure Time (DT), Arrival Time (AT))

In S2, the attribute DT can be either the departure gate time or the takeoff time. Similarly, AT can be either the arrival gate time or the landing time.

Consider clustering the attributes of S1 and S2. There are multiple ways to cluster the attributes and they correspond to different mediated schemas. A few are listed as follows:

Med1({FN}, {DT, DGT, TT}, {AT, AGT, LT})

Med2({FN}, {DT, DGT}, {TT}, {AT, LT}, {AGT})

Med3({FN}, {DT, DGT}, {TT}, {AT, AGT}, {LT})

Med4({FN}, {DT, TT}, {DGT}, {AT, LT}, {AGT})

Med5({FN}, {DT}, {DGT}, {TT}, {AT}, {AGT}, {LT})

None of the listed mediated schemas is perfect. Schema Med1 groups together multiple attributes from S1. Schema Med2 seems inconsistent because Departure Time is grouped with Departure Gate Time while Arrival Time is grouped with Landing Time. Schemas Med3, Med4 and Med5 are partially correct but none of them captures the fact that Departure time and Arrival time can be either gate time, or takeoff time and landing time.

As a result, none of the listed mediated schemas will return ideal answers for all user queries, even if perfect schema mappings exist. For example, using Med1 prohibits returning correct answers for queries that contain both Departure Gate Time and Takeoff Time, because they are taken to be the same attribute. As another example, consider a query that contains Departure Time and Arrival Time. Using Med3 or Med4 as the mediated schema will unnecessarily favor takeoff time and landing time over gate time, or vice versa. A system with Med2 will incorrectly favor answers that return the departure gate time together with arrival landing time. A system with Med5 may either miss information from sources that provide DGT, TT, AGT, LT, or have the same problems as using Med2-Med4.

As a solution, a probabilistic mediated schema can be constructed for all clusterings that are most likely to be true, and each clustering is associated with a probability. For example, a probabilistic mediated schema can be constructed to include Med3 and Med4, each with probability 0.6 and 0.4 respectively.

| Possible Mediated Schema | Probability |
|---|---|
| Med3({FN}, {DT, DGT}, {TT}, {AT, AGT}, {LT}) | 0.6 |
| Med4({FN}, {DT, TT}, {DGT}, {AT, LT}, {AGT}) | 0.4 |

Probabilistic mediated schemas are formally defined as follows. Consider a set of source schemas $\{S_1, \ldots, S_n\}$. Denote the attributes in schema $S_i$, $i \in [1, n]$, by $\overline{A}(S_i)$, and the set of all source attributes as $\mathcal{A}$. That is, $\mathcal{A} = \overline{A}(S_1) \cup \ldots \cup \overline{A}(S_n)$. Denote a mediated schema for the set of sources $\{S_1, \ldots, S_n\}$ by $\text{Med} = \{\mathbf{A}_1, \ldots, \mathbf{A}_m\}$, where each $\mathbf{A}_i$, $i \in [1, m]$, is called a *mediated attribute*. The mediated attributes are *sets* of attributes from the sources, (i.e., $\mathbf{A}_i \subseteq \mathcal{A}$); for each $i, j \in [1, m]$, $i \neq j$, it holds that $\mathbf{A}_i \cap \mathbf{A}_j = \emptyset$. As stated before, if a query contains an attribute $A \in \mathbf{A}_i$, $i \in [1, m]$, then when answering the query $A$ is replaced everywhere with $\mathbf{A}_i$.

A *probabilistic mediated schema (p-med-schema)* consists of a set of mediated schemas, each with a probability indicating the likelihood that the schema correctly describes the domain of the sources.

**Definition 2.1** (Probabilistic Mediated Schema) [Das Sarma et al. 2008] Let $\{S_1, \ldots, S_n\}$ be a set of schemas. A *probabilistic mediated schema (p-med-schema) for* $\{S_1, \ldots, S_n\}$ is a set

$$\text{pMed} = \{(\text{Med}_1, \Pr(\text{Med}_1)), \ldots, (\text{Med}_l, \Pr(\text{Med}_l))\},$$

where

- for each $i \in [1, l]$, $\text{Med}_i$ is a mediated schema for $S_1, \ldots, S_n$, and for each $i, j \in [1, l]$, $i \neq j$, $\text{Med}_i$ and $\text{Med}_j$ correspond to different clusterings of the source attributes in $\mathcal{A}$; and

- $\Pr(\text{Med}_i) \in (0, 1]$, and $\Sigma_{i=1}^{l} \Pr(\text{Med}_i) = 1$.

Das Sarma et al. [2008] propose an algorithm for creating a probabilistic mediated schema for source schemas $S_1, \ldots, S_n$: first construct the multiple mediated schemas $\text{Med}_1, \ldots, \text{Med}_l$ in pMed, and then assign each of them a probability.

Two pieces of information available in the source schemas can serve as evidence for attribute clustering: (1) pairwise similarity of source attributes; and (2) statistical co-occurrence properties of source attributes. The first piece of information indicates when two attributes are likely to be similar, and is used for creating multiple mediated schemas. One can apply a collection of attribute matching modules to compute pairwise attribute similarity. The similarity $s(a_i, a_j)$ between two source attributes $a_i$ and $a_j$ measures how closely the two attributes represent the same real-world concept. The second piece of information indicates when two attributes are likely to be different, and is used for assigning probabilities to each of the mediated schemas.

For the example schemas S1 and S2, pairwise string similarity and dictionary matching would indicate that attribute DT can be similar to both DGT and TT because of attribute-name similarity and value similarity. However, since the first source schema contains DGT and TT together, they cannot refer to the same concept. Hence, the first schema suggests DGT is different from TT, making it less likely for clustering DT, DGT, TT all together.

More specifically, given source schemas $S_1, \ldots, S_n$, the p-med-schema pMed is created in three steps. First, compute similarity between attributes. Put attributes whose similarity is above a threshold $\tau + \epsilon$ into the same cluster, and call a pair of attributes whose similarity falls in $[\tau - \epsilon, \tau + \epsilon]$ an *uncertain pair*. Second, create a mediated schema for every subset of uncertain pairs, where each pair of attributes in the subset are put in the same cluster. The resulting sets of mediated schemas form the possible mediated schemas in the probabilistic mediated schema. Finally, consider a source schema $S_i$, $i \in [1, n]$, as consistent with a possible mediated schema $\text{Med}_j$, $j \in [1, l]$, if no two attributes in $\overline{A}(S_i)$ occur in a cluster represented by a mediated attribute in $\text{Med}_j$. For each possible mediated schema, count the number of source schemas consistent with it and compute its probability proportional to the count.

## Probabilistic Schema Mappings

Schema mappings describe the relationship between the contents of the sources and that of the mediated data. In many applications it is impossible to provide all schema mappings upfront. Probabilistic schema mappings can capture uncertainty on mappings between schemas. We again start with an illustrative example, then formally define probabilistic schema mappings, and describe how they are generated at the end.

**Example 2.2**   Continue with Example 2.1. Consider the mapping between S1 and the mediated schema Med3. A semi-automatic attribute-matching tool may generate four possible mappings between S1 and Med3, each in the form of attribute matchings as only single-table schemas are considered. They are shown as follows, where DDGT ={ DT, DGT } and AAGT ={ AT, AGT }.

| | Possible Mapping Between S1 and Med3 | Probability |
|---|---|---|
| $M_1$ | {(FN, FN), (DGT, DDGT), (TT, TT), (AGT, AAGT), (LT, LT)} | 0.64 |
| $M_2$ | {(FN, FN), (DGT, DDGT), (TT, TT), (AGT, LT), (LT, AAGT)} | 0.16 |
| $M_3$ | {(FN, FN), (DGT, TT), (TT, DDGT), (AGT, AAGT), (LT, LT)} | 0.16 |
| $M_4$ | {(FN, FN), (DGT, TT), (TT, DDGT), (AGT, LT), (LT, AAGT)} | 0.04 |

Whereas the four mappings all map S1.FN to Med3.FN, they map other attributes in the source and the mediated schemas differently. For example, mapping $M_1$ maps S1.DGT to Med3.DDGT, whereas $M_3$ maps S1.DGT to Med3.TT. To capture the uncertainty about which mapping is correct, instead of discarding some of the possible mappings arbitrarily or according to intervention of domain experts, all mappings are kept for query answering and each is assigned a probability indicating its likelihood of being true.

Similarly, there is a probabilistic mapping between S1 and Med4, where DTT ={ DT, TT } and ALT ={ AT, LT }.

| | Possible Mapping Between S1 and Med4 | Probability |
|---|---|---|
| $M_5$ | {(FN, FN), (DGT, DGT), (TT, DTT), (AGT, AGT), (LT, ALT)} | 0.64 |
| $M_6$ | {(FN, FN), (DGT, DGT), (TT, DTT), (AGT, ALT), (LT, AGT)} | 0.16 |
| $M_7$ | {(FN, FN), (DGT, DTT), (TT, DGT), (AGT, AGT), (LT, ALT)} | 0.16 |
| $M_8$ | {(FN, FN), (DGT, DTT), (TT, DGT), (AGT, ALT), (LT, AGT)} | 0.04 |

Before defining probabilistic schema mappings, let us first review non-probabilistic schema mappings. The goal of a schema mapping is to specify the semantic relationships between a *source schema S* and a *target schema T* (e.g., mediated schema). The schema mapping considered in this section is of a limited form: it contains one-to-one matching between attributes in $S$ and attributes in $T$.

Intuitively, a probabilistic schema mapping describes a probability distribution of a set of *possible* schema mappings between a source schema and a target schema.

**Definition 2.2** (Probabilistic Mapping)    [Dong et al. 2009c] Let $S$ and $T$ be relational schemas, each containing a single relational table. A *probabilistic mapping (p-mapping)*, $pM$, between source $S$ and target $T$ is a set $pM = \{(M_1, \Pr(M_1)), \ldots, (M_l, \Pr(M_l))\}$, such that

- for $i \in [1, l]$, $M_i$ is a one-to-one attribute matching between $S$ and $T$, and for every $i, j \in [1, l]$, $i \neq j$, $M_i$ and $M_j$ are different; and

- $\Pr(M_i) \in (0, 1]$ and $\sum_{i=1}^{l} \Pr(M_i) = 1$.

Das Sarma et al. [2008] propose an algorithm for creating a p-mapping. First, compute *weighted matchings* between each pair of source attribute and target attribute. These weighted matchings are created by applying a set of existing attribute matching techniques. The weights are normalized to range $[0, 1]$. Denote the weighted matching between the $i$-th source attribute and the $j$-th target attribute as $m_{i,j} = ((i, j), w_{i,j})$, where $w_{i,j}$ is the weight of matching $(i, j)$.

Although weighted matchings indicate the degree of similarity between pairs of attributes, they do not indicate *which* target attribute a source attribute should map to. For example, a target attribute Arrival Time can be similar both to the source attribute Arrival Gate Time and to Landing Time, so it makes sense to map either of them to Arrival Time in a schema mapping. In fact, given a set of weighted matchings, there could be a *set* of p-mappings that are *consistent with* it.

**Definition 2.3** (Consistent P-mapping)    [Das Sarma et al. 2008] A p-mapping $pM$ is *consistent with* a weighted matching $m_{i,j}$ between a pair of source attribute and target attribute if the sum of the probabilities of all mappings $M \in pM$ containing matching $(i, j)$ equals $w_{i,j}$; that is,

$$w_{i,j} = \sum_{M \in pM, (i,j) \in M} \Pr(M).$$

A p-mapping is *consistent with* a set of weighted matchings **m** if it is consistent with each weighted matching in $m \in \mathbf{m}$.

Given a set of weighted matchings, there can be an infinite number of p-mappings that are consistent with it. The following example illustrates this.

**Example 2.3**    Consider a source schema S(A,B) and a target schema T(A',B'). Assume the following weighted matchings between source and target attributes: $w_{A,A'} = 0.6$ and $w_{B,B'} = 0.5$ (the rest are 0). There are an infinite number of p-mappings that are consistent with this set of weighted matchings and the following table lists two.

| P-mapping | Possible Mapping | Probability |
|---|---|---|
| $pM_1$ | $M_1$: $\{(A, A'), (B, B')\}$ | 0.3 |
| | $M_2$: $\{(A, A')\}$ | 0.3 |
| | $M_3$: $\{(B, B')\}$ | 0.2 |
| | $M_4$: Ø | 0.2 |
| $pM_2$ | $M_1'$: $\{(A, A'), (B, B')\}$ | 0.5 |
| | $M_2'$: $\{(A, A')\}$ | 0.1 |
| | $M_3'$: Ø | 0.4 |

In a sense, $pM_1$ seems better than $pM_2$ because it assumes that the similarity between A and A' is independent of the similarity between B and B'.

In the general case, among the many p-mappings that are consistent with a set of weighted matchings **m**, the best is the one with the *maximum entropy*; that is, the p-mapping whose probability distribution obtains the maximum value of $\sum_{i=1}^{l} -p_i * \log p_i$. In Example 2.3, $pM_1$ obtains the maximum entropy.

The intuition behind maximum entropy is that when selecting among multiple possible distributions on a set of exclusive events, the one that does not favor any of the events over the others is preferred. Hence, the distribution that does not *introduce new information* not known *a priori* is preferred. The principle of maximum entropy is widely used in other areas such as natural language processing.

In summary, a p-mapping can be created in three steps. First, generate the weighted matchings between every pair of attributes in the source schema $S$ and the target schema $T$. Second, enumerate all possible one-to-one schema mappings between $S$ and $T$ that contain a subset of matchings in **m**, denoted by $M_1, \ldots, M_l$. Third, assign probabilities to the mappings by maximizing the entropy of the result p-mapping; in other words, solve the following constraint optimization problem:

$$\text{Maximize} \sum_{k=1}^{l} -p_k * \log p_k \quad \text{subject to:}$$

1. $\forall k \in [1, l], 0 \le p_k \le 1,$

2. $\sum_{k=1}^{l} p_k = 1, \quad \text{and}$

3. $\forall i, j: \sum_{k \in [1,l], (i,j) \in M_k} p_k = w_{i,j}.$

## Query Answering

Before discussing query answering with respect to a p-med-schema and p-mappings, we first need to define the semantics of p-mappings. Intuitively, a probabilistic schema mapping models the uncertainty about which of the mappings in $pM$ is the correct one. When a schema matching system produces a set of candidate matches, there are two ways to interpret the uncertainty: (1) a single mapping in $pM$ is the correct one and it applies to all the data in $S$, or (2) several mappings are partially correct and each is suitable for a subset of tuples in $S$, although it is not known which mapping is the right one for a specific tuple.

Query answering is defined under both interpretations. The first interpretation is referred to as the *by-table* semantics and the second one is referred to as the *by-tuple* semantics of probabilistic mappings. Note that one cannot argue for one interpretation over the other; the needs of the application should dictate the appropriate semantics. The next example illustrates the two semantics.

**Example 2.4**   Continue with Example 2.2 and consider an instance of S1 as follows.

| FN | DGT | TT | LT | AGT |
|----|-----|-----|-----|-----|
| 49 | 18:45 | 18:53 | 20:45 | 20:50 |
| 53 | 15:30 | 15:40 | 20:40 | 20:50 |

Recall that users can compose queries using any attribute in the source. Now consider query $Q$: SELECT AT FROM Med3, where Med3 is given in Example 2.1. Consider the p-mapping in

Example 2.2. Under the by-table semantics, each possible mapping is applied on all tuples in S1 and it generates the following answer.

| By-table Answer (AT) | Probability | | | | |
|---|---|---|---|---|---|
| | $M_1$ | $M_2$ | $M_3$ | $M_4$ | p-mapping |
| 20:50 | 0.64 | — | 0.16 | — | 0.64+0.16=0.8 |
| 20:45 | — | 0.16 | — | 0.04 | 0.16+0.04=0.2 |
| 20:40 | — | 0.16 | — | 0.04 | 0.16+0.04=0.2 |

In contrast, under the by-tuple semantics, different possible mappings are applied on different tuples in S1 and it generates the following answer (details skipped).

| By-tuple Answer (AT) | Probability |
|---|---|
| 20:50 | 0.96 |
| 20:45 | 0.2 |
| 20:40 | 0.2 |

The definition for query answering with respect to p-mappings is a natural extension for query answering with respect to normal mappings, reviewed next. A mapping defines a relationship between instances of $S$ and instances of $T$ that are *consistent* with the mapping.

**Definition 2.4** (Consistent Target Instance)   [Abiteboul and Duschka 1998] Let $M$ be a schema mapping between source $S$ and target $T$ and $D_S$ be an instance of $S$.

An instance $D_T$ of $T$ is said to be *consistent with $D_S$ and $M$*, if for each tuple $t_S \in D_S$, there exists a tuple $t_T \in D_T$, such that for every attribute matching $(a_s, a_t) \in M$, the value of $a_s$ in $t_S$ is the same as the value of $a_t$ in $t_T$.

For a relation mapping $M$ and a source instance $D_S$, there can be an infinite number of target instances that are consistent with $D_S$ and $M$. Denote by $\overline{D_T}(D_S, M)$ the set of all such target instances. The set of answers to a query $Q$ is the intersection of the answers on all instances in $\overline{D_T}(D_S, M)$.

**Definition 2.5** (Certain Answer)   [Abiteboul and Duschka 1998] Let $M$ be a relation mapping between source $S$ and target $T$. Let $Q$ be a query over $T$ and let $D_S$ be an instance of $S$.

A tuple $t$ is said to be a *certain answer of $Q$ with respect to $D_S$ and $M$*, if for every instance $D_T \in \overline{D_T}(D_S, M)$, $t \in Q(D_T)$.

These notions can be generalized to the probabilistic setting, beginning with the by-table semantics. Intuitively, a p-mapping $pM$ describes a set of possible worlds, each with a possible mapping $M \in pM$. In by-table semantics, a source table can fall in one of the possible worlds;

that is, the possible mapping associated with that possible world applies to the whole source table. Following this intuition, target instances that are *consistent with* the source instance are defined as follows.

**Definition 2.6** (By-table Consistent Instance)    [Dong et al. 2009c] Let $pM$ be a p-mapping between source $S$ and target $T$ and $D_S$ be an instance of $S$.

An instance $D_T$ of $T$ is said to be *by-table consistent with* $D_S$ *and* $pM$, if there exists a mapping $M \in pM$ such that $D_T$ is consistent with $D_S$ and $M$.

In the probabilistic context, a probability is assigned to every answer. Intuitively, the certain answers are considered in isolation with respect to each possible mapping. The probability of an answer $t$ is the sum of the probabilities of the mappings for which $t$ is deemed to be a certain answer. By-table answers are defined as follows.

**Definition 2.7** (By-table Answer)    [Dong et al. 2009c] Let $pM$ be a p-mapping between source $S$ and target $T$. Let $Q$ be a query over $T$ and let $D_S$ be an instance of $S$.

Let $t$ be a tuple. Let $\overline{m}(t)$ be the subset of mappings in $pM$, such that for each $M \in \overline{m}(t)$ and for each $D_T \in \overline{D_T}(D_S, M)$, $t \in Q(D_T)$.

Let $p = \sum_{M \in \overline{m}(t)} \Pr(M)$. If $p > 0$, then $(t, p)$ is a *by-table answer of* $Q$ *with respect to* $D_S$ *and* $pM$.

Under the possible-world notions, in by-tuple semantics, different tuples in a source table can fall in different possible worlds; that is, different possible mappings associated with those possible worlds can apply to the different source tuples.

Formally, the key difference in the definition of by-tuple semantics from that of by-table semantics is that a consistent target instance is defined by a mapping *sequence* that assigns a (possibly different) mapping in **M** to each source tuple in $D_S$. (Without losing generality, in order to compare between such sequences, some order is assigned to the tuples in the instance).

**Definition 2.8** (By-tuple Consistent Instance)    [Dong et al. 2009c] Let $pM$ be a p-mapping between source $S$ and target $T$ and let $D_S$ be an instance of $S$ with $d$ tuples.

An instance $D_T$ of $T$ is said to be *by-tuple consistent with* $D_S$ *and* $pM$, if there is a sequence $\langle M^1, \ldots, M^d \rangle$ such that $d$ is the number of tuples in $D_S$ and for every $1 \leq i \leq d$,

- $M^i \in pM$, and

- for the $i^{th}$ tuple of $D_S$, $t_i$, there exists a target tuple $t'_i \in D_T$ such that for each attribute matching $(a_s, a_t) \in M^i$, the value of $a_s$ in $t_i$ is the same as the value of $a_t$ in $t'_i$.

Given a mapping sequence $seq = \langle M^1, \ldots, M^d \rangle$, denote by $\overline{D_T}(D_S, seq)$ the set of all target instances that are consistent with $D_S$ and $seq$. Note that if $D_T$ is by-table consistent with $D_S$ and $M$, then $D_T$ is also by-tuple consistent with $D_S$ and a mapping sequence in which each mapping is $M$.

One can think of every sequence of mappings $seq = \langle M^1, \ldots, M^d \rangle$ as a separate event whose probability is $\Pr(seq) = \Pi_{i=1}^{d} \Pr(M^i)$. If there are $l$ mappings in $pM$, then there are $l^d$ sequences of length $d$, and their probabilities add up to 1. Denote by $\mathbf{seq}_d(pM)$ the set of mapping sequences of length $d$ generated from $pM$.

**Definition 2.9** (By-tuple Answer)   [Dong et al. 2009c] Let $pM$ be a p-mapping between source $S$ and target $T$. Let $Q$ be a query over $T$ and $D_S$ be an instance of $S$ with $d$ tuples.

Let $t$ be a tuple. Let $\overline{seq}(t)$ be the subset of $\mathbf{seq}_d(pM)$, such that for each $seq \in \overline{seq}(t)$ and for each $D_T \in \overline{D_T}(D_S, seq)$, $t \in Q(D_T)$.

Let $p = \sum_{seq \in \overline{seq}(t)} \Pr(seq)$. If $p > 0$, then $(t, p)$ is a *by-tuple answer of $Q$ with respect to $D_S$ and $pM$.*

The set of by-table answers for $Q$ with respect to $D_S$ is denoted by $Q^{table}(D_S)$ and the set of by-tuple answers for $Q$ with respect to $D_S$ is denoted by $Q^{tuple}(D_S)$.

In the case of by-table semantics, answering queries is conceptually simple. Given a p-mapping $pM$ between source $S$ and target $T$ and an SPJ query $Q$ on $T$, compute the certain answers of $Q$ under each of the mappings $M \in pM$. Attach the probability $\Pr(M)$ to every certain answer under $M$. If a tuple is an answer to $Q$ under multiple mappings in $pM$, then add up the probabilities of the different mappings.

To extend the by-table query-answering strategy to by-tuple semantics, one would need to compute the certain answers for every *mapping sequence* generated by $pM$. However, the number of such mapping sequences is exponential in the size of the input data. In fact, it is proved that in general, answering SPJ queries in by-tuple semantics with respect to schema p-mappings is hard.

**Theorem 2.1**   [Dong et al. 2009c] Let $pM$ be a p-mapping and let $Q$ be an SPJ query.

- Answering $Q$ with respect to $pM$ in by-table semantics is in PTIME in the size of the data and the mapping.

- The problem of finding the probability for a by-tuple answer to $Q$ with respect to $pM$ is #P-complete in the size of the data and is in PTIME in the size of the mapping.

*Proof.*  PTIME complexity is obvious. #P-hardness for by-tuple semantics in the size of the data can be proved by reducing the problem of counting the number of variable assignments that satisfy a bipartite monotone 2DNF boolean formula to the problem of finding the query answers.   ∎

Finally, consider the semantics of query answering with respect to a p-med-schema and a set of p-mappings, each for a possible mediated schema. Intuitively, to compute query answers, one should first answer the query with respect to each possible mediated schema, and then for each answer tuple take the sum of its probabilities weighted by the probabilities of the mediated schemas. The formal definition for by-table semantics is as follows; the definition for by-tuple semantics is similar.

**Definition 2.10** (Query Answer Under P-med-schema and P-mappings)    [Das Sarma et al. 2008] Let $S$ be a source schema and pMed $= \{(\text{Med}_1, \text{Pr}(\text{Med}_1)), \ldots, (\text{Med}_l, \text{Pr}(\text{Med}_l))\}$ be a p-med-schema. Let $\mathbf{pM} = \{pM(\text{Med}_1), \ldots, pM(\text{Med}_l)\}$ be a set of p-mappings where $pM(\text{Med}_i)$ is the p-mapping between $S$ and $\text{Med}_i$. Let $D_S$ be an instance of $S$ and $Q$ be a query.

Let $t$ be a tuple. Let $\text{Pr}(t|\text{Med}_i)$, $i \in [1, l]$, be the probability of $t$ in the answer of $Q$ with respect to $\text{Med}_i$ and $pM(\text{Med}_i)$. Let $p = \Sigma_{i=1}^{l} \text{Pr}(t|\text{Med}_i) * \text{Pr}(\text{Med}_i)$. If $p > 0$, then $(t, p)$ is a by-table answer with respect to pMed and $\mathbf{pM}$.

All answers are denoted by $Q_{\mathbf{M},\mathbf{pM}}(D_S)$.

**Example 2.5**    Consider the instance of S1 in Example 2.4 and query $Q$: SELECT AT FROM M. Under the by-table semantics, the answers with respect to pMed in Example 2.1 and $\mathbf{pM}$ in Example 2.2 are shown as follows.

| By-table answer (AT) | Med3 | Med4 | Final Probability |
|:---:|:---:|:---:|:---:|
| 20:50 | 0.8 | 0.2 | 0.8*0.6+0.2*0.4=0.56 |
| 20:45 | 0.2 | 0.8 | 0.2*0.6+0.8*0.4=0.44 |
| 20:40 | 0.2 | 0.8 | 0.2*0.6+0.8*0.4=0.44 |

Such answers have two advantages: (1) answers with departure gate time and arrival gate time and answers with takeoff time and landing time are treated equally, and (2) answers with the correct correlation between departure time and arrival time are favored.

## Main Results

Das Sarma et al. [2008] evaluate the proposed techniques on web tables crawled in five domains, where each domain contains 50–800 web tables (i.e., data sources). The major results are as follows.

1. Comparing with an integration system where schema mappings are manually specified, the proposed method obtains an F-measure over 0.9 in query answering on every domain.

2. The proposed method significantly improves the PR-curve over keyword search (for the same recall, the precision often doubles), showing the benefit of leveraging the structure information in a probabilistic manner.

3. Using a probabilistic mediated schema obtains better results than using a deterministic mediated schema.

4. System setup time increases linearly in the number of data sources, and finished in roughly 3.5 minutes for the domain with 817 data sources.

## 2.2.2 PAY-AS-YOU-GO USER FEEDBACK

A dataspace system starts with best-effort service by probabilistic schema alignment. As more queries arrive, it would find the candidates where a precise mapping can help most and ask users or domain experts to manually verify these mappings. There can be far too many candidates that can benefit from user feedback; soliciting feedback for all of them is expensive and often unnecessary. The challenge is thus to decide which is the best order to confirm candidate matches.

Jeffery et al. [2008] propose solving this problem using a decision-theoretic approach. The key concept from decision theory used here is the *value of perfect information (VPI)* [Russell and Norvig 2010], which quantifies the potential benefit of determining the true value for some unknown. We next explain in detail how the concept of VPI is applied in deciding the ordering of candidate mappings for feedback.

### Benefit of Confirming a Matching

Let $\Omega$ be a dataspace containing a set of data sources and matchings that are known between a pair of attributes, a pair of entities, and a pair of values. Let $\Lambda$ be a set of candidate matches not contained in $\Omega$. Denote the *utility* of the dataspace $\Omega$ with respect to $\Lambda$ by $U(\Omega, \Lambda)$. The utility is aggregated over a set of queries in the workload $\mathbf{Q}$ that have been observed in the query log. Each query $Q_i$ is associated with a weight $w_i$, decided by the frequency of the query or the importance of the query. For each query $Q_i$, its result quality over $\Omega$ and $\Lambda$ is denoted by $r(Q, \Omega, \Lambda)$. The utility of $\Omega$ with respect to $\Lambda$ is computed as follows:

$$U(\Omega, \Lambda) = \sum_{(Q_i, w_i) \in \mathbf{Q}} w_i \cdot r(Q_i, \Omega, \Lambda). \tag{2.1}$$

Assume no query involves negation and only confirmed matchings are used to answer a query, then knowing more mappings will improve the coverage of the answers. Accordingly, $r(Q, \Omega, \Lambda)$ represents the coverage of the answers using the current dataspace $\Omega$ over that using the dataspace enriched by the user feedback on $\Lambda$, denoted by $\Omega \cup \Lambda^p$ ($\Lambda^p \subseteq \Lambda$ are the correct matchings according to user feedback).

$$r(Q, \Omega, \Lambda) = \frac{|Q(\Omega)|}{|Q(\Omega \cup \Lambda^p)|}. \tag{2.2}$$

Now consider the benefit of confirming a candidate match $\lambda \in \Lambda$. There are two possible outcomes from the feedback: either $\lambda$ is confirmed as correct or it is disconfirmed as incorrect. Denote the two possible resulting dataspaces by $\Omega_\lambda^+$ and $\Omega_\lambda^-$ respectively. Assume with probability $p$ the matching is correct; the probability can be computed according to the confidence from the automatic matching results. The benefit of confirming $\lambda$ can be computed using the following difference:

$$Benefit(\lambda) = U(\Omega_\lambda^+, \Lambda \setminus \{\lambda\}) \cdot p + U(\Omega_\lambda^-, \Lambda \setminus \{\lambda\}) \cdot (1-p)$$

$$- U(\Omega, \Lambda). \tag{2.3}$$

### Approximating the Benefit

Computing the benefit of confirming a matching $\lambda$ requires estimating the coverage of a query, in turn requiring the knowledge of the dataspace after user feedback on $\Lambda$, which is unknown. The utility can be approximated by assuming that $\Lambda$ contains only the mapping $\lambda$. Then Eq. (2.2) can be rewritten as follows:

$$r(Q, \Omega, \Lambda) = \frac{|Q(\Omega)|}{|Q(\Omega \cup \{\lambda\})|} \cdot p + \frac{|Q(\Omega)|}{|Q(\Omega)|} \cdot (1-p)$$

$$= \frac{|Q(\Omega)|}{|Q(\Omega \cup \{\lambda\})|} \cdot p + (1-p). \tag{2.4}$$

On the other hand, since $\Lambda = \{\lambda\}$, it holds that

$$U(\Omega_\lambda^+, \Lambda \setminus \{\lambda\}) = U(\Omega_\lambda^-, \Lambda \setminus \{\lambda\}) = \sum_{(Q_i, w_i) \in \mathbf{Q}} w_i \cdot 1 = 1. \tag{2.5}$$

Putting them together, the benefit can be rewritten as follows:

$$Benefit(\lambda) = \sum_{(Q_i, w_i) \in \mathbf{Q}} w_i \left( p + (1-p) - (\frac{|Q(\Omega)|}{|Q(\Omega \cup \{\lambda\})|} \cdot p + (1-p)) \right)$$

$$= \sum_{(Q_i, w_i) \in \mathbf{Q}} w_i \cdot p \left( 1 - \frac{|Q(\Omega)|}{|Q(\Omega \cup \{\lambda\})|} \right) \tag{2.6}$$

Finally, since it is assumed that $\Lambda = \{\lambda\}$, only queries that contain one of the elements in $\lambda$ need to be considered, as other queries will not be affected. Denote such queries by $\mathbf{Q}_\lambda$; thus,

$$Benefit(\lambda) = \sum_{(Q_i, w_i) \in \mathbf{Q}_\lambda} w_i \cdot p \left( 1 - \frac{|Q(\Omega)|}{|Q(\Omega \cup \{\lambda\})|} \right). \tag{2.7}$$

Order the matchings by their benefits and user feedback should be obtained first on high-benefit matchings.

**Example 2.6**  Consider an instance of S1 in Example 2.4, denoted by $D(\text{S1})$, and Med3 in Example 2.1. Consider a candidate attribute matching $\lambda = (\text{AGT, AAGT})$ with probability 0.8 being true.

Assume only two queries have been observed relevant to λ. Query $Q_1$: SELECT AT FROM Med3 has weight 0.9; query $Q_2$: SELECT AGT FROM Med3 has weight 0.5.

For $Q_1$, without matching λ no answer can be obtained from $D(\text{S1})$; thus, $|Q_1(\Omega)| = 0$. Once λ is known, all answers can be obtained and so $|Q_1(\Omega \cup \{\lambda\})| = 1$. For $Q_2$, however, even without matching λ all answers can still be obtained from $D(\text{S1})$; thus, $|Q_2(\Omega)| = |Q_2(\Omega \cup \{\lambda\})| = 1$. Applying Eq. (2.7), the benefit of λ is

$$Benefit(m) = 0.9 * 0.8 * \left(1 - \frac{0}{1}\right) + 0.5 * 0.8 * \left(1 - \frac{1}{1}\right) = 0.72.$$

## Main Results
Jeffery et al. [2008] evaluate the proposed algorithm on a data set derived from *Google Base* (http://base.google.com). There are two major results.

1. The proposed method is effective: after confirming the top 10% of the candidate matchings, it improves the coverage by 17.2%, and after confirming the top 20% matchings, it already reaches 95% of the potential benefit obtained by getting feedback on all candidate matchings.

2. The proposed approximation is significantly better than baseline methods that sum the weights, count the number of affected tuples, or use a random ordering. Its performance is close to using an oracle that already knows the results of running the entire query load.

## 2.3    ADDRESSING THE VARIETY AND VOLUME CHALLENGES

The proliferation of the web provides huge volume of structured data; realizing the full potential of such data requires seamless integration. However, the data are at web scale, the border between the different domains is fuzzy and the variety within each domain is huge, and at every moment a new web source may appear or an existing web source may disappear. All these present big challenges for schema alignment.

This section describes recent progress in integrating two types of structured data on the web. Section 2.3.1 describes integrating deep web data, and Section 2.3.2 describes integrating tabular data on the web. We describe how the proposed methods address the *volume* and *variety* challenges in big data.

### 2.3.1    INTEGRATING DEEP WEB DATA
The *deep web* refers to data stored in underlying databases and queried by HTML forms. As an example, Figure 2.4 shows the web form to search flights at Orbitz.com. Cafarella et al. [2011] estimated that deep web data generated more than 1 B web pages.

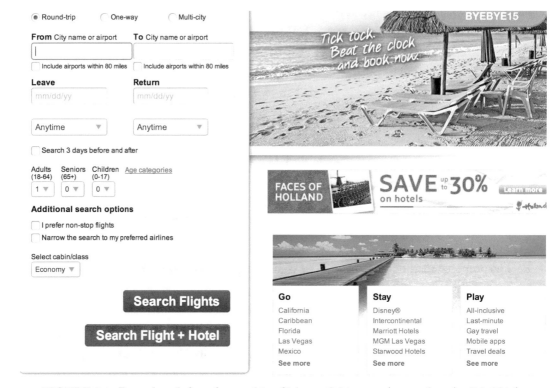

FIGURE 2.4: Example web form for searching flights at Orbitz.com (accessed on April 1, 2014).

There are two common approaches for offering access to deep web data. The first is a data integration solution that builds vertical search engines. Chuang and Chang [2008] propose building holistic schema matching for web forms. The hypothesis is that there is an underlying domain schema, and each source populates its data by projecting on a subset of attributes and selecting a subset of tuples. As a result, discovering schema matching can be achieved by constructing a *complete* domain schema that best describes all input data, and each attribute in this domain schema is essentially a group of attributes from different sources that have the same semantic meaning. This approach shares some similarity with constructing probabilistic mediated schema described in Section 2.2; we skip the details here.

The second approach is *surfacing*. Madhavan et al. [2008] propose pre-computing the most relevant form submissions for all interesting HTML forms. The URLs resulting from these submissions are generated off-line and indexed like any other HTML webpage. This approach allows seamless inclusion of deep-web data in web search: when a user decides from the snippet of search results that some deep-web content is relevant, she would click on the answer and be directed to the underlying web site for fresh content. We next describe this technique in more detail.

There are two key problems to solve in surfacing the deep web. First, one needs to decide which form inputs to fill when submitting queries to a form. Second, one needs to find appropriate values to fill in these inputs. HTML forms typically have more than one input and hence a naive strategy of enumerating the entire Cartesian product of all possible inputs can result in a very large number of URLs being generated. Crawling too many URLs would drain the resources of a web crawler and pose an unreasonable load on web servers hosting the HTML forms. On the other hand, among the Cartesian product, very likely a large number of the result pages are empty and hence useless from an indexing standpoint. For example, Madhavan et al. [2008] show that a particular search form on cars.com has 5 inputs and a Cartesian product yields over 240M URLs, but there are only 650K cars on sale.

Consider modeling the content behind a web form as a database $D$ with a single table of $m$ attributes, and the web form $F_D$ that is used to query $D$ as having $n$ inputs: $X_1, \ldots, X_n$. A form submission takes values for each of the inputs and returns a subset of the records in $D$. The notion of *query templates* designates a subset of the inputs of $F_D$ as *binding* inputs and the rest as *free* inputs. Multiple form submissions can be generated by assigning different values to the binding inputs. In the example web form, one may use From, To, Leave, and Return as binding inputs, and set default values for the rest of the free inputs.

Now the problem of surfacing a deep-web site can be divided into two subproblems.

1. Selecting an appropriate set of query templates.

2. Selecting appropriate input values for the binding inputs; that is, instantiating the query template with actual values. For a select menu, use all values in the menu; for a text input, the values need to be predicted without prior knowledge of the domains of the values.

## Selecting Query Templates

When selecting templates, it is desirable to select templates that do not contain any presentation inputs as binding inputs, because these templates retrieve the same underlying records as the corresponding template without the presentation inputs. In addition, it is desirable to use the correct dimension (i.e., the number of binding variables); too many dimensions increases crawling traffic and may produce many results that are empty, whereas too few dimensions may return too many records and go beyond the limit that the website allows for retrieval per query.

A query template is evaluated based on the *distinctness* of the web pages resulting from the form submissions it generates. If the number of distinct web pages is small in comparison with the

---

**Algorithm 2.1:  ISIT: Incremental search for informative query templates [Madhavan et al. 2008]**

**Input:** web form $F$.

**Output:** set $\mathbf{T}$ of informative templates.

1    $\mathbf{I} = \textsc{GetCandidateInputs}(F)$
2    $\mathbf{Q} = \{T \mid T.\text{binding} = \{I\}, I \in \mathbf{I}\}$
3    $\mathbf{T} = \emptyset$
4    **while** $\mathbf{Q} \neq \emptyset$ **do**
5        $T = \textsc{Pop}(\mathbf{Q})$
6        **if** $\textsc{CheckInformative}(T, F)$ **then**
7            $\mathbf{T} = \mathbf{T} \cup \{T\}$
8            $\mathbf{Q} = \mathbf{Q} \cup \{T' \mid T'.\text{binding} = T.\text{binding} \cup \{I\}, I \notin T.\text{binding}\}$
9        **endif**
10    **endwhile**

---

number of form submissions, it is very likely that either the template includes a presentation input, or the template dimension is too high and many answer pages have no record. A template is considered *informative* if the generated pages are sufficiently distinct. Specifically, a *signature* is computed for the contents of the answer web pages and a template is deemed to be uninformative if the percentage of signatures over all submissions is lower than a threshold $\tau$. The details of signature generation are less important; however, they should be agnostic to HTML formatting, record ordering, and tolerant to minor differences in page contents (e.g., advertisements).

**Definition 2.11** (Informative query template)    [Madhavan et al. 2008] Let $T$ be a query template and Sig be a function that computes signatures for HTML pages. Let $G$ be the set of all answer pages from possible submissions according to $T$ and $S = \{\text{Sig}(p) \mid p \in G\}$.

    Template $T$ is *informative* if $\frac{|S|}{|G|} \geq \tau$. The ratio $\frac{|S|}{|G|}$ is called the *distinctness fraction*.

    Algorithm ISIT shows how to find informative templates. Start with candidate templates of dimension 1: for binding inputs choose values from select menus and for the text boxes; for free inputs use default values (line 2). For each candidate, check if it is informative (line 6). An informative candidate will be recorded for returning (line 7), and augmented by increasing the dimension by 1 (line 8). Terminate when there are no informative templates of a given dimension (line 4).

    Note that it is possible that none of the one-dimensional query templates is informative but there exist informative two-dimensional templates. In our example, only if one specifies both From and To does the web form search return meaningful results; in other words, for any one-dimensional template, $|S| = 0$. A practical solution is to test templates of dimension two when none of the one-dimensional templates is deemed informative.

## Generating Input Values

A large number of HTML forms have text boxes. In addition, some forms with select menus require valid values in their text boxes before any result can be retrieved. Consider *generic* text boxes where the words entered in the text box are used to retrieve all documents in a backend text database that contain those words. An iterative probing approach can be applied to identify the candidate keywords for a text box.

At a high level, the algorithm proceeds in three steps.

1. Start by finding an initial seed set of words as values for the text box and construct a query template with the text box as the single binding input. To cover all possible languages, select the seeds from the words on the form page.

2. Generate the corresponding form submissions and extract additional keywords from the resulting documents. The extracted keywords are then used to update the candidate values for the text box.

3. Repeat Step 2 until either not being able to extract further keywords, or reaching an alternate stopping condition (e.g., reaching the maximum number of iterations or the maximum number of extracted keywords). On termination, a subset of the candidate keywords is chosen as the set of values for the text box.

In the example in Figure 2.4, there are city names such as *Las Vegas* on the entrance webpage of Orbitz.com and they can be used as input for From and To. From the results the algorithm would iteratively extract more city names, such as from connection cities.

## Main Results

Madhavan et al. [2008] evaluate the proposed algorithm on a sample of 500,000 HTML forms and the major results are as follows.

1. Algorithm ISIT effectively generates templates. As the number of inputs increases, the number of possible templates increases exponentially; however, the number of templates ISIT tests increases only linearly, and so does the number of templates found to be informative.

2. Testing informativeness can reduce the number of generated URLs per form by an order of magnitude.

3. The proposed method for generating input values can achieve good coverage of the underlying database.

4. Generating values only for text boxes can retrieve many more records than using only select menus, showing the important role of value generation for text boxes.

## 2.3.2    INTEGRATING WEB TABLES

*Web tables* refer to relational data in tabular form on the web. As an example, Figure 2.5 shows a web table about major airlines of the world. Cafarella et al. [2008a] estimate that after filtering out tables that are used for page layout or other non-relational reasons, there are 154M distinct web tables from English-language documents in Google's main index (Section 1.2.5).

**The World's biggest Airlines**

| Airline | Passengers (in million) 2009 | Passengers (in million) 2010 | Main Hub IATA code | Headquarter/ City | Country |
|---|---|---|---|---|---|
| **Africa/Middle East** | | | | | |
| Emirates Airline | 27,454 | 31,422 | Dubai International Airport | Dubai | United Arab Emirates |
| Qatar Airways | 10,212 | 12,392 | Doha International Airport | Doha | Qatar |
| Saudi Arabian Airlines | 18,334 | 18,172 | Jeddah-King Abdulaziz International | Jeddah | Saudi Arabia |
| **Asia/Pacific** | | | | | |
| AirAsia | 14,253 | 16,055 | Kuala Lumpur International Airport | Kuala Lumpur | Malaysia |
| Air China | 39,841 | 46,241 | Beijing Capital International Airport | Beijing | China |
| Air New Zealand Group | 12,368 | 12,324 | Auckland Airport | Auckland | New Zealand |
| ANA - All Nippon Airways | 44,562 | 45,743 | Narita International Airport (IATA code: NRT) | Tokyo | Japan |
| Asiana Airlines | 12,372 | 13,944 | Incheon International Airport | Seoul | South Korea |
| Cathay Pacific | 24,558 | 26,796 | Hong Kong International Airport | Hong Kong | China |

FIGURE 2.5:  Example web table (Airlines) with some major airlines of the world (accessed on April 1, 2014).

Web tables are different from deep web data: they are HTML tables that are already crawlable without filling in any form; typically each web table is small. The two sets of data intersect, but neither contains the other. Web tables are also different from relational databases. Web tables do not have clearly specified schemas; the semantics are often encoded in the column caption, which can sometimes be missing. Also, not every row necessarily corresponds to a tuple in a relational database; in the example in Figure 2.5, two rows indicate the regions for the airlines in the rows below them.

Three topics have been studied for leveraging web table data. The first is keyword search on web tables, where the goal is to return highly relevant tables in answers to a keyword search [Cafarella et al. 2008a, Pimplikar and Sarawagi 2012]. The second is to find relevant tables, where the goal is to return tables that have similar or complementary data to the table edited by the user, to possibly provide reference [Das Sarma et al. 2012]. The third is to extract knowledge from web tables, where the goal is to extract (entity, property, value) triples that can be used to populate knowledge bases [Limaye et al. 2010, Suchanek et al. 2011, Venetis et al. 2011, Zhang and Chakrabarti 2013]. We next describe techniques for each topic.

Note that similar problems have been studied for web lists [Elmeleegy et al. 2011, Gupta and Sarawagi 2009]; we skip the details in this book.

## Keyword Search on Web Tables

The goal of keyword search on web tables is to accept user keyword queries and rank web tables by relevance. Cafarella et al. [2008a] propose a linear regression model and Pimplikar and Sarawagi [2012] propose a graphical model to solve the problem. Here we describe the techniques for the WebTables search engine [Cafarella et al. 2008a].

Ranking for web tables poses a unique set of challenges: frequent words in the webpage that contains a web table may be different from what the web table describes; attribute labels in the web tables are extremely important to understand the table but may not appear frequently; even a webpage with high quality in general may contain tables of varying quality. As a result, a naive ranking strategy that simply returns the webpages that best match the keyword search does not work well. To address these challenges, Cafarella et al. [2008a] propose two ranking functions that do not rely on existing search engines.

**FeatureRank** considers a set of relation-specific features listed in Table 2.1. It numerically combines the different feature scores using a linear regression estimator. The estimator was trained on a training set containing more than a thousand *(q, relation)* pairs, each judged by two human judges with a score in [1, 5] indicating the relevance. The two most heavily weighted features are the number of hits in each table's header and the number of hits in each table's leftmost column. The former fits the intuition that attribute labels form a strong

TABLE 2.1: Selected text-derived features used in search rankers. The most important features are in italic [Cafarella et al. 2008a]

No. of rows

No. of columns

Has-header?

No. of NULLs in table

Document-search rank of source page

*No. of Hits on header*

*No. of Hits on leftmost column*

No. of Hits on second-to-leftmost column

No. of Hits on table body

---

indicator of a table's subject matter. The latter indicates that values in the leftmost column often act as a "semantic key", providing a useful summary of the contents of a table row.

**SchemaRank** is the same as FEATURERANK, except that it also includes a score indicating the coherence of a schema as a feature. Intuitively, a *coherent schema* is one where the attributes are all tightly related to one another. For example, a schema that consists of the attributes gate and terminal is coherent, but one with gate and address is much less coherent.

Coherency is measured by *Pointwise Mutual Information (PMI)*, which is often used in computational linguistics and web text search to quantify how strongly two items are related [Turney 2001]. The PMI of the schema is computed as the average PMI of every pair of attributes in the schema, which is computed from the frequency of each attribute and the frequency of co-occurrences of two attributes. Formally, let $A_1$ and $A_2$ be two attributes. Denote by $p(A_i)$ the fraction of unique schemas containing $A_i$ and by $p(A_1, A_2)$ the fraction of unique schemas containing both $A_1$ and $A_2$. Compute the PMI of a schema $S$ with attributes $\overline{A}$ as follows:

$$PMI(S) = \text{Avg}_{A_1, A_2 \in \overline{A}, A_1 \neq A_2} \log \frac{p(A_1, A_2)}{p(A_1) \cdot p(A_2)}. \tag{2.8}$$

**Example 2.7** Consider four web tables with the following schemas.

T1(FI, SDT, SAT)

T2(FI, SDT, SAT, ADT, AAT)

T3(FI, FC, F)

T4(AC, AN, ACI, ACO)

For attributes SDT and SAT, the PMI is computed as follows. According to the schemas, $p(\text{SDT}) = 0.5$, $p(\text{SAT}) = 0.5$, $p(\text{SDT, SAT}) = 0.5$; thus, $PMI(\text{SDT, SAT}) = \log \frac{0.5}{0.5 * 0.5} = 1$.

On the other hand, for attributes FI and SDT, $p(\text{FI}) = 0.75$, $p(\text{SDT}) = 0.5$, $p(\text{FI, SDT}) = 0.5$; thus, $PMI(\text{FI, SDT}) = \log \frac{0.5}{0.5 * 0.75} = 0.42$. Intuitively, SDT is more coherent with SAT than with FI.

Finally, the coherence for T1 is $\text{Avg}\{1, 0.42, 0.42\} = 0.61$.

**Main results.** Cafarella et al. [2008a] show that FEATURERANK significantly improves over using web search ranking, whereas SCHEMARANK obtains even better results than FEATURERANK.

### Finding Related Web Tables

Das Sarma et al. [2012] describe a framework for discovering tables in a corpus that are related to a given table. This problem is challenging for two reasons. First, the schemas of web tables are partial at best and extremely heterogeneous. In some cases the crucial aspects of the schema that are needed for reasoning about relatedness are embedded in text surrounding the tables or textual descriptions attached to them. Second, one needs to consider different ways and degrees to which data can be related. The following example illustrates the latter challenge.

**Example 2.8**   Consider the two CapitalCity tables in Figure 2.6. One of them lists major cities in Asia and the other lists cities in Africa. They are related: their schemas are identical, and they provide complementary sets of entities. Their *union* would produce a meaningful table.

On the other hand, consider these two tables and the Airlines table in Figure 2.5. The Airlines table describes major airlines and their headquarter cities. Some of the cities, such as *Doha*, are capital cities and information such as population is provided in the CapitalCity tables. The *join* of these tables would produce a meaningful table.

In general, two tables are considered as related to each other if they can be viewed as results to queries over the same (possibly hypothetical) original table. In particular, consider two most common types of related tables: *entity complement* and *schema complement*, resulting from applying different *selection* or *projection* conditions in similar structured queries, respectively, over the same underlying virtual table. In a sense, finding related tables can be viewed as reverse-engineering vertical/horizontal fragmentation in distributed databases. They are formally defined as follows.

**Definition 2.12** (Entity complement)   [Das Sarma et al. 2012] Let $T_1$ and $T_2$ be two tables. They are *entity complement* if there exists a coherent virtual table $T$, such that $Q_1(T) = T_1$ and $Q_2(T) = T_2$, where

1. $Q_i$ takes the form $Q_i(T) = \sigma_{P_i(X)}(T)$, where $X$ contains a set of attributes in $T$ and $P_i$ is a selection predicate over $X$;

**Capital Cities and States of Asia**

| Capital City | Satellite View/Map | Citizens | Country |
|---|---|---|---|
| Abu Dhabi (Abu Zabi, Abu Zaby (ae)) | Abu Dhabi Map | 260,000 | United Arab Emirates |
| Amman | Amman Map | 965,000 | Jordan |
| Ankara (Angora) | Ankara Map | 2,900,000 | Turkey |
| Ashgabat (Ashkhabad, Asgabat (tk), Ashabad (rus)) | Ashgabat Map | 410,000 | Turkmenistan |
| Astana | Astana Map | 1,176,000 | Kazakhstan |
| Baghdad | Baghdad Map | 3,900,000 | Iraq |
| Baku | Baku Map | 1,150,000 | Azerbaijan |
| Bandar Seri Begawan | Bandar Seri Begawan Map | 55,000 | Brunei |
| Bangkok (Krung Thep) | Bangkok Map | 5,900,000 | Thailand |
| Beijing (Peking) | Beijing Map | 7,400,000 | China |
| Beirut (Bayrut, Beiroût (lb) | Beirut Map | 480,000 | Lebanon |
| Bishkek (Biskek) | Bishkek Map | 590,000 | Kyrgyzstan |
| Colombo Kotte (administrative) | Colombo Map | 620,000 | Sri Lanka |
| Damascus (Dimashq) | Damascus Map | 1,600,000 | Syria |
| Dhaka | Dhaka Map | 3,400,000 | Bangladesh |
| Dili | Dili Map | 50,000 | Timor_Leste |
| Doha (Ad Dawhah, Al-Dawhah) | Doha Map | 220,000 | Qatar |

(a)

**Capital cities and states of Africa**

| Capital City | Searchable map and satellite view | Citizens | Country |
|---|---|---|---|
| Abuja | Abuja Map | 300,000 | Nigeria |
| Accra | Accra Map | 600,000 | Ghana |
| Addis Ababa (Addis Abeba) | Addis Ababa Map | 2,400,000 | Ethiopia |
| Algiers (Alger, El Djazâir, Al Jaza'ir) | Algiers Map | 1,600,000 | Algeria |
| Antananarivo | Antananarivo Map | 370,000 | Madagascar |
| Asmara (Asmera) | Asmara Map | 360,000 | Eritrea |
| Bamako | Bamako Map | 700,000 | Mali |
| Bangui | Bangui Map | 480,000 | Central Africa |
| Banjul | Banjul Map | 52,000 | Gambia |
| Bissau | Bissau Map | 120,000 | Guinea-Bissau |
| Brazzaville | Brazzaville Map | 620,000 | Congo (Brazzaville) |
| Bujumbura | Bujumbura Map | 240,000 | Burundi |

(b)

FIGURE 2.6: Two web tables (CapitalCity) describing major cities in Asia and in Africa from nationsonline.org (accessed on April 1, 2014).

2.  $T_1 \cup T_2$ covers all entities in $T$ and $T_1 \neq T_2$; and

3.  optionally, each $Q_i$ renames or projects a set of attributes and both include the key attribute $X$.

**Definition 2.13** (Schema complement)   [Das Sarma et al. 2012] Let $T_1$ and $T_2$ be two tables. They are *schema complement* if there exists a coherent virtual table $T$, such that $Q_1(T) = T_1$ and $Q_2(T) = T_2$, where

1.  $Q_i$ takes the form $Q_i(T) = \Pi_{A_i}(T)$, where $A_i$ is the set of attributes (with optionally renaming) to be projected;

2.  $A_1 \cup A_2$ covers all attributes in $T$, $A_1 \cap A_2$ covers the key attribute in $T$, and $A_1 \neq A_2$;

3.  optionally, each $Q_i$ applies a fixed selection predicate $P$ over the set of key attributes.

Formally, the problem of finding related tables is defined as follows.

**Definition 2.14** (Finding related tables)   [Das Sarma et al. 2012] Let $\mathcal{T}$ be a corpus of tables, $T$ be a query table, $k$ be a constant. The problem selects $k$ tables $T_1, \ldots, T_k \in \mathcal{T}$ with the highest relatedness score of entity complement (schema complement) with $T$.

Several criteria can be considered in finding related tables. For entity complement tables, there are three criteria.

**Entity consistency.**   A related table $T'$ should have the same type of entities as $T$, as required by the coherence of the virtual table $T$ and closeness of $Q_1$ and $Q_2$ in Definition 2.12. For example, entities in the two tables in Figure 2.6 are both capital cities in the world. Das Sarma et al. [2012] use reference sources such as *Freebase* [Bollacker et al. 2008] to decide type of entities for type comparison.

**Entity expansion.**   $T'$ should substantially add new entities to those in $T$, as required by the second bullet in Definition 2.12. For example, entities in the two tables in Figure 2.6 are capital cities from different continents. Das Sarma et al. [2012] measure this by set comparison.

**Schema consistency.**   The two tables should have similar (if not the same) schemas, thereby describing similar properties of the entities, as required by the third bullet in Definition 2.12. Das Sarma et al. [2012] apply state-of-the-art schema mapping techniques to obtain a schema consistency score.

For schema complement, there are two criteria.

**Coverage of entity set.**   $T'$ should consist of most of the entities in $T$, if not all of them. This is required by the third bullet in Definition 2.13. Das Sarma et al. [2012] compute this metric by first applying entity mapping (or mapping entities in both tables to a reference data source such as *Freebase*), and then computing the coverage of $T'$ regarding entities in $T$.

**Benefit of additional attributes.**  $T'$ should contain additional attributes that are not contained in $T$'s schema. This is required by the second bullet in Definition 2.13. Das Sarma et al. [2012] quantify the benefit by combining the *consistency* and *number* of $T''$s additional attributes, where the former can be computed using metrics similar to $PMI$ introduced in Section 2.3.2.

**Main results.** Das Sarma et al. [2012] experimented on Wikipedia tables. They show the effectiveness of their selection criteria and also show that the number of related tables roughly follows a power-law distribution.

## Extracting Knowledge from Web Tables

Web tables contain structured data that are often carefully edited and so of high quality. Each row in a web table typically presents an entity, each column typically presents a property of the entities, and each cell typically presents the value for the corresponding property of the corresponding entity. It is desirable to extract such structured information from the web and the results can be used to facilitate search or populate knowledge bases.

As a first step towards knowledge extraction, there has been a lot of work describing annotating entities, types, and relationships in web tables [Limaye et al. 2010, Suchanek et al. 2011, Venetis et al. 2011, Zhang and Chakrabarti 2013]. Here we describe the graphical-model based solution proposed in [Limaye et al. 2010]. This approach assumes an external catalog such as *Freebase* and the goal is to annotate each table in the following ways.

- Annotate each column of the table with one or more types. If a column is deemed not to have any type in the catalog, determine that as well.

- Annotate each pair of columns with a binary relation in the catalog. If two columns are not involved in any binary relation in the catalog, determine that as well.

- Annotate each table cell with an entity ID in the catalog when applicable.

The solution models the table annotation problem using a number of interrelated random variables following a suitable joint distribution, represented by a probabilistic graphical model as shown in Figure 2.7. The task of annotation then amounts to searching for an assignment of values to the variables that maximizes the joint probability. We next describe the graphical model in more detail.

**Variables.** There are three variables, shown as follows.

$t_c$    the type of column $c$
$b_{cc'}$ the relation between column pairs $c$ and $c'$
$e_{rc}$ the entity label for a cell in row $r$ and column $c$

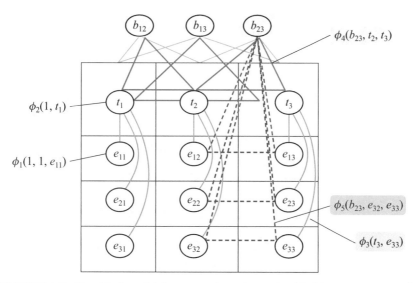

FIGURE 2.7: Graphical model for annotating a 3x3 web table [Limaye et al. 2010].

**Features.** Intuitively, assigning values to the variables $t_c$, $b_{cc'}$, and $e_{rc}$ needs to take into consideration several signals. Following the framework of graphical models, these signals are represented as *features*, and models are trained to learn how to combine these signals with suitable weights. These features and weights are used to define *potential* functions over subsets of variables, and the product of these potentials gives the joint distribution over all variables. The following table lists the five types of features.

| | |
|---|---|
| $\phi_1(r, c, e_{rc})$ | Captures whether the text for cell $(r, c)$ matches the entity $e_{rc}$. |
| $\phi_2(c, t_c)$ | Captures whether the header text for column $c$ describes a property of type $t_c$. |
| $\phi_3(t_c, e_{rc})$ | Captures whether the entity $e_{rc}$ for row $r$ and column $c$ has type $t_c$ for column $c$. |
| $\phi_4(b_{cc'}, t_c, t_{c'})$ | Captures whether the relation $b_{cc'}$ between columns $c$ and $c'$ is compatible with the types $t_c$ and $t_{c'}$. |
| $\phi_5(b_{cc'}, e_{rc}, e_{rc'})$ | Captures whether the relation $b_{cc'}$ between the two cells at $(r, c)$ and $(r, c')$ is compatible with the two entities $e_{rc}$ and $e_{rc'}$. |

**Main results.** Limaye et al. [2010] experiment on annotating web tables using *YAGO* schema and entities [Suchanek et al. 2007]. They show that the graphical model obtains a higher accuracy than baseline methods including least common ancestor and majority voting.

CHAPTER 3

# Record Linkage

The second component of data integration is *record linkage*. Even after the schemas of different sources have been aligned, when different sources provide values for the same attribute of the same entity, these values may differ due to mis-typing, multiple naming conventions, and so on. To illustrate, in our Flights example in Chapter 1, flight numbers are represented in source Airline2 using digits (e.g., *53* in $r_{32}$), while they are represented in source Airfare4 using alphanumerics (e.g., *A2-53* in $r_{64}$). Similarly, airports are represented in source Airline2 using 3-letter codes (e.g., *EWR* and *SFO* in $r_{32}$), but as descriptive strings in Airfare4.Flight (e.g., *Newark Liberty* and *San Francisco* in $r_{64}$). These representational differences make it hard to link records $r_{32}$ and $r_{64}$, even though they refer to the same entity. The goal of record linkage is to decide which records refer to the same entity, and which refer to different entities.

In traditional record linkage, the goal is typically to link millions of records obtained from tens to hundreds of data sources; thus, a brute force approach that compares every pair of records is infeasible. Section 3.1 presents a quick tour of traditional record linkage, highlighting the role that each of blocking, pairwise matching, and clustering plays in the process, before focusing on the impact of the various facets of BDI on record linkage.

The big data environment makes the record linkage problem even more challenging: the number of data sources available for integration is now in the millions, a vast number of which are unstructured sources with textual data; the data in these sources dynamically change, and have a lot of representational differences and errors. These challenges in volume, velocity, variety and veracity of big data call for new record linkage techniques.

Section 3.2 discusses two techniques that have been proposed to address the challenge of *volume*: one where MapReduce is used to effectively parallelize record linkage, and the other which analyzes the results of blocking to reduce the number of pairwise matchings performed.

Then, Section 3.3 shows that incremental record linkage is necessary to effectively address the challenge of *velocity*, and describes recent techniques that allow efficient incremental linkage under insertions, deletions and modifications of records.

Section 3.4 describes a record linkage approach to address the *variety* challenge of BDI, for the case where unstructured text snippets need to be linked to structured data.

Finally, Section 3.5 presents record linkage techniques to address the *veracity* challenge, for two scenarios: one where entities evolve over time requiring record linkage to be time-aware, and the other that shows promising results in the presence of both erroneous data and multiple representations of the same attribute value.

## 3.1    TRADITIONAL RECORD LINKAGE: A QUICK TOUR

We first formally define the problem of record linkage in data integration. Let $\mathcal{E}$ denote a set of entities in a domain, described using a set of attributes $\mathcal{A}$. Each entity $E \in \mathcal{E}$ is associated with zero, one or more values for each attribute $A \in \mathcal{A}$. We consider a set of data sources $\mathcal{S}$. For each entity in $\mathcal{E}$, a source $S \in \mathcal{S}$ provides zero, one or more records over the attributes $\mathcal{A}$, where each record provides at most one value for an attribute.[1] We consider atomic values (string, number, date, time, etc.) as attribute values, and allow multiple representations of the same value, as well as erroneous values, in records. The goal of record linkage is to take the records provided by the sources as input and decide which records refer to the same entity.

**Definition 3.1** (Record Linkage)    Consider a set of data sources $\mathcal{S}$, providing a set of records $\mathcal{R}$ over a set of attributes $\mathcal{A}$. *Record linkage* computes a partitioning $\mathcal{P}$ of $\mathcal{R}$, such that each partition in $\mathcal{P}$ identifies the records in $\mathcal{R}$ that refer to a distinct entity.

**Example 3.1**    Consider our illustrative Flights domain. The entities in that domain are individual flights, which are associated with attributes Airline (AL), Flight Number (FN), Departure Airport (DA), Departure Date (DD), Departure Time (DT), Arrival Airport (AA), Arrival Date (AD), and Arrival Time (AT).

A sample input set of records $r_{211}$-$r_{215}$, $r_{221}$-$r_{224}$, $r_{231}$-$r_{233}$ for record linkage is shown in Table 3.1. These may have been obtained from multiple sources, but schema alignment can be assumed to have been successfully performed.

Record linkage computes a partitioning, where records $r_{211}$-$r_{215}$ refer to the same entity (depicted using the shared yellow color), $r_{221}$-$r_{224}$ refer to the same entity (depicted using the shared red color), and $r_{231}$-$r_{233}$ refer to the same entity (depicted using the shared green color). Erroneous attribute values are depicted in bold font and red color (e.g., Arrival Date of record $r_{212}$, Airline of $r_{214}$). Small differences between the values of Departure Time in records that refer to the same entity are often acceptable (e.g., *15:30*, *15:37*, *15:28*, and *15:25* in $r_{221}$-$r_{224}$); similarly for Arrival Time. This is because the records come from different sources that may use independent observers (e.g., airline pilot, airport control tower) or slightly different semantics (e.g., gate departure time, takeoff time); this is common in real sources.

---

1. This relies on the schemas of the sources having been aligned.

TABLE 3.1: Sample Flights records

|  | AL | FN | DA | DD | DT | AA | AD | AT |
|---|---|---|---|---|---|---|---|---|
| $r_{211}$ | A2 | 53 | SFO | 2014-02-08 | 15:35 | EWR | 2014-02-08 | 23:55 |
| $r_{212}$ | A2 | 53 | SFO | 2014-02-08 | 15:25 | EWR | 2014-02-08 | 00:05 |
| $r_{213}$ | A2 | 53 | SFO | 2014-02-08 | 15:27 | EWR | 2014-02-09 | 00:09 |
| $r_{214}$ | A1 | 53 | SFO | 2014-02-08 | 15:15 | EWR | 2014-02-08 | 23:30 |
| $r_{215}$ | A2 | 53 | SFO | 2014-03-08 | 15:27 | EWR | 2014-02-08 | 23:55 |
| $r_{221}$ | A2 | 53 | SFO | 2014-03-09 | 15:30 | EWR | 2014-03-09 | 23:45 |
| $r_{222}$ | A2 | 53 | SFO | 2014-03-09 | 15:37 | EWR | 2014-03-09 | 23:40 |
| $r_{223}$ | A2 | 53 | SFO | 2014-03-09 | 15:28 | EWR | 2014-03-09 | 23:37 |
| $r_{224}$ | A2 | 53 | SFO | 2014-03-08 | 15:25 | EWR | 2014-03-09 | 23:35 |
| $r_{231}$ | A1 | 49 | EWR | 2014-02-08 | 18:45 | SFO | 2014-02-08 | 21:40 |
| $r_{232}$ | A1 | 49 | EWR | 2014-02-08 | 18:30 | SFO | 2014-02-08 | 21:37 |
| $r_{233}$ | A1 | 49 | EWR | 2014-02-08 | 18:30 | SAN | 2014-02-08 | 21:30 |

FIGURE 3.1: Traditional record linkage: three steps.

Record linkage consists of three main steps: blocking, pairwise matching, and clustering, depicted in Figure 3.1. We will describe each of these steps in more detail next, but it is worth keeping in mind that pairwise matching and clustering are used to ensure the *semantics* of record linkage, while blocking is used to achieve *scalability*.

### 3.1.1    PAIRWISE MATCHING

The basic step of record linkage is *pairwise matching*, which compares a pair of records and makes a local decision of whether or not they refer to the same entity. A variety of techniques have been proposed for this step.

*Rule-based* approaches [Hernández and Stolfo 1998, Fan et al. 2009] have been commonly used for this step in practice, and apply domain knowledge to make the local decision. For example, in the illustrative example shown in Table 3.1, a useful rule that can achieve pairwise matching of $r_{211}$ and $r_{212}$, while ensuring that $r_{211}$ and $r_{221}$ do not match, might be:

If two records share the values of Airline, Flight Number, Departure Airport, and Arrival Airport, and also share either the value of Departure Date or Arrival Date, then declare a match; otherwise, declare a non-match.

The advantage of this approach is that the rule can be tailored to effectively deal with complex matching scenarios. However, a key disadvantage of this approach is that it requires considerable domain knowledge as well as knowledge about the data to formulate the pairwise matching rule, rendering it ineffective when the records contain errors. For example, the above rule is inadequate to achieve pairwise matching of $r_{211}$ and $r_{214}$ (since $r_{214}$ has an incorrect value of Airline), while it incorrectly matches records $r_{215}$ and $r_{224}$ (since both records have the same incorrect value of Departure Date).

*Classification-based* approaches have also been used for this step since the seminal paper by Fellegi and Sunter [1969], wherein a classifier is built using positive and negative training examples, and the classifier decides whether a pair of records is a match or a non-match; it is also possible for the classifier to output a possible-match, in which case the local decision is turned over to a human. Such classification-based machine learning approaches have the advantage that they do not require significant domain knowledge about the domain and the data, only knowledge of whether a pair of records in the training data refers to the same entity or not. A disadvantage of this approach is that it often requires a large number of training examples to accurately train the classifier, though active learning based variations [Sarawagi and Bhamidipaty 2002] are often effective at reducing the volume of training data needed.

Finally, *distance-based* approaches [Elmagarmid et al. 2007] apply distance metrics to compute dissimilarity of corresponding attribute values (e.g., using Levenstein distance for computing dissimilarity of strings, and Euclidean distance for computing dissimilarity of numeric attributes), and take the weighted sum as the record-level distance. Low and high thresholds are used to declare matches, non-matches and possible matches. A key advantage of this approach is that the domain knowledge is limited to formulating distance metrics on atomic attributes, which can be potentially reused for a large variety of entity domains. A disadvantage of this approach is that it is a blunt hammer, which often requires careful parameter tuning (e.g., what should the weights on individual attributes be for the weighted sum, what should the low and high thresholds be), although machine learning approaches can often be used to tune the parameters in a principled fashion.

**Example 3.2**   Consider the set of records shown in Table 3.1, and the following simple distance-based measure with thresholding for pairwise distance between records.

If corresponding attribute values are the same for a pair of records, the distance between them is 0, else the distance between them is 1. Using weight 1 for each of the attributes Airline, Flight Number, Departure Airport, Departure Date, Arrival Airport, and Arrival Date, and weight 0 for each of

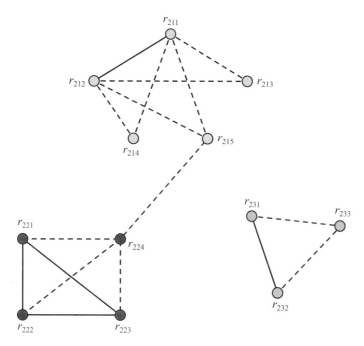

FIGURE 3.2: Pairwise matching graph.

the attributes Departure Time and Arrival Time, compute the record-level distance as the weighted sum of the corresponding attribute-level distances. If the distance between two records is at most 1 (low threshold) then declare a match; otherwise, declare a non-match.

A graph showing the pairwise distance between records is depicted in Figure 3.2. The solid lines indicate that the distance between the corresponding records is 0, and the dashed lines indicate that the distance between the corresponding records is 1.

## 3.1.2 CLUSTERING

The local decisions of match or non-match made by the pairwise matching step may not be globally consistent. For example, there is an inconsistency if pairwise matching declares that record pair $R_1$ and $R_2$ match, record pair $R_2$ and $R_3$ match, but record pair $R_1$ and $R_3$ do not match. In such a scenario, the purpose of the *clustering* step is to reach a globally consistent decision of how to partition the set of all records such that each partition refers to a distinct entity, and different partitions refer to different entities.

This step first constructs a pairwise matching graph $G$, where each node corresponds to a distinct record $R \in \mathcal{R}$, and there is an undirected edge $(R_1, R_2)$ if and only if the pairwise matching step declares a match between $R_1$ and $R_2$. A clustering of $G$ partitions the nodes into pairwise disjoint subsets based on the edges that are present in $G$. There exists a wealth of literature on clustering algorithms for record linkage [Hassanzadeh et al. 2009]. These clustering algorithms tend not to constrain the number of clusters in the output, since the number of entities in the data set is typically not known *a priori*.

One of the simplest graph clustering strategies efficiently clusters graph $G$ into connected components by a single scan of the edges in the graph [Hernández and Stolfo 1998]. Essentially, this strategy places a high trust on the local match decision, so even a few erroneous match decisions can significantly alter the results of record linkage. Example 3.3 illustrates this scenario.

At the other extreme, a robust but expensive graph clustering algorithm is *correlation clustering* [Bansal et al. 2004]. The goal of correlation clustering is to find a partition of nodes in $G$ that minimizes *disagreements* between the clustering and the edges in $G$, as follows. For each pair of nodes in the same cluster that are not connected by an edge, there is a *cohesion penalty* of 1; for each pair of nodes in different clusters that are connected by an edge, there is a *correlation penalty* of 1. Correlation clustering seeks to compute the clustering that minimizes the overall sum of the penalties (i.e., the disagreements). It has been proved that correlation clustering is NP-complete [Bansal et al. 2004], and many efficient approximation algorithms have been proposed for this problem (e.g., Bansal et al. 2004, Charikar et al. 2003).

**Example 3.3**  Continue with Example 3.2, and the pairwise matching graph shown in Figure 3.2. First, observe that the set of local decisions made by pairwise matching are globally inconsistent.

Second, clustering the graph into connected components would incorrectly declare that the nine records $r_{211}$-$r_{224}$ all refer to the same entity, because of the spurious edge between $r_{215}$ and $r_{224}$.

Third, the use of correlation clustering could correctly obtain three clusters of records, corresponding to the three flights: $r_{211}$-$r_{215}$, $r_{221}$-$r_{224}$, and $r_{231}$-$r_{233}$. This solution has a cohesion penalty of 3 (due to the missing edges $(r_{213}, r_{214})$, $(r_{213}, r_{215})$, $(r_{214}, r_{215})$ in the first cluster) and a correlation penalty of 1 (due to the extra edge $(r_{215}, r_{224})$ between the first and the second cluster), for an overall sum of penalties of 4. This is the minimum total penalty among all clusterings of this graph. For example, the total penalty of the connected components clustering is 22.

### 3.1.3  BLOCKING

Pairwise matching and clustering together ensure the desired semantics of record linkage, but may be quite inefficient and even infeasible for a large set of records. The main source of inefficiency is that pairwise matching appears to require a quadratic number of record pair comparisons to decide which record pairs are matches and which are non-matches. When the number of records is even moderately large (e.g., millions), the number of pairwise comparisons becomes prohibitively large.

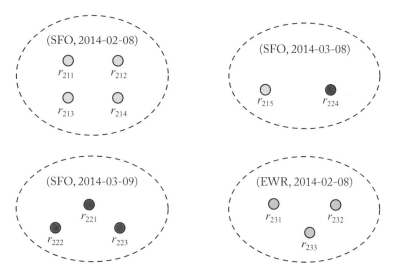

FIGURE 3.3: Use of a single blocking function.

Blocking was proposed as a strategy to scale record linkage to large data sets [Bitton and DeWitt 1983, Hernández and Stolfo 1998]. The basic idea is to utilize a *blocking function* on the values of one or more attributes to partition the input records into multiple small blocks, and restrict the subsequent pairwise matching to records in the same block.

**Example 3.4** Consider the records in Table 3.1. They could be partitioned by using a blocking function that is the composition of values of the attributes (Departure Airport, Departure Date). Figure 3.3 illustrates the partitioning of records achieved using this blocking function.

The advantage of this strategy is that it can significantly reduce the number of pairwise comparisons needed, and make record linkage feasible and efficient even for large data sets. In our example, the number of pairwise comparisons would reduce from 66 (when comparing every pair of 12 records) to 13.

The disadvantage of this strategy is *false negatives*: if there are incorrect values or multiple representations in the value of any attribute used by the blocking function, records that ought to refer to the same entity may end up with different blocking key values, and hence could not be discovered to refer to the same entity by subsequent pairwise matching and clustering steps. For example, record $r_{215}$ has an incorrect value for the Departure Date attribute, and does not get correctly clustered with records $r_{211}$-$r_{214}$ subsequently, if the blocking function of Example 3.4 is used.

The key to addressing this disadvantage is to allow *multiple blocking functions*. Hernández and Stolfo [1998] were the first to make this observation, and showed that using multiple blocking

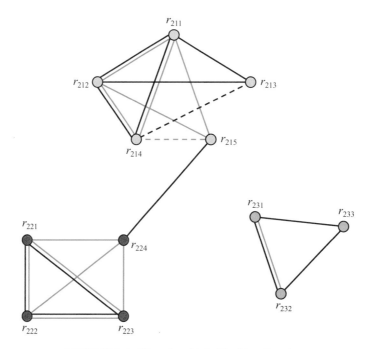

FIGURE 3.4: Use of multiple blocking functions.

functions could result in high quality record linkage without necessarily incurring a high cost. In general, such blocking functions create a set of overlapping blocks that balance the recall of record linkage (i.e., absence of false negatives) with the number of comparisons incurred by pairwise matching. For example, $q$-grams[2] blocking [Gravano et al. 2001] creates blocks of records that share at least one $q$-gram. Similarly, the Canopy method [McCallum et al. 2000] employs a computationally cheap similarity metric for building high-dimensional, overlapping blocks.

**Example 3.5**   Consider again the records in Table 3.1. Although the use of (Departure Airport, Departure Date) as a blocking function can lead to false negatives, as shown in Example 3.4, adding an additional bi-gram, such as (Arrival Airport, Arrival Date), as a blocking function would resolve the false negatives.

Figure 3.4 illustrates the pairwise comparisons that would be performed using both blocking functions. The edges in black connect record pairs that would be compared under the (Departure Airport, Departure Date) blocking function, and the edges in blue connect record pairs that would be compared under the (Arrival Airport, Arrival Date) blocking function. Comparing with Figure 3.2,

---

2. A $q$-gram of a string value is a substring of length $q$. A $q$-gram of a set of values is a subset of size $q$.

one can see that every pair of records that should match would be compared using at least one of these two blocking functions. Further, only two record pairs that do not match (($r_{213}$, $r_{214}$) and ($r_{214}$, $r_{215}$), shown using dashed lines) are compared using these blocking functions. Note that the non-matching record pair ($r_{213}$, $r_{215}$) would not be compared using either blocking function.

## 3.2  ADDRESSING THE VOLUME CHALLENGE

Even with the use of blocking, record linkage for big data sets can take several hours or even days [Köpcke et al. 2010]. In this section, we present two complementary techniques that have been proposed to address this problem.

The first uses the MapReduce (MR) programming model, which has been highly effective in parallelizing data-intensive computing in cluster environments with thousands of nodes, to parallelize the blocking step of record linkage [Kolb et al. 2012]. The second analyzes the graph of record pairs compared when multiple blocking functions are used, and identifies the most promising set of pairwise matchings to perform [Papadakis et al. 2014].

### 3.2.1  USING MAPREDUCE TO PARALLELIZE BLOCKING

We first present a brief description of the MapReduce programming model, before describing the technique of Kolb et al. [2012], which uses MapReduce to speed up the blocking step of record linkage.

### MapReduce: A Brief Description

In the MapReduce programming model [Dean and Ghemawat 2004, Li et al. 2014], computation is expressed using two user-defined functions.

map: $value_1 \rightarrow list(key_2, value_2)$.

The map function is called for each input $value_1$, and produces a list of ($key_2$, $value_2$) pairs; this function can be executed in parallel on disjoint partitions of the input data.

Each output ($key_2$, $value_2$) pair of the map function is assigned to a unique reducer by a partition function, based on $key_2$ and the number of available reducers. Consequently, all ($key$, $value$) pairs with $key = key_2$ would be assigned to the same reducer.

reduce: ($key_2$, $list(value_2)$) $\rightarrow list(value_3)$.

The reduce function is called for each $key_2$ that is assigned to a reducer, and can access the list of all associated values $list(value_2)$ using a grouping function. This function can also be executed in parallel for different ($key_2$, $list(value_2)$) pairs.

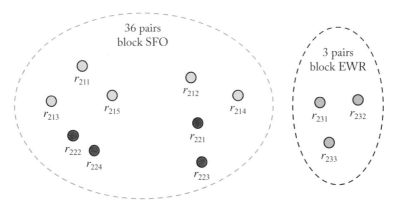

FIGURE 3.5: Using MapReduce: a basic approach.

## Using MapReduce: A Basic Approach

A basic approach to using MapReduce for record linkage is to: (i) read the input records, and use map functions in parallel to redistribute the input records among several reducers based on the blocking key; and (ii) perform pairwise matching on all records in a block using a reduce function, processing different blocks in parallel. Such a basic MapReduce implementation is susceptible to severe load imbalances due to *skewed* block sizes, limiting the speedup that can be achieved.

**Example 3.6** Consider using MapReduce to perform record linkage on the records in Table 3.1. Assume that the 12 records are blocked based on the value of attribute Departure Airport. The straightforward approach to using MapReduce would proceed as follows.

The nine records $r_{211}$-$r_{224}$ are mapped to one reducer based on the value SFO of attribute Departure Airport, and the three records $r_{231}$-$r_{233}$ are mapped to a second reducer based on the value EWR of attribute Departure Airport. The first reducer calls the reduce function on nine records: pairwise matching compares 36 pairs of records. The second reducer calls the reduce function on three records: pairwise matching compares only three pairs of records. Figure 3.5 illustrates this approach.

Due to the skewed block sizes, there is a significant load imbalance between the two reducers, and the speedup achieved over a sequential implementation is only 1.083 (i.e., $(36 + 3)/\max\{36, 3\}$) with two reducers.

## Using MapReduce: Load Balancing

Kolb et al. [2012] propose two strategies to balance the load among reducers for MapReduce-based record linkage: BLOCKSPLIT and PAIRRANGE.

The first strategy, BLOCKSPLIT, achieves load balancing by generating one or more logical *match* tasks for each block, and greedily distributing the logical match tasks to the physical reducers. It is based on three key ideas.

- First, a preprocessing MapReduce job determines the distribution of block sizes, to identify where load balancing would be needed.

- Second, BLOCKSPLIT processes small blocks (where the number of pairwise comparisons is no larger than the average workload that would need to be processed by a reducer to achieve a balanced load) within a single match task. Large blocks are split into smaller sub-blocks, which are processed using match tasks of two types: individual sub-blocks are processed akin to small blocks, and pairs of distinct sub-blocks are processed by match tasks that evaluate the cross-product of the two sub-blocks. This guarantees that all the pairwise comparisons in the original block will be computed by the (set of) match tasks.

- Third, BLOCKSPLIT determines the number of comparisons for each match task, and assigns match tasks to reducers to implement a greedy load balancing heuristic.

Since a record in a large block may need to participate in multiple match tasks, BLOCKSPLIT replicates such records, taking advantage of the ability of the map function to compute a list of $(key_2, value_2)$ pairs from a single input $value_1$, where the different $key_2$ values encode the nature of the match tasks that the record participates in.

**Example 3.7**    Consider again the records in Table 3.1, and assume that they are split into two groups according to an arbitrary input partitioning $\mathcal{P}$: records $r_{211}$, $r_{213}$, $r_{215}$, $r_{222}$, $r_{224}$, and $r_{232}$ are in group $P_0$, and records $r_{212}$, $r_{214}$, $r_{221}$, $r_{223}$, $r_{231}$, and $r_{233}$ are in group $P_1$.

The pre-processing MapReduce job determines the distribution of block sizes for each group in the input partition, resulting in the following distribution.

| Block Key | Partition Group | Size |
|:---:|:---:|:---:|
| SFO | $P_0$ | 5 |
| SFO | $P_1$ | 4 |
| EWR | $P_0$ | 1 |
| EWR | $P_1$ | 2 |

The block with blocking key EWR has three records, and three pairwise comparisons need to be performed on this block. The block with blocking key SFO has 9 records, and 36 pairwise comparisons need to be performed on this block. If record linkage needs to be conducted using two reducers, the block with blocking key EWR is considered as a small block, and the one with blocking key SFO is considered as a large block, and split into sub-blocks as illustrated in Figure 3.6.

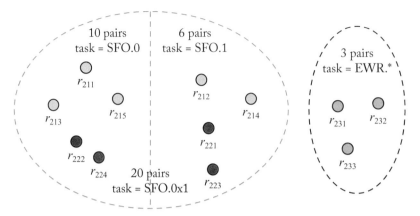

FIGURE 3.6:  Using MapReduce: BLOCKSPLIT.

To achieve this split, the map function first processes the records as described in the following table.

| Input $value_1$ | Partition Group | Output $list(key_2, value_2)$ |
|---|---|---|
| $r_{211}$ | $P_0$ | $[(SFO.0, r_{211}), (SFO.0x1, r_{211}^0)]$ |
| $r_{213}$ | $P_0$ | $[(SFO.0, r_{213}), (SFO.0x1, r_{213}^0)]$ |
| $r_{215}$ | $P_0$ | $[(SFO.0, r_{215}), (SFO.0x1, r_{215}^0)]$ |
| $r_{222}$ | $P_0$ | $[(SFO.0, r_{222}), (SFO.0x1, r_{222}^0)]$ |
| $r_{224}$ | $P_0$ | $[(SFO.0, r_{224}), (SFO.0x1, r_{224}^0)]$ |
| $r_{232}$ | $P_0$ | $[(EWR.*, r_{232})]$ |
| $r_{212}$ | $P_1$ | $[(SFO.1, r_{212}), (SFO.0x1, r_{212}^1)]$ |
| $r_{214}$ | $P_1$ | $[(SFO.1, r_{214}), (SFO.0x1, r_{214}^1)]$ |
| $r_{221}$ | $P_1$ | $[(SFO.1, r_{221}), (SFO.0x1, r_{221}^1)]$ |
| $r_{223}$ | $P_1$ | $[(SFO.1, r_{223}), (SFO.0x1, r_{223}^1)]$ |
| $r_{231}$ | $P_1$ | $[(EWR.*, r_{231})]$ |
| $r_{233}$ | $P_1$ | $[(EWR.*, r_{233})]$ |

The reduce function groups together $(key_2, value_2)$ pairs with the same $key_2$ value, and computes the number of comparisons to be performed based on the nature of the match task encoded in the $key_2$ value, as described in the following table.

| Input $(key_2, list(value_2))$ | Match Task | No. of Comparisons |
|---|---|---|
| $(SFO.0, [r_{211}, r_{213}, r_{215}, r_{222}, r_{224}])$ | sub-block matching | 10 |
| $(SFO.1, [r_{212}, r_{214}, r_{221}, r_{223}])$ | sub-block matching | 6 |
| $(SFO.0x1, [r_{211}^0, r_{213}^0, r_{215}^0, r_{222}^0, r_{224}^0$ $r_{212}^1, r_{214}^1, r_{221}^1, r_{223}^1])$ | cross-product matching | 20 |
| $(EWR.*, [r_{231}, r_{232}, r_{233}])$ | small block matching | 3 |

Finally, BLOCKSPLIT assigns the match tasks to the two available reducers, based on a greedy load balancing heuristic: reducer 0 is assigned match task $SFO.0x1$, which incurs 20 comparisons, reducer 1 is assigned match tasks $SFO.0$, $SFO.1$, and $EWR.*$, which together incur 19 comparisons. The speedup obtained with this assignment is 1.95 (i.e., $(20 + 19)/\max\{20, 19\}$), which is close to the ideal speedup of 2 with two reducers.

Since BLOCKSPLIT is dependent on the input partitioning, and uses a greedy load balancing heuristic, it does not guarantee load balancing, though it is quite effective as the previous example illustrates. The second strategy proposed by Kolb et al. [2012], PAIRRANGE, guarantees load balancing by assigning a very similar number of pairwise matchings to each reduce task. It is based on three key ideas.

- First, a preprocessing MapReduce job determines the distribution of block sizes, as for BLOCKSPLIT.

- Second, PAIRRANGE implements a *virtual global enumeration* of all records and relevant pairwise matchings based on the computed block size distribution. The enumeration scheme is used by a map function to identify the pairwise matchings that are processed by each reduce task.

- Third, to achieve load balancing, PAIRRANGE splits the range of all pairwise matchings into $r$ (almost) equal size ranges, and assigns the $k$'th range to the $k$'th reduce task.

As in BLOCKSPLIT, PAIRRANGE replicates input records, taking advantage of the ability of the map function to compute a list of $(key_2, value_2)$ pairs from a single input $value_1$.

**Example 3.8**   Consider again the records in Table 3.1, and assume that block size distributions are given, and the same input partitioning is used as in BLOCKSPLIT. The virtual global enumeration of all records and pairwise matchings is illustrated in Table 3.2.

First, the records in the block with blocking key SFO are virtually enumerated (randomly) in the order $r_{211}, r_{213}, r_{215}, r_{222}, r_{224}, r_{212}, r_{214}, r_{221}, r_{223}$; this is illustrated by assigning them

TABLE 3.2: Virtual global enumeration in PAIRRANGE

| | | Blocking key SFO | | | | | | | | | | Blocking key EWR | |
|---|---|---|---|---|---|---|---|---|---|---|---|---|---|
| | | $r_{211}$ | $r_{213}$ | $r_{215}$ | $r_{222}$ | $r_{224}$ | $r_{212}$ | $r_{214}$ | $r_{221}$ | | | $r_{232}$ | $r_{231}$ |
| | | 0 | 1 | 2 | 3 | 4 | 5 | 6 | 7 | | | 9 | 10 |
| $r_{213}$ | 1 | 0 | | | | | | | | | | | |
| $r_{215}$ | 2 | 1 | 8 | | | | | | | $r_{231}$ | 10 | 36 | |
| $r_{222}$ | 3 | 2 | 9 | 15 | | | | | | $r_{233}$ | 11 | 37 | 38 |
| $r_{224}$ | 4 | 3 | 10 | 16 | 21 | | | | | | | | |
| $r_{212}$ | 5 | 4 | 11 | 17 | 22 | 26 | | | | | | | |
| $r_{214}$ | 6 | 5 | 12 | 18 | 23 | 27 | 30 | | | | | | |
| $r_{221}$ | 7 | 6 | 13 | 19 | 24 | 28 | 31 | 33 | | | | | |
| $r_{223}$ | 8 | 7 | 14 | 20 | 25 | 29 | 32 | 34 | 35 | | | | |

numbers 0–8 in Table 3.2. Since every pair of records in this block needs to be compared, the pairwise matchings can also be virtually enumerated, by leveraging the numbers assigned to each of the records participating in the pairwise matchings. Thus, the pairwise matching $(r_{211}, r_{213})$, corresponding to the records with numbers 0 and 1, is assigned the smallest number 0; $(r_{211}, r_{215})$ is assigned the next number 1; and so on, until the last pairwise matching $(r_{221}, r_{223})$, corresponding to the record with numbers 7 and 8, is assigned the largest number 35.

In the next step, the records in the block with blocking key EWR are virtually enumerated (randomly) in the order $r_{232}, r_{231}, r_{233}$; this is illustrated by assigning them numbers 9–11 in Table 3.2. Then, all pairwise matchings involving these records are also enumerated in the virtual global enumeration; this is illustrated by assigning them numbers 36–38.

Finally, if there are only two reducers, PAIRRANGE achieves load balancing by splitting the range [0, 38] into two almost equally sized ranges, [0, 19] (indicated in green color in Table 3.2) and [20, 38] (indicated in purple color in Table 3.2), and assigns these two ranges of pairwise matchings to the two different reducers.

## Main Results

Kolb et al. [2012] experimentally evaluate the various load balancing strategies on real-world data sets, and compare them with the basic approach to using MapReduce for record linkage. Their main results are as follows.

1. Both BLOCKSPLIT and PAIRRANGE are stable across all data skews, with a small advantage for PAIRRANGE due to its somewhat more uniform workload distribution.

   In comparison, the basic strategy is not robust because a higher data skew increases the number of pairs of the largest block, which can make it an order of magnitude or more slower than either BLOCKSPLIT or PAIRRANGE.

2. Both BLOCKSPLIT and PAIRRANGE can take advantage of an increasing number of reduce tasks, and are able to evenly distribute the workload across reduce tasks and nodes. BLOCK-SPLIT is shown to be preferable for smaller data sets, otherwise PAIRRANGE has a better performance.

### 3.2.2    META-BLOCKING: PRUNING PAIRWISE MATCHINGS

Papadakis et al. [2014] consider the problem of identifying the most promising set of pairwise matchings to perform when the set of all pairwise matchings suggested by the use of a blocking method is still too large for efficient record linkage.

As discussed in Section 3.1.3, blocking methods that allow multiple overlapping blocks have the advantage of reducing false negatives (i.e., missed matches). Such methods are especially important in the presence of schematic heterogeneity, where the lack of schema alignment suggests the use of blocking keys in a schema-agnostic fashion. This issue is illustrated in the following example.

**Example 3.9**    Consider the five records $r'_{211}$-$r'_{215}$ shown in Table 3.3. These records refer to the same entity, and contain the same information as the corresponding records $r_{211}$-$r_{215}$ in Table 3.1. However, the schemas of the records in Table 3.3 have not been properly aligned, and the values in green and in bold font indicate misaligned values (while values in red and in bold font indicate erroneous data, as in Table 3.1).

For example, records $r'_{211}$ and $r'_{215}$ contain the value EWR in the same column as the value SFO in records $r'_{212}$-$r'_{214}$. Whether this column is assumed to be the Departure Airport or the Arrival Airport, such inconsistencies would cause problems for traditional record linkage, which assumes schematic homogeneity. In particular, even if one used multiple blocking keys on the values of (column 4, column 5) and (column 7, column 8), which is analogous to the multiple blocking keys used in Example 3.5, subsequent pairwise matching would only be able to compare record pairs $(r'_{212}, r'_{214})$, $(r'_{211}, r'_{215})$ and $(r'_{213}, r'_{214})$, making it impossible to link all five records, even though they refer to the same entity.

If, however, blocking was done on the (multiple) values of (Airport, Date), *independent* of the columns in which these values occur, then every pair of records among the five records $r'_{211}$-$r'_{215}$ would undergo pairwise matching (which would also need to be schema-agnostic to correctly

TABLE 3.3: Sample Flights records with schematic heterogeneity

| | | | | | | | | | |
|---|---|---|---|---|---|---|---|---|---|
| $r'_{211}$ | A2 | 53 | EWR | 2014-02-08 | 15:35 | SFO | 2014-02-08 | 23:55 |
| $r'_{212}$ | A2 | 53 | SFO | 2014-02-08 | 00:05 | EWR | 2014-02-08 | 00:05 |
| $r'_{213}$ | A2 | 53 | SFO | 2014-02-09 | 15:27 | EWR | 2014-02-08 | 00:09 |
| $r'_{214}$ | A1 | 53 | SFO | 2014-02-08 | 15:15 | EWR | 2014-02-08 | 23:30 |
| $r'_{215}$ | A2 | 53 | EWR | 2014-03-08 | 23:55 | SFO | 2014-02-08 | 15:27 |
| $r'_{221}$ | A2 | 53 | EWR | 2014-03-09 | 15:30 | SFO | 2014-03-09 | 23:45 |
| $r'_{222}$ | A2 | 53 | SFO | 2014-03-09 | 23:40 | EWR | 2014-03-09 | 15:37 |
| $r'_{223}$ | A2 | 53 | SFO | 2014-03-09 | 15:28 | EWR | 2014-03-09 | 23:37 |
| $r'_{224}$ | A2 | 53 | EWR | 2014-03-08 | 23:35 | SFO | 2014-03-09 | 15:25 |
| $r'_{231}$ | A1 | 49 | SFO | 2014-02-08 | 18:45 | EWR | 2014-02-08 | 21:40 |
| $r'_{232}$ | A1 | 49 | EWR | 2014-02-08 | 18:30 | SFO | 2014-02-08 | 21:37 |
| $r'_{233}$ | A1 | 49 | EWR | 2014-02-08 | 18:30 | SAN | 2014-02-08 | 21:30 |

declare record matches), and subsequent clustering would determine that they all refer to the same entity.

## Using Multiple Blocking Keys: Inefficiency

Example 3.9 showed that, in the presence of schema heterogeneity in big data, the use of multiple blocking keys in a schema-agnostic fashion is essential to achieve high recall. However, it can result in considerable inefficiency: many pairs of *non-matching* records may end up being compared because of the schema-agnostic use of blocking keys. This issue is illustrated in the following example.

**Example 3.10**   Example 3.5 showed how the use of multiple blocking functions such as (Departure Airport, Departure Date) and (Arrival Airport, Arrival Date) would avoid the problem of false negatives associated with the use of either blocking key.

In the presence of schema heterogeneity, it is unclear which values correspond to Departure Airport and Arrival Airport, and which values correspond to Departure Date and Arrival Date. To get the benefits of multiple blocking functions, one would need to block on multiple values, regardless of the columns in which these values occur. Figure 3.7 illustrates the different (overlapping) blocks that would be created when blocking on *possible* (Airline), (Flight Number), (Departure Airport, Departure Date), and (Arrival Airport, Arrival Date) values; only blocks that have more than one record are shown in the figure.

The use of schema-agnostic blocking ends up comparing many more non-matching record pairs. As can be seen from Figure 3.7, non-matching record pairs $(r'_{211}, r'_{231})$ and $(r'_{213}, r'_{232})$ would

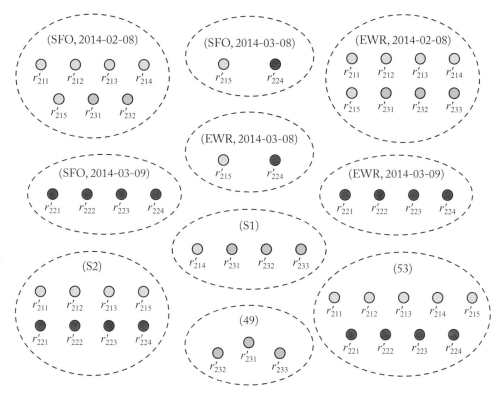

FIGURE 3.7: Using schema agnostic blocking on multiple values.

end up being compared, since these records occur in the blocks (SFO, 2014-02-08) and (EWR, 2014-02-08). Note that these record pairs would *not* have been compared at all for the same set of blocking functions in the absence of schema heterogeneity, as in Table 3.1. Thus, the use of schema-agnostic blocking can increase the number of non-matching record pairs that undergo pairwise comparison.

## Meta-blocking: Improving Efficiency

Papadakis et al. [2014] propose *meta-blocking* as an approach to address the problem identified previously. They aim to identify the most promising pairs of records for pairwise comparison, based on a given set of blocks, thereby (i) performing significantly fewer pairwise comparisons, while (ii) maintaining a high recall. Meta-blocking is independent of the choice of blocking functions used, but is especially useful when the underlying blocking functions perform schema-agnostic blocking.

Meta-blocking first builds an edge-weighted *blocking graph*, $G_B$, for a given set of blocks $\mathcal{B}$, where the nodes of $G_B$ are the records that occur in at least one block of $\mathcal{B}$, and (undirected) edges connect pairs of records that co-occur in at least one block. Papadakis et al. [2014] propose several edge weighting schemes, and pruning schemes, as follows.

- The edge weights are intended to balance the cost and benefit of actually performing the pairwise comparison between the records that are connected by the edge.

- The pruning schemes identify and remove edges in the blocking graph that have a low likelihood of a match. Pairwise comparisons are performed only for the edges that remain in the blocking graph after pruning.

A simple edge weighting strategy is the Common Blocks Scheme (CBS), where the weight of an edge is the number of common blocks in which the two records co-occur. A more sophisticated strategy is the Aggregate Reciprocal Comparisons Scheme (ARCS), where the weight of an edge is the sum of the reciprocal cardinalities of their common blocks; the intuition is that the more records a block contains, the less likely they are to match.

Papadakis et al. [2014] propose pruning schemes that compose a pruning algorithm and a pruning criterion. Two pruning algorithms, edge-centric (EP) and node-centric (NP), are identified, where EP algorithms select the most globally promising edges, while NP algorithms select the edges that are the most locally promising for each node. Two pruning criteria, weight-based (W) and cardinality-based (C), are identified, where weight-based pruning eliminates edges whose weight is below an identified threshold, while cardinality-based pruning retains the top-k edges. By combining the pruning algorithm and the pruning criterion, four pruning schemes—WEP, CEP, WNP and CNP—are identified.

We illustrate an edge weighting strategy and some pruning schemes in the following example.

**Example 3.11**   Consider the set of blocks depicted in Figure 3.7, for the records in Table 3.3.

Figure 3.8 depicts the blocking graph for the CBS edge weighting strategy, where nodes of the same color indicate records that refer to the same entity. The solid edges have a weight of 3 or 4 (i.e., the corresponding records co-occur in 3 or 4 blocks). For example, the records $(r'_{211}, r'_{213})$ co-occur in the four blocks (SFO, 2014-02-08), (EWR, 2014-02-08), (A2), and (53), while the records $(r'_{214}, r'_{231})$ co-occur in the three blocks (SFO, 2014-02-08), (EWR, 2014-02-08), and (A1). The dashed edges have a weight of 1 or 2 (i.e., the corresponding records co-occur in 1 or 2 blocks). For example, the records $(r'_{211}, r'_{233})$ co-occur in only one block (EWR, 2014-02-08), while the records $(r'_{211}, r'_{222})$ co-occur in the two blocks (A2) and (53). There are a total of 54 edges in the graph, of which 22 are solid edges, and 32 are dashed edges. The average edge weight in this blocking graph is 136/54 = 2.52.

If the WEP (weight-based, edge-centric pruning) scheme was used with a weight threshold of the average edge weight, all the edges with weight 1 or 2 (i.e., the dashed edges) would get

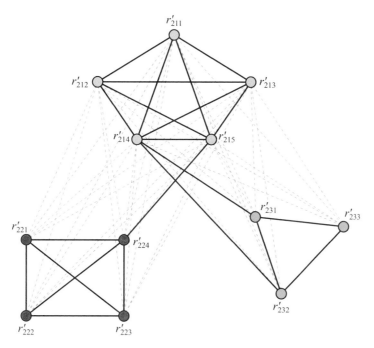

FIGURE 3.8: Using meta-blocking with schema agnostic blocking.

pruned out. Only the 22 edges with a weight of 3 or 4 (i.e., the solid edges) would undergo pairwise comparison.

If the CEP (cardinality-based, edge-centric pruning) scheme was used with a cardinality threshold of at least 22, all the solid edges would be retained and undergo pairwise comparison. With a lower cardinality threshold, e.g., 13, some matching record pairs may not undergo pairwise comparison, leading to a lower recall.

## Main Results

Papadakis et al. [2014] experimentally evaluate various edge weighting strategies and pruning schemes to demonstrate the benefits of meta-blocking over conventional blocking methods. Their data sets and code are publicly available at http://sourceforge.net/projects/erframework (accessed on October 1, 2014), and their main results are as follows.

1. Meta-blocking significantly improves blocking efficiency, often by 1-2 orders of magnitude, while preserving a high recall.

    The main reasons are that (i) the construction of the blocking graph uses low-cost edge weight computation, instead of the more expensive pairwise comparison, and (ii) a large number of (non-matching) record pairs are pruned, and hence not compared in a pairwise fashion.

2. Edge-centric pruning typically outperforms node-centric pruning in efficiency, discarding more superfluous pairwise comparisons, while maintaining a high recall when the fraction of matching record pairs is expected to be low. In this case, the high weighted edges are more likely to correspond to the matching record pairs.

3. Weight-based pruning typically achieves a better recall than cardinality-based pruning. Depending on the threshold, the latter can be much more efficient than the former, but this is achieved with a moderate loss in recall.

4. Among the proposed edge weighting schemes, ARCS consistently achieves the highest performance. This is because ARCS downweights the co-occurrence of records in high cardinality blocks, which is analogous to the use of IDF (inverse document frequency) in document search.

## 3.3    ADDRESSING THE VELOCITY CHALLENGE

In the big data era, many of the data sources are very dynamic and the number of data sources is also rapidly exploding. This high velocity of data updates can quickly make previous linkage results obsolete. Since it is expensive to perform batch record linkage each time there is a data update, it would be ideal to perform *incremental record linkage*, to be able to quickly update existing linkage results when data updates arrive.

### 3.3.1    INCREMENTAL RECORD LINKAGE

While there has been a significant body of work on record linkage in the literature over the past few decades, incremental record linkage has started to receive attention only in recent years [Whang and Garcia-Molina 2010, Whang and Garcia-Molina 2014, Gruenheid et al. 2014].

The main focus of the works by Whang and Garcia-Molina [2010], Whang and Garcia-Molina [2014] is the evolution of pairwise matching rules over time. Whang and Garcia-Molina [2014] briefly discuss the case of evolving data, and identify a *general incremental* condition under which incremental record linkage can be easily performed using the batch linkage method. Gruenheid et al. [2014] address the general case where the batch linkage algorithm may not be general incremental, and propose incremental techniques that explore the trade-offs between quality of the linkage results and efficiency of the incremental algorithms.

### Challenges for Incremental Linkage

Recall that record linkage computes a partitioning $\mathcal{P}$ of the input records $\mathcal{R}$, such that each partition in $\mathcal{P}$ identifies the records in $\mathcal{R}$ that refer to the same entity.

A natural thought for incremental linkage is that each inserted record is compared with existing clusters, then either put it into an existing cluster (i.e., referring to an already known entity), or create a new cluster for it (i.e., referring to a new entity). However, linkage algorithms can make mistakes and the extra information from the data updates can often help identify and fix such mistakes, as illustrated next with an example.

**Example 3.12**    Table 3.4 shows the records from the Flights domain, organized according to the order in which the date updates arrived, where $\overline{\text{Flights}_0}$ is the initial set of records, and $\Delta\overline{\text{Flights}_1}$ and $\Delta\overline{\text{Flights}_2}$ are two updates.

Assume that the initial set of records $\overline{\text{Flights}_0}$ consists of seven records—$r_{213}$, $r_{214}$, $r_{215}$, $r_{224}$, $r_{231}$, $r_{232}$, and $r_{233}$. Figure 3.9 illustrates the pairwise matching graph obtained by applying the same pairwise similarity as in Example 3.2, and the result of record linkage by applying correlation clustering on this graph. Note that this partitioning makes several mistakes due to the errors in the data.

- Records $r_{215}$ and $r_{224}$ are in the same cluster, even though they refer to different entities. This happens because of the erroneous values of Departure Date in both records.

- Records $r_{213}$, $r_{214}$, and $r_{215}$ are in different clusters, even though they refer to the same entity. This happens because the pairwise similarity measure does not declare any match between pairs of these records, again because of the erroneous values in these records.

TABLE 3.4:  Flights records and updates

|  |  | AL | FN | DA | DD | DT | AA | AD | AT |
|---|---|---|---|---|---|---|---|---|---|
| Flights$_0$ | $r_{213}$ | A2 | 53 | SFO | 2014-02-08 | 15:27 | EWR | 2014-02-09 | 00:09 |
|  | $r_{214}$ | **A1** | 53 | SFO | 2014-02-08 | 15:15 | EWR | 2014-02-08 | 23:30 |
|  | $r_{215}$ | A2 | 53 | SFO | **2014-03-08** | 15:27 | EWR | 2014-02-08 | 23:55 |
|  | $r_{224}$ | A2 | 53 | SFO | **2014-03-08** | 15:25 | EWR | 2014-03-09 | 23:35 |
|  | $r_{231}$ | A1 | 49 | EWR | 2014-02-08 | 18:45 | SFO | 2014-02-08 | 21:40 |
|  | $r_{232}$ | A1 | 49 | EWR | 2014-02-08 | 18:30 | SFO | 2014-02-08 | 21:37 |
|  | $r_{233}$ | A1 | 49 | EWR | 2014-02-08 | 18:30 | **SAN** | 2014-02-08 | 21:30 |
| $\Delta$Flights$_1$ | $r_{221}$ | A2 | 53 | SFO | 2014-03-09 | 15:30 | EWR | 2014-03-09 | 23:45 |
|  | $r_{222}$ | A2 | 53 | SFO | 2014-03-09 | 15:37 | EWR | 2014-03-09 | 23:40 |
|  | $r_{223}$ | A2 | 53 | SFO | 2014-03-09 | 15:28 | EWR | 2014-03-09 | 23:37 |
| $\Delta$Flights$_2$ | $r_{211}$ | A2 | 53 | SFO | 2014-02-08 | 15:35 | EWR | 2014-02-08 | 23:55 |
|  | $r_{212}$ | A2 | 53 | SFO | 2014-02-08 | 15:25 | EWR | **2014-02-08** | 00:05 |

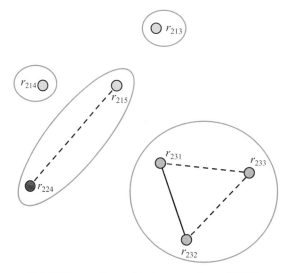

FIGURE 3.9: Record linkage results on $\overline{\text{Flights}}_0$.

Now consider the update $\Delta\overline{\text{Flights}}_1$, shown in Table 3.4, which consists of records $r_{221}$, $r_{222}$, and $r_{223}$. Figure 3.10 illustrates the pairwise matching graph, and the result of batch record linkage by applying correlation clustering on this graph. Note that the extra information from this update has helped identify and fix the previous mistake of putting $r_{215}$ and $r_{224}$ in the same cluster. Clearly, this error could not have been fixed if an inserted record is either added to an existing cluster or used to create a new cluster.

Finally, consider the update $\Delta\overline{\text{Flights}}_2$, shown in Table 3.4, which consists of records $r_{211}$ and $r_{212}$. Figure 3.11 illustrates the pairwise matching graph, and the result of batch record linkage by applying correlation clustering on this graph. This contains three clusters, and fixes the previous mistake of putting $r_{213}$, $r_{214}$, and $r_{215}$ in separate clusters.

### Optimal Incremental Algorithms

The goal of incremental linkage is two-fold. First, incremental linkage should be *much faster* than conducting batch linkage, especially when the number of operations in the update $\Delta\overline{R}$ is small. Second, incremental linkage should obtain results of *similar quality* to batch linkage.

Note that correlation clustering algorithms operate on individual nodes and edges of the graph, rather than on clusters, so they are *not* general incremental. Hence, the techniques of Whang and Garcia-Molina [2014] are not applicable in the previous example. For this reason, we focus attention on the incremental record linkage algorithms proposed by Gruenheid et al. [2014] in this section.

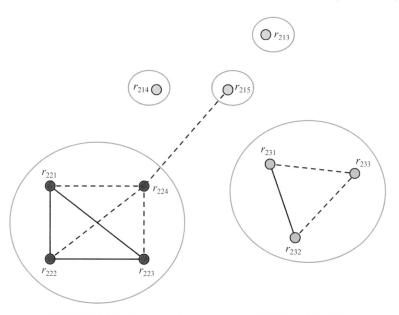

FIGURE 3.10: Record linkage results on $\overline{\mathsf{Flights}}_0 + \Delta\overline{\mathsf{Flights}}_1$.

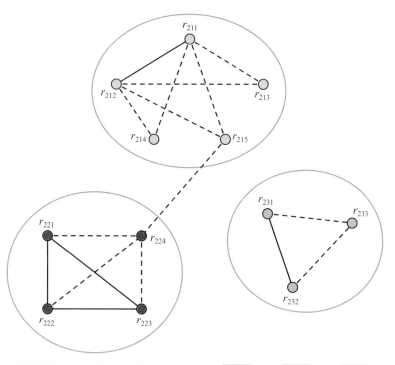

FIGURE 3.11: Record linkage results on $\overline{\mathsf{Flights}}_0 + \Delta\overline{\mathsf{Flights}}_1 + \Delta\overline{\mathsf{Flights}}_2$.

Gruenheid et al. propose two incremental algorithms, CONNECTEDCOMPONENT and ITER-ATIVE, that apply correlation clustering on subsets of the records, rather than all records, but are guaranteed to find an optimal solution.

The CONNECTEDCOMPONENT algorithm considers only the clusters in the previous record linkage result that are directly or indirectly connected to the nodes in the update $\Delta \overline{R}$. Correlation clustering is applied on this subgraph $G$, and the new result of record linkage is obtained from the previous result by replacing the old clusters of $G$ by the new clusters.

The ITERATIVE algorithm starts with the clusters in the previous record linkage result that are *directly* connected to the nodes in the update $\Delta \overline{R}$, and expands it only when necessary. Intuitively, it proceeds in three steps.

1. Obtain the clusters that are directly connected to the update $\Delta \overline{R}$, and put each of its connected subgraphs into a queue.

2. For each connected subgraph $G$ in the queue, dequeue it, and find its optimal clustering $\overline{C}$. For each cluster $C \in \overline{C}$ that did not exist in the previous clustering, find other clusters that are directly connected to it, and put this connected subgraph $G_1$ into the queue, taking care to remove duplicates and merge with overlapping subgraphs in the queue.

3. Repeat Step 2 until the queue is empty.

**Theorem 3.1** [Gruenheid et al. 2014] CONNECTEDCOMPONENT and ITERATIVE give optimal results for incremental record linkage if optimal algorithms are used for correlation clustering.

The proof of this theorem is based on establishing that correlation clustering satisfies a variety of desirable properties, including *locality*, *exchangeability*, *separability*, and *monotonicity* [Gruenheid et al. 2014]. The optimality of CONNECTEDCOMPONENT relies only on locality and monotonicity, while the optimality of ITERATIVE relies on all the properties being satisfied.

Correlation clustering is an NP-complete problem, hence optimal algorithms for correlation clustering are not feasible for big data [Bansal et al. 2004]. However, a variety of polynomial-time approximation algorithms have been proposed for correlation clustering (e.g., Bansal et al. 2004, Charikar et al. 2003), and any of these algorithms can be used within the framework of CONNECTEDCOMPONENT and ITERATIVE. While the resulting algorithms do not have any optimality guarantees, Gruenheid et al. [2014] show that they obtain good quality results in practice.

**Example 3.13** Consider the records in Table 3.4, and the clustering of $\overline{\text{Flights}_0}$ shown in Figure 3.9.

Let us consider the case when the records $r_{221}$, $r_{222}$, and $r_{223}$ in the update $\Delta \overline{\text{Flights}_1}$ are added. These records are (directly or indirectly) connected only to the cluster in Figure 3.9 that contains $r_{224}$ and $r_{215}$. Hence, CONNECTEDCOMPONENT applies correlation clustering on these five records, and obtains two clusters, one containing $r_{221}$-$r_{224}$, the other containing only $r_{215}$. ITERATIVE performs the same actions in this case. The resulting clustering of $\overline{\text{Flights}}_0 + \Delta \overline{\text{Flights}}_1$ is shown in Figure 3.10.

Now consider the case when the records $r_{211}$ and $r_{212}$ in the update $\Delta \overline{\text{Flights}}_2$ are added. These records are (directly or indirectly) connected to the four clusters in Figure 3.10 that contain $r_{213}$, $r_{214}$, $r_{215}$, and $r_{221}$-$r_{224}$. Hence, CONNECTEDCOMPONENT applies correlation clustering on these nine records, and obtains two clusters, one containing $r_{211}$-$r_{215}$, and the other containing $r_{221}$-$r_{224}$.

In this case, ITERATIVE does something different from CONNECTEDCOMPONENT, although the final result is identical. Note that the records in the update $\Delta \overline{\text{Flights}}_2$ are directly connected only to the three clusters in Figure 3.10 that contain $r_{213}$, $r_{214}$, and $r_{215}$. Hence, ITERATIVE first applies correlation clustering on the five records $r_{211}$-$r_{215}$, and obtains a single cluster that contains all five records. Since this is a new cluster, which is directly connected to the cluster in Figure 3.10 that contains $r_{221}$-$r_{224}$, ITERATIVE next applies correlation clustering on the nine records $r_{211}$-$r_{224}$. Since this results in the same two clusters as before, ITERATIVE terminates. The resulting clustering of $\overline{\text{Flights}}_0 + \Delta \overline{\text{Flights}}_1 + \Delta \overline{\text{Flights}}_2$ is shown in Figure 3.11.

Note that, in this example, ITERATIVE does more work than CONNECTEDCOMPONENT. However, if the first iteration of ITERATIVE (applying correlation clustering on the five records $r_{211}$-$r_{215}$) had resulted in no change to the singleton cluster containing $r_{215}$, ITERATIVE would have terminated after the first iteration, doing strictly less work than CONNECTEDCOMPONENT.

## Greedy Incremental Algorithms

In general, the CONNECTEDCOMPONENT algorithm may require considering an unnecessarily big subgraph when the pairwise similarity graph is well connected, while the ITERATIVE algorithm may require repeated efforts in examining quite a few subgraphs before convergence, as shown in Example 3.13. Further, both algorithms operate at the coarse granularity of connected subgraphs of the graph, which can be even larger than individual clusters.

Gruenheid et al. [2014] also propose a polynomial-time GREEDY algorithm, where the clustering in each later round is incrementally built upon the clustering of the previous round. Specifically, each time a cluster in the queue is examined, the algorithm considers three possible operations on the cluster, and chooses the best option (the one with the lowest penalty value, as in correlation clustering).

- MERGE the cluster with one neighboring cluster.

- SPLIT the cluster into two clusters, by examining one record at a time and deciding whether splitting it out of the cluster generates a better clustering.

- MOVE some nodes of the cluster to a neighboring cluster, or move some nodes of a neighboring cluster into the given cluster.

We illustrate the operation of the GREEDY algorithm using an example next.

**Example 3.14**   Consider the records in Table 3.4, and the clustering of $\overline{\text{Flights}}_0$ shown in Figure 3.9.

When the records $r_{221}$, $r_{222}$, and $r_{223}$ in the update $\Delta\overline{\text{Flights}}_1$ are added, each of these records is first put into the queue separately. A series of MERGE operations is then performed to result in a single cluster containing these three records: the intra-cluster penalty of this cluster is 0, since each pair of records in the cluster is a match according to the pairwise similarity measure used. Finally, a MOVE operation is performed to move record $r_{224}$ from the previous cluster containing $r_{224}$ and $r_{215}$ into the cluster containing records $r_{221}$, $r_{222}$, and $r_{223}$. The GREEDY algorithm then terminates, with the clustering shown in Figure 3.10.

Similarly, when the records $r_{211}$ and $r_{212}$ in the update $\Delta\overline{\text{Flights}}_2$ are added to the clustering shown in Figure 3.10, a series of greedy MERGE operations would end up with the clustering where all records that refers to the same entity are in the same cluster, and records that refer to different entities are in different clusters. This is shown in Figure 3.11.

## Main Results

Gruenheid et al. [2014] experimentally evaluate the various incremental linkage algorithms to demonstrate their benefits over batch linkage as well as naive incremental linkage algorithms. Their main results are as follows.

1. The incremental record linkage algorithms significantly improve over batch linkage on efficiency (often by 1-2 orders of magnitude) without sacrificing linkage quality.

2. The CONNECTEDCOMPONENT algorithm is always better than batch record linkage for all update sizes as it solely modifies those clusters that are (directly or indirectly) connected to the update.

3. The iterative approaches, ITERATIVE (with the polynomial time algorithm that provides an approximation for correlation clustering [Bansal et al. 2004]) and GREEDY, are best applied to updates that affect a small portion of the pairwise matching graph, i.e., when the update has a local rather than global impact.

4. The GREEDY algorithm is shown to be the most robust in noisy environments, obtained by varying the parameters of a synthetic data set generator.

## 3.4   ADDRESSING THE VARIETY CHALLENGE

The big data era has a large variety of domains, sources, and data, as illustrated in Chapter 1. Ideally, schema alignment (as described in the previous chapter) should have resolved schematic heterogeneity across the sources, and the task of record linkage could assume schematic homogeneity among the sources. In practice, though, schema alignment is not easy, especially when entities, relationships and ontologies need to be extracted from text snippets.

### 3.4.1    LINKING TEXT SNIPPETS TO STRUCTURED DATA

Many applications see a need to link text snippets with embedded attribute values, and sometimes attribute names along with other text, to structured records. We will illustrate both the challenging aspects of the problem, and the intricacy of the presented technique using an example from our Flights domain.

### Challenges

One approach to link a text snippet to the structured data is to use information extraction techniques on the text snippet to obtain a structured, properly segmented record [Cortez and da Silva 2013], and then use the techniques discussed in previous sections for the linkage. However, this may not be straightforward for text snippets that are terse, with grammatically ill-formed text in the snippet. Motivated by the need to link unstructured product offers from tens of thousands of online merchants to a known shopping catalog with structured product information, Kannan et al. [2011] consider this linkage problem. They propose a novel approach to link the text snippets to the structured data in a way that makes effective use of the data in the structured records for this purpose. The following example identifies some of the challenges that need to be overcome.

**Example 3.15**    Let the structured data consist of only records $r_{211}$, $r_{221}$, and $r_{231}$ from Table 3.1, reproduced in Table 3.5 for convenience. Consider the following text snippet, containing booking information for a flight ticket.

> PNR TWQZNK for A2 flight 53 SFO 2014-02-08 (15:30 hrs) to EWR fare class Q $355.55 confirmed.

It is evident that this booking information text snippet is a good match for record $r_{211}$ in Table 3.5. However, being able to link them requires overcoming several challenges.

TABLE 3.5:  Sample Flights records from Table 3.1

|        | AL | FN | DA  | DD         | DT    | AA  | AD         | AT    |
|--------|----|----|-----|------------|-------|-----|------------|-------|
| $r_{211}$ | A2 | 53 | SFO | 2014-02-08 | 15:35 | EWR | 2014-02-08 | 23:55 |
| $r_{221}$ | A2 | 53 | SFO | 2014-03-09 | 15:30 | EWR | 2014-03-09 | 23:45 |
| $r_{231}$ | A1 | 49 | EWR | 2014-02-08 | 18:45 | SFO | 2014-02-08 | 21:40 |

- First, the text snippet does not always contain attribute names. For example, SFO could match Departure Airport or Arrival Airport.

- Second, the attribute values present in the text snippet may match exactly or approximately, or even be erroneous. For example, 15:30 in the text snippet matches the Departure Time of $r_{221}$ exactly, and that of $r_{211}$ approximately.

- Third, the text snippet does not contain all the attribute values from the structured records, i.e., one has to deal with missing data. For example, there is no information about the arrival date or arrival time into EWR in the text snippet.

- Fourth, the text snippet may contain attribute values that are not present in the structured data. For example, it contains information about fare class (Q) and price ($355.55), which are not present in the structured record.

## Solution

Kannan et al. [2011] take a supervised learning approach to the linkage problem and find the structured record that has the highest probability of match to the given unstructured text snippet. The matching function is learned in an offline stage, based on a small training set of text snippets, each of which has been matched to a unique structured record. In the subsequent online stage, new text snippets are matched one at a time, by choosing the best matched structured record amongst the candidates by applying the learned matching function. The key components of the offline and online stages are the *semantic parsing* strategy for the text snippets, and the *matching function* for quantifying the quality of the match.

Semantic parsing of a text snippet is used both in the offline and online stages, and consists of three steps: *tagging* strings in the text snippet with attribute names, identifying *plausible parses* based on the tags, and finally obtaining an *optimal parse* of the text snippet for each candidate structured record.

**Tagging.** Let $\mathcal{A}$ denote the attribute names in the structured data. An inverted index is built on the structured records such that, for each string $v$, the inverted index returns the set of attribute names in $\mathcal{A}$ associated with string $v$ in the structured records.

Tagging of the text snippet is accomplished by examining all token level $q$-grams (e.g., up to $q = 4$) in the snippet and associating it with the set of all attribute names, using the inverted index.

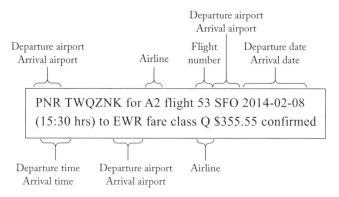

FIGURE 3.12: Tagging of text snippet.

**Plausible Parse.**   Given the tagging, a plausible parse of a text snippet is defined to be a particular combination of all attributes identified in the tagging step such that each attribute is associated with at most one value.[3]

 Multiple plausible parses arise because of ambiguities in the data. Typically, only a small number of parses are plausible.

**Optimal Parse.**   When the text snippet is paired with a structured record, one of the plausible parses of the text snippet is optimal, based on the learned matching function.

 Different parses of the text snippet may be optimal for different structured records. Each of these is evaluated, and the structured record that has the highest match probability with the text snippet is returned.

We illustrate the semantic parsing strategy using an example next.

**Example 3.16**   Figure 3.12 shows the tagging of our example text snippet, using a large structured database that contains (among others) the records in Table 3.5. As can be seen, three distinct strings PNR, SFO, and EWR have been tagged with the two attributes Departure Airport and Arrival Airport, since these are all valid airport codes. In this text snippet, the intent of PNR is passenger name record and the tagging indicates the ambiguity in the data. However, strings such as $355.55 in the text snippet are not tagged since the structured data do not contain any attributes with pricing information.

---

3. Not associating an identified attribute with a value is needed since the text snippet may not contain all attributes from the structured data, and may contain attributes not present in the structured data.

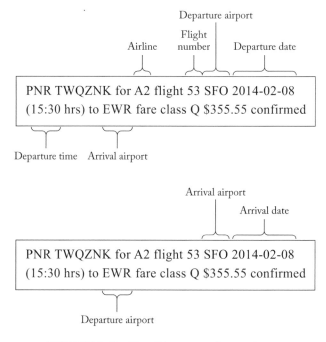

FIGURE 3.13:  Plausible parses of text snippet.

The tagging of the text snippet shown in Figure 3.12 has multiple plausible parses, due to the ambiguity of the terse text snippet. Figure 3.13 shows two of the plausible parses. The plausible parse at the top of the figure has associated the attribute Departure Airport with the value SFO, and the attribute Arrival Airport with the value EWR. The plausible parse at the bottom of the figure has reversed the associations. The plausible parse at the top of the figure has values for the attributes Airline, Flight Number and Departure Time. The plausible parse at the bottom of the figure has no values for these attributes; this captures the possibility that the strings such as A2, 53, and 15:30 may not refer to attributes present in the structured data.

Kannan et al. [2011] present a matching function that can provide a probabilistic score of matching between the text snippet and the structured record. In addition to ensuring that it takes into account the match in values of certain attributes, the matching function also needs to (i) penalize mismatches more than missing values, and (ii) learn the relative importance among these attributes.

For the former criterion, a *similarity feature vector* is designed for determining the similarity levels between corresponding attributes, where

(i) A feature value is 1 if the attribute values in the text snippet and structured record match; for numeric values (such as Departure Time), approximation is allowed in measuring similarity.

(ii)  A feature value is −1 if the attribute values mismatch.

(iii)  A feature value is 0 if the attribute value is missing.

For the latter criterion, binary logistic regression is used to learn the weights of each feature, given labeled data of good and bad matches. The logistic regression learns a mapping from the similarity feature vector to a binary label.

**Example 3.17**   Continue with Example 3.16. The plausible parse at the top of Figure 3.13 is the optimal parse for record $r_{211}$, with the similarity feature vector having value 1 for each of the attributes Airline, Flight Number, Departure Airport, Departure Date, Departure Time (allowing for numeric approximation), and Arrival Airport, and value 0 for all the other attributes.

Similarly, the plausible parse at the bottom of the figure is the optimal parse for record $r_{231}$ in Table 3.5, with the similarity feature vector having value 1 for each of the attributes Departure Airport, Arrival Airport, and Arrival Date.

Among these, record $r_{211}$ has a higher match probability with the text snippet, and is returned.

## Main Results
Kannan et al. [2011] experimentally evaluate several variants of their matching function in order to study its characteristics, and also identify product categories where their technique resulted in at least 85% precision in matching. Their system is deployed and used to match all the offers received by Bing Shopping to the Bing product catalog. Their main results are as follows.

1. They observe that there is a positive correlation between the price of products in a category and the data quality of the structured data and unstructured product offers. In particular, the product categories that do not pass the desired threshold of 85% precision are low price categories (e.g., accessories).

2. They show that the quality of the matching function improves when the weights of each feature are learned, compared to assuming that the features are weighted equally. This is especially true in the presence of low data quality, when certain combinations of few features provide spurious matches.

3. They demonstrate a significant gain in F-measure when missing attributes are treated differently from mismatched values. This is especially true for low economic value categories, where missing attributes are more common.

4. Finally, they provide evidence for the scalability of their method, especially in conjunction with the use of blocking functions where (i) they use a classifier to categorize product offers into categories, and limit matching to product specifications in the same category; and (ii) they identify candidates with at least one high-weighted feature.

## 3.5   ADDRESSING THE VERACITY CHALLENGE

The different sources that provide records about the entities in a domain often represent the same attribute value in different ways, some provide erroneous values, and when the records are about the entities at different points in time, some of the erroneous values may just be out-of-date values. Record linkage seeks to partition the records into clusters and identify the records that refer to the same entity, *despite* the multiple representations of a value, erroneous and out-of-date attribute values. The task of resolving conflicts and identifying the correct values for each of the attributes of the entities is done during data fusion (described in detail in Chapter 4), which is performed after record linkage.

While this separation of tasks enables sophisticated methods to be developed for each of these tasks independently, it faces the problem that erroneous and out-of-date values in the records may prevent correct record linkage. In this section, we present two record linkage techniques to address this veracity challenge: one that focuses on out-of-date values, and another that effectively deals with erroneous values.

### 3.5.1   TEMPORAL RECORD LINKAGE

In this section, we describe a technique proposed by Li et al. [2011], which identifies out-of-date attribute values using a model of entity evolution over time, to enable linkage over temporal records. Subsequent works by Chiang et al. [2014a], Chiang et al. [2014b] developed more detailed probabilistic models to capture entity evolution, and faster algorithms for performing temporal record linkage.

### Challenges & Opportunities

We first illustrate the challenges faced by linkage over temporal records, using the following example. We then highlight the new opportunities available to temporal record linkage that enable an elegant solution to this problem.

**Example 3.18**   Consider again the Flights domain, but this time consider traveller flight profiles, as in Table 3.6.

The 12 records refer to three entities, with record ids depicted in yellow, red, and green colors. Record $r_{260}$ describes $E_1$: *James Robert*, in *sales* from *Toronto* in *1991*. Records $r_{270}$-$r_{274}$ describe $E_2$: *James Michael Robert*, an *engineer* from *San Francisco* from *2004*, who moved to *New York* as an *engineer* in *2009* and became a *manager* in *2010* in *New York*; he used a shorter version of his name in *2004-2005*; this representational variation is depicted in blue color in bold font. Finally, records $r_{280}$-$r_{285}$ describe $E_3$: *Robert James*, a *programmer* in *Chicago* from *2004*, who became a *manager* in *2008* in *Chicago*, then moved to *Seattle* later that year. Each of the records also lists names of co-travellers. This clustering of records, corresponding to the ground truth due to entity evolution is shown in Figure 3.14.

TABLE 3.6: Traveller flight profiles

| | Name | Profession | Home Airport | Co-travellers | Year |
|---|---|---|---|---|---|
| $r_{260}$ | James Robert | Sales | Toronto | Brown | 1991 |
| $r_{270}$ | James Robert | Engineer | San Francisco | Smith, Wesson | 2004 |
| $r_{271}$ | James Robert | Engineer | San Francisco | Smith | 2005 |
| $r_{272}$ | James Michael Robert | Engineer | San Francisco | Smith, Wollensky | 2007 |
| $r_{273}$ | James Michael Robert | Engineer | New York | Smith, Wollensky | 2009 |
| $r_{274}$ | James Michael Robert | Manager | New York | Wollensky | 2010 |
| $r_{280}$ | Robert James | Programmer | Chicago | David, Black | 2004 |
| $r_{281}$ | Robert James | Programmer | Chicago | Black | 2006 |
| $r_{282}$ | Robert James | Manager | Chicago | Larry, David | 2008 |
| $r_{283}$ | Robert James | Manager | Seattle | John, David | 2008 |
| $r_{284}$ | Robert James | Manager | Seattle | John, Long | 2009 |
| $r_{285}$ | Robert James | Manager | Seattle | John | 2010 |

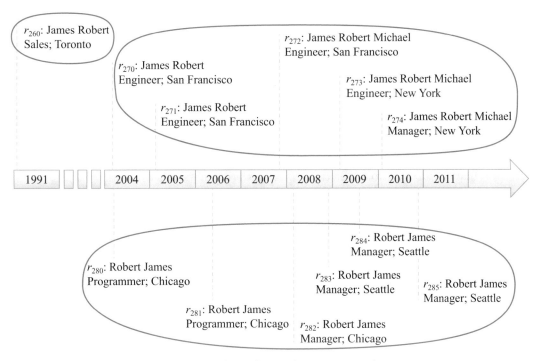

FIGURE 3.14: Ground truth due to entity evolution.

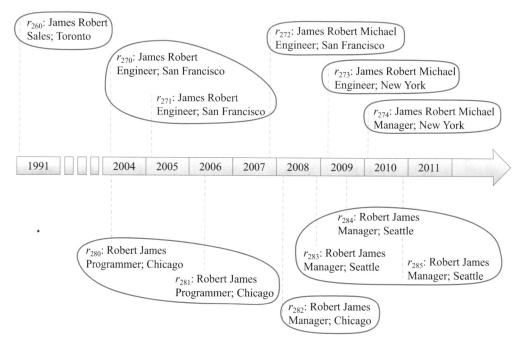

FIGURE 3.15: Linkage with high value consistency.

If linkage is performed based on high value consistency on Name, Profession, and Home Airport, the records in entities $E_2$ and $E_3$ may be split, as records for each of them can have different values for these attributes. This clustering of records is shown in Figure 3.15.

Finally, if linkage is performed based only on high similarity of Name, all the records in entities $E_1$ and $E_3$ along with some of the records in entity $E_2$ may be merged, as their names share the same set of words. This clustering of records is shown in Figure 3.16.

It is quite challenging to obtain the desired clustering of records without taking into account the possibility of evolution of entities over time.

Despite the challenges faced by linkage over temporal records, temporal information does present additional opportunities for linkage.

- First, entities typically evolve *smoothly*, with only a few attribute values of an entity changing at any given time.

  Consider again the example in Table 3.6. In 2009, person $E_2$ changed his Home Airport, but his Profession and Co-travellers remained the same; the following year, $E_2$ changed his Profession, but his Home Airport remained the same, and his Co-travellers had an overlap.

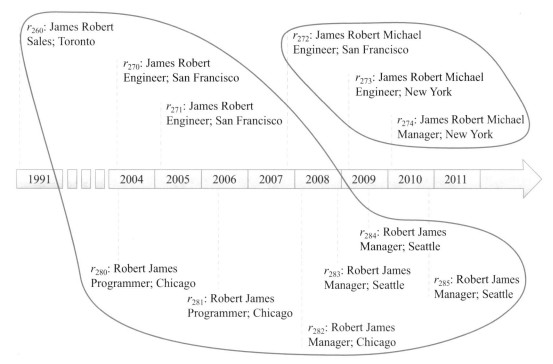

FIGURE 3.16:  Linkage with only name similarity.

- Second, entity evolution over time is typically *not erratic*.

    In the example in Table 3.6, records $r_{270}$, $r_{280}$, $r_{271}$, $r_{281}$, $r_{282}$ are very unlikely to all refer to the same entity (see Figure 3.16), as a person is very unlikely to change his profession back and forth over many years.

- Third, in case the data set is fairly complete, records that refer to the same real-world entity typically (though not necessarily) observe *continuity*, or similarity in time gaps between adjacent records.

    In the example in Table 3.6, one is less confident that record $r_{260}$ refers to the same person as records $r_{270}$-$r_{274}$, given the big time gap between $r_{260}$ and $r_{270}$ and the small time gaps between adjacent record pairs in $r_{270}$-$r_{274}$.

These opportunities provide clues to a possible solution for temporal record linkage, and we next describe the solution strategy proposed by Li et al. [2011].

Disagreement and Agreement Decays

Recall from Section 3.1 that record linkage consists of three steps: blocking, pairwise matching and clustering. Li et al. [2011] propose improvements in the second and third steps of linkage for records with timestamps. Here, we present their approach for pairwise matching; subsequently, we'll describe their temporal clustering strategy.

When performing pairwise matching, traditional linkage techniques reward high similarity between attribute values, and penalize low similarity between attribute values. This is not necessarily appropriate for temporal record linkage. First, as time elapses, attribute values of an entity may evolve. For example, in Table 3.6, the values of attributes Profession and Home Airport change for entities $E_2$ and $E_3$ over time. Second, as time elapses, different entities are increasingly likely to share the same attribute values. For example, in Table 3.6, records $r_{260}$ and $r_{270}$ share the same name, after a time gap of 13 years, even though they refer to distinct persons.

A key insight by Li et al. [2011] is that the notion of *time decay*, often used in data analytics to reduce the impact of older records on analysis results [Cohen and Strauss 2003], can be used effectively to capture the effect of time elapse on attribute value evolution. They propose two types of decay, *disagreement decay* and *agreement decay*, defined as follows.

**Definition 3.2** (Disagreement Decay)   [Li et al. 2011] Consider an attribute $A \in \mathcal{A}$ and a time gap $\Delta T$. The *disagreement decay* of $A$ over $\Delta T$, denoted by $d^{\neq}(A, \Delta T)$, is the probability that an entity changes its $A$-value within time $\Delta T$.

**Definition 3.3** (Agreement Decay)   [Li et al. 2011] Consider an attribute $A \in \mathcal{A}$ and a time gap $\Delta T$. The *agreement decay* of $A$ over $\Delta T$, denoted by $d^{=}(A, \Delta T)$, is the probability that two different entities have the same $A$-value within time $\Delta T$.

It is easy to see that both disagreement and agreement decays are in $[0, 1]$, and monotonically non-decreasing as a function of their second argument $\Delta T$. Intuitively, the disagreement decay is used to reduce the penalty for value disagreement, while the agreement decay is used to reduce the reward for value agreement, over a long time period. More formally, this is done by defining the pairwise similarity between two records $R_1$ and $R_2$ as

$$sim(R_1, R_2) = \frac{\Sigma_{A \in \mathcal{A}} dw_A(s(R_1.A, R_2.A), \Delta T) * s(R_1.A, R_2.A)}{\Sigma_{A \in \mathcal{A}} dw_A(s(R_1.A, R_2.A), \Delta T)}$$

where $dw_A(s(), \Delta T)$ denotes the decayed weight of attribute $A$ with value similarity $s()$ and time gap $\Delta T = |R_1.T - R_2.T|$. When the value similarity $s()$ is low, $dw_A(s(), \Delta T)$ is set to $w_A * (1 - d^{\neq}(A, \Delta T))$; when the value similarity $s()$ is high, $dw_A(s(), \Delta T)$ is set to $w_A * (1 - d^{=}(A, \Delta T))$, where $w_A$ is the non-decayed weight of attribute $A$.

Li et al. [2011] also describe ways to learn the disagreement and agreement decays empirically from a labeled data set.

We next illustrate how the use of disagreement and agreement decays effectively capture the effect of time elapse on attribute value evolution.

**Example 3.19** (Linkage with Entity Evolution)    Consider the records in Table 3.6. Let the record similarity function be the weighted average similarity of the four attributes Name, Profession, Home Airport and Co-travellers, with non-decayed weights 0.4, 0.2, 0.2 and 0.2, respectively. Let the value similarity function be the Jaccard similarity (ratio of the size of the intersection of two sets to the size of their union) of the sets of tokens in the two attribute values.

In the absence of any disagreement or agreement decays, the similarity of records $r_{280}$ and $r_{282}$ would be $(0.4 * 1 + 0.2 * 0 + 0.2 * 1 + 0.2 * 0.33)/(0.4 + 0.2 + 0.2 + 0.2) = 0.666$.

These two records have a time gap of 4 years. Suppose the low value similarity threshold is 0.25, and the high value similarity threshold is 0.75, and the following values for the disagreement and agreement decays have been learned: $d^{\neq}$(Profession, 4) = 0.8 (i.e., the probability that a person changes her profession within 4 years is 0.8), $d^{=}$(Name, 4) = 0.001 (i.e., the probability that two different persons have the same name in 4 years is 0.001), and $d^{=}$(HomeAirport, 4) = 0.01 (i.e., the probability that two different persons have the same home airport in 4 years is 0.01). Also, suppose that there are no disagreement or agreement decays for Co-travellers. Then, the decayed similarity of records $r_{280}$ and $r_{282}$ would be $(0.4 * 0.999 * 1 + 0.2 * 0.2 * 0 + 0.2 * 0.99 * 1 + 0.2 * 0.33)/(0.4 * 0.999 + 0.2 * 0.2 + 0.2 * 0.99 + 0.2) = 0.792$, which is higher than the non-decayed similarity between these two records.

## Temporal Clustering

We now describe the temporal clustering strategy of Li et al. [2011]. Together with the approach for refining pairwise matching with disagreement and agreement decays, it provides a complete solution for temporal record linkage.

Their key intuition is that, unlike traditional clustering techniques that are time-agnostic, considering the time order of records can often provide important clues for correct record linkage. In Table 3.6, for example, records $r_{270}$-$r_{272}$ and $r_{273}$-$r_{274}$ may refer to the same person, even though the decayed similarity between records $r_{272}$ and $r_{274}$ is low, because the time periods of $r_{270}$-$r_{272}$ (years *2004–2007*) and $r_{273}$-$r_{274}$ (years *2009–2010*) do not overlap. On the other hand, records $r_{270}$-$r_{272}$ and $r_{280}$-$r_{282}$ are very likely to refer to different persons even though the decayed similarity between $r_{270}$ and $r_{282}$ is high, because the records interleave and their occurrence periods highly overlap.

Li et al. [2011] propose a variety of temporal clustering methods that process records in time order and accumulate evidence over time to enable global decision making.

- *Early binding* makes eager decisions and either creates a new cluster or merges a record with a previously created cluster with which it has a high (decayed) record similarity.

- *Late binding* compares a record with each previously created cluster and computes a probability of merging, but makes the clustering decision after processing all the records.

- *Adjusted binding* augments early or late binding, and improves on them by also comparing a record with clusters created later, and adjusting the clustering results.

## Main Results

Li et al. [2011] solve the temporal record linkage problem, and experimentally evaluate their techniques on real-world data sets, including the DBLP data set. Their main results are as follows.

1. The two key components of *decay* and *temporal clustering* are both important for obtaining good linkage results, improving in F-measure over traditional record linkage methods by up to 43% on the DBLP data set.

   Applying decay alone on baseline methods increases the recall a lot, but it is at the price of a considerable drop in precision. Applying temporal clustering alone on baseline methods considers the time order in clustering and continuity computation, so it can increase the recall quite a bit (though not as much as applying decay alone) without reducing the precision as much. Applying both components together provides the best F-measure, obtaining both high precision and high recall.

2. *Adjusted binding* is shown to be the best temporal clustering method.

   Early binding has a lower precision as it makes local decisions to merge records with previously formed clusters, while late binding has a lower recall as it is conservative in merging records that have high decayed similarity but low non-decayed similarity. Adjusted binding significantly improves in recall over both methods by comparing early records with clusters formed later, without sacrificing the precision much.

3. Finally, the proposed combination of decay and temporal clustering obtains good results on hard cases in DBLP (such as the records for authors named Wei Wang), often fixing errors made in DBLP.

## 3.5.2    RECORD LINKAGE WITH UNIQUENESS CONSTRAINTS

In this section, we present a record linkage technique proposed by Guo et al. [2010], which shows promising results in the presence of both erroneous data and multiple representations of the same attribute value.

## Challenges

We first illustrate the challenges faced by record linkage in such a scenario, using the following example.

TABLE 3.7:  Airline business listings

|  | Name | Phone | Address | Source |
|---|---|---|---|---|
| $r_{206}$ |  | xxx-1255 | 1 Main Street | $S_{10}$ |
| $r_{207}$ |  | xxx-9400 | 1 Main Street |  |
| $r_{208}$ | SmileAir Inc | xxx-0500 |  |  |
| $r_{216}$ | SkyAir Corp | xxx-1255 | 1 Main Street | $S_{11}$ |
| $r_{217}$ |  | xxx-9400 | 1 Main Street |  |
| $r_{218}$ | SmileAir Inc | xxx-0500 | 2 Summit Avenue |  |
| $r_{226}$ | SkyAir Corp | xxx-1255 | 1 Main Street | $S_{12}$ |
| $r_{227}$ | SkyAir Corp | xxx-9400 | 1 Main Street |  |
| $r_{228}$ | SmileAir Inc | xxx-0500 | 2 Summit Avenue |  |
| $r_{236}$ | SkyAir Corp | xxx-1255 | 1 Main Street | $S_{13}$ |
| $r_{237}$ | SkyAir Corp | xxx-9400 | 1 Main Street |  |
| $r_{238}$ | SmileAir Inc | xxx-0500 | 2 Summit Avenue |  |
| $r_{246}$ | SkyAir Corp | xxx-1255 | 1 Main Street | $S_{14}$ |
| $r_{247}$ | SkyAir Corp | xxx-9400 | 1 Main Street |  |
| $r_{248}$ | SmileAir Inc | xxx-0500 | 2 Summit Avenue |  |
| $r_{256}$ | SkyAir Corp | **xxx-2255** | 1 Main Street | $S_{15}$ |
| $r_{257}$ | SmileAir Inc | xxx-0500 | 2 Summit Avenue |  |
| $r_{266}$ |  | xxx-1255 | 1 Main Street | $S_{16}$ |
| $r_{267}$ | SmileAir Inc | xxx-0500 | 2 Summit Avenue |  |
| $r_{276}$ |  | xxx-1255 | 1 Main Street | $S_{17}$ |
| $r_{277}$ | SmileAir Inc | xxx-0500 | 2 Summit Avenue |  |
| $r_{286}$ | SmileAir Inc | xxx-0500 | 2 Summit Avenue | $S_{18}$ |
| $r_{296}$ |  | **xxx-0500** | **2 Summit Avenue** | $S_{19}$ |
| $r_{297}$ | SmileAir Inc | xxx-0500 | 2 Summit Avenue |  |

**Example 3.20**  Consider again the Flights domain, but this time consider airline business listings as in Table 3.7. The 24 records are provided by 10 sources, $S_{10}$-$S_{19}$, and refer to two entities, with record ids depicted in yellow and green colors. Representational variations are depicted in blue color in bold font, while erroneous values are depicted in red color in bold font.

To illustrate that erroneous values may prevent correct linking, a straightforward linkage may link $r_{296}$ (provided by $S_{19}$) with the *SmileAir Inc* records, as they share phone and address, while failing to link them with the *SA Corp* records from $S_{16}$ and $S_{17}$, let alone the *SkyAir Corp* records.

If one realizes that $r_{296}$ confuses between *SkyAir* and *SmileAir* and provides wrong values, there is a higher likelihood to obtain correct linkage results.

To illustrate that linkage in such cases benefits from looking at global evidence, not just local evidence, for the resolution of conflicts, suppose all *SA Corp* records have been correctly linked with other *SkyAir Corp* records; then the fact that *xxx-0500* is provided by more sources for *SmileAir Inc* provides further evidence that it is incorrect for *SkyAir Corp*.

### Linkage + Fusion

In general, an entity may have multiple values for an attribute. However, many domains often have attributes that satisfy *uniqueness* constraints, that is, each entity has at most one value for an attribute and each value is associated with at most one entity. (This *hard constraint* can be relaxed to a *soft constraint* by allowing for a few exceptions.) Such constraints hold for attributes like business name, phone, address, and so on, as in Table 3.7.

Guo et al. [2010] address the following problem to enable robust record linkage in the presence of erroneous attribute values: *Given a set $S$ of independent data sources providing a set of records $\mathcal{R}$, and a set of (hard or soft) uniqueness constraints, (i) partition $\mathcal{R}$ into subsets of records that refer to the same entity and (ii) discover the true values (if any) and different representations of each true value under the uniqueness constraints.*

They propose an approach to record linkage that combines it with the data fusion step, to identify incorrect values and differentiate them from alternate representations of the correct value during the record linkage step itself, thereby obtaining better linkage results. For this purpose, they consider a finer granularity version of the pairwise matching graph, where individual attribute values are nodes in the graph, and edges are binary associations between values in the records to be linked, labeled with the sources that provide this association.

**Definition 3.4** (*K*-Partite Graph Encoding)    [Guo et al. 2010] Let $S$ be a set of data sources, providing a set of records $\mathcal{R}$ over a set of attributes $\mathcal{A}$, with uniqueness constraints over $k$ attributes $A_1, \ldots, A_k \in \mathcal{A}$. The *k-partite graph encoding* of $(S, \mathcal{R})$ is an undirected graph $G = (\overline{V}_1, \ldots, \overline{V}_k, \overline{L})$, such that:

- each node in $\overline{V}_i$, $i \in [1, k]$, is a value of attribute $A_i$, provided by a source in $\overline{S}$;
- each edge $(V_i, V_j) \in \overline{L}$, $V_i \in \overline{V}_i$, $V_j \in \overline{V}_j$, $i, j \in [1, k]$, $i \neq j$, represents the existence of at least one record $R$ with value $V_i$ in attribute $A_i$ and value $V_j$ in attribute $A_j$; this edge is labeled with the set of all sources that provide such records.

**Example 3.21**    Figure 3.17 shows the 3-partite graph encoding of the data set in Table 3.7.

Solutions to the problem that Guo et al. [2010] tackle can be naturally encoded on the *k*-partite graph by (i) clustering the nodes of $\overline{V}_i$ such that each cluster represents a unique value of

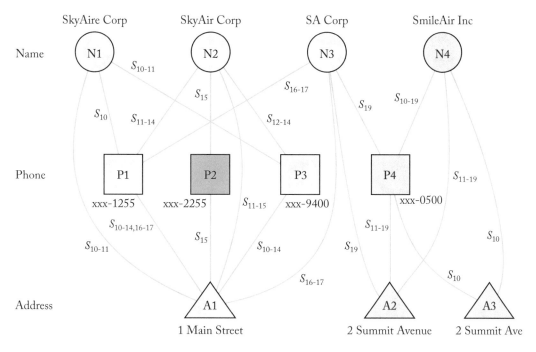

FIGURE 3.17: *K*-partite graph encoding.

$A_i$, and (ii) associating an edge between clusters if and only if they belong to the same entity in $\mathcal{E}$. We present the solutions obtained under hard and soft uniqueness constraints next, followed by a discussion of the linkage technique with hard constraints.

**Example 3.22** Figure 3.18 shows the solution obtained under hard uniqueness constraints on the *k*-partite graph shown in Figure 3.17.

Note that it has correctly identified N1, N2, and N3 as alternate representations of the same name, and A2 and A3 as alternate representations of the same address. Under the hard uniqueness constraints, an entity can have at most one name, one phone and one address associated with it, and each name, phone and address can be associated with at most one entity. This allows erroneous values to be identified. Since there are only two entities in the final clustering, phones P2 and P3 are not associated with any name or address.

While we skip a discussion of the linkage technique with soft uniqueness constraints, the solution obtained under these constraints is shown in Figure 3.19. Note that since some entities can have more than one attribute value in this case, phones P1 and P3 are associated with the same entity, since there is enough evidence in the input records for this linkage result.

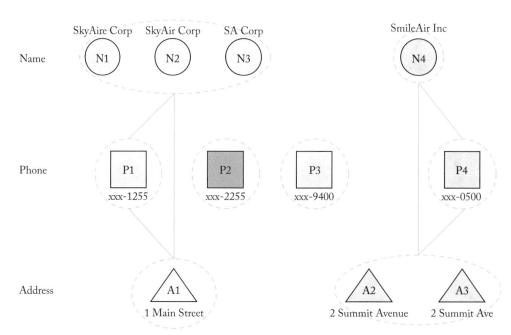

FIGURE 3.18:  Linkage with hard constraints.

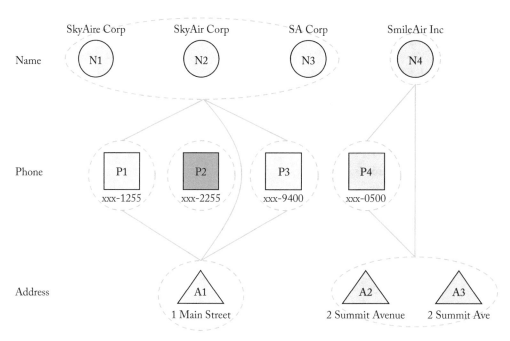

FIGURE 3.19:  Linkage with soft constraints.

## Linkage with Hard Constraints

In the case of hard uniqueness constraints, Guo et al. [2010] reduce the problem to a $k$-partite graph clustering problem. For this clustering task, they use the Davies-Bouldin index [Davies and Bouldin 1979] (DB-index), which balances high intra-cluster cohesion with low inter-cluster correlation.

Formally, given a clustering $C = \{C_1, \ldots, C_n\}$, its DB-index is defined as

$$\text{Avg}_{i=1}^{n} \left( \max_{j \in [1,n], j \neq i} \frac{d(C_i, C_i) + d(C_j, C_j)}{d(C_i, C_j)} \right)$$

where $d(C_i, C_j)$ defines the distance between $C_i$ and $C_j$. When $i = j$, the distance is the complement of the cohesion of $C_i$; otherwise the distance is the complement of the correlation between $C_i$ and $C_j$. The goal is to obtain a clustering with the minimum DB-index.

To compute the cluster distance, Guo et al. [2010] average the similarity distance between value representations of the same attribute, and the association distance between value representations of different attributes.

Since finding an optimal DB-index clustering is intractable, Guo et al. [2010] propose a *hill climbing* algorithm that (i) first generates an initial clustering using the well-known Hungarian algorithm [Kuhn 2010] to find the one-to-one matching with the strongest associations (the sum of the number of supporting sources on the selected edges), and then (ii) iteratively examines each node and re-assigns it to its best cluster greedily, until convergence.

## Main Results

Guo et al. [2010] solve their linkage problem for hard uniqueness constraints and soft uniqueness constraints, and experimentally evaluate their solutions on real-world data sources that provide business listings. Their main results are as follows.

1. The proposed combination of record linkage and data fusion is shown to have better accuracy (F-measure) than techniques that apply linkage and fusion separately.

   In particular, applying record linkage followed by data fusion can enforce uniqueness, but is unable to identify false values from the beginning, so can mis-cluster during the record linkage step.

2. The use of record linkage with soft constraints improves F-measure by a significant amount, since real data often have exceptions to the hard constraint.

In particular, the use of hard constraints has good precision, but the recall of the solution suffers compared to the recall under soft constraints.

3. Finally, the proposed combination of record linkage and data fusion is scalable in conjunction with the use of simple blocking techniques, with the overall execution time growing linearly in the size of the data.

CHAPTER 4

# BDI: Data Fusion

The third component of data integration is *data fusion*. Even when different sources provide information for the same attribute of the same entity, they may provide conflicting values. Such conflicts can arise because of mis-typing, incorrect calculations, out-of-date information, inconsistent interpretations of the semantics, and sometimes rumors. The problem can be exacerbated by data sharing and plagiarism between different sources. As an example, consider the scheduled departure time for *Flight 49* departing from *EWR* on *2014-04-05*. Data source Airline1 provides *18:20*, which is the scheduled time for the airplane to leave the gate (typical interpretation for departure time); and source Airfare4 provides *18:05*, which was the scheduled time for the same flight before *2014-04-01*. Providing conflicting and incorrect data in data integration can be confusing, misleading, and sometimes even harmful. The goal of data fusion is to decide which value truly reflects the real world. In this example, one wishes to find out that *18:20* is the real scheduled departure time, so the passengers can better plan their trip.

Data fusion is a fairly new area compared with schema alignment and record linkage. Traditionally, data integration mainly integrated enterprise data, which are fairly clean, so data fusion is often rule based and the research focus is more of improving the efficiency, as overviewed in Section 4.1.

With the recent rapid growth and expansion of web sources, many of which have low-to-medium quality, a vast volume of conflicting data are introduced into the web. Section 4.2 describes more advanced fusion models in addressing such *veracity* of big data; such models are typically applied offline in creating data warehouses.

Section 4.3 addresses the *volume* of big data for both *offline fusion* and *online fusion*. For offline fusion, a MapReduce based implementation of an advanced model is described. For online fusion applied at query answering time, which has the benefit of being able to capture fast changes in the data: an algorithm is described that returns estimated results according to partially retrieved data, and refines the results after obtaining data from more sources.

Section 4.4 addresses the *velocity* of big data by introducing *dynamic data fusion*: instead of assuming a static world, dynamic data fusion considers the evolution of the world and changes of true values over time, and tries to decide for each data value not only its correctness but also the period of the time for which it is correct.

Finally, as previous chapters have shown, there can be a large heterogeneity from different sources in terms of schema and entity reference, so it is not safe to assume well-aligned data as input for data fusion. Section 4.5 describes how to address the *variety* of big data by applying multiple techniques for schema alignment and record linkage, and resolving disagreements between those techniques and between data sources holistically.

## 4.1    TRADITIONAL DATA FUSION: A QUICK TOUR

This section formally defines the problem of data fusion. Sections 4.3–4.5 extend the definition for more complex applications.

Consider a set of *data sources* $S$ and a set of *data items* $D$. A data item represents a particular aspect of a real-world entity, such as the scheduled departure time of a flight; in a relational database, a data item corresponds to a cell in a table. For each data item $D \in \mathcal{D}$, a source $S \in \mathcal{S}$ can (but not necessarily) provide a *value*; the value can be atomic (e.g., scheduled departure time), a set of values (e.g., a set of phone numbers), or a list of values (e.g., a list of book authors).

Among different values provided for a data item, one is consistent with the real world thus *true*, and the rest are *false*. In case the provided value is a set or list of atomic values, a value is considered as true if all of its atomic values are correct and the set or list is complete (and the order is preserved for a list). The goal of data fusion is to find for each data item $D \in \mathcal{D}$ the true value.

**Definition 4.1** (Data Fusion)    Let $\mathcal{D}$ be a set of data items. Let $\mathcal{S}$ be a set of data sources, each providing values for a subset of data items in $\mathcal{D}$. *Data fusion* decides the true value for each data item in $\mathcal{D}$.

**Example 4.1**    Consider the five data sources in Table 4.1. They provide information on the scheduled departure time for five flights on *2014-04-01*.

Source S1 provides all correct times. Source S2 provides the correct times for most of the flights; however, sometimes it has mis-typing (e.g., *21:49* instead of *21:40* for *Flight 4*) and sometimes it uses the take-off time (e.g., *19:18* instead of *19:02* for *Flight 1*) thus is internally inconsistent. Source S3 has not updated its data and still provides the scheduled departure times for the period of *2014-01-01* to *2014-03-31*. Sources S4 and S5 copy the data from S3, while S5 makes an error during copying.

Data fusion aims at finding the correct scheduled departure time for each flight; that is, the times provided by source S1.

TABLE 4.1: Five data sources provide information on the scheduled departure time of five flights. False values are in italics. Only S1 provides all true values.

|          | S1    | S2    | S3    | S4    | S5    |
|----------|-------|-------|-------|-------|-------|
| Flight 1 | 19:02 | *19:18* | 19:02 | 19:02 | *20:02* |
| Flight 2 | 17:43 | 17:43 | *17:50* | *17:50* | *17:50* |
| Flight 3 | 9:20  | 9:20  | 9:20  | 9:20  | 9:20  |
| Flight 4 | 21:40 | *21:49* | *20:33* | *20:33* | *20:33* |
| Flight 5 | 18:15 | 18:15 | *18:22* | *18:22* | *18:22* |

Early approaches to data fusion methods were typically rule based, such as using the observed value from the most recently updated source, taking the average, maximum, or minimum for numerical values, or applying voting to take the value provided by the largest number of data sources. They focus on improving efficiency with the use of database queries (surveyed by Bleiholder and Naumann, 2008). However, such rule-based fusion is often inadequate when large veracity exists, as illustrated next.

**Example 4.2** Continue with the motivating example in Example 4.1. First consider the three sources S1, S2, and S3. For all flights except *Flight 4*, a majority voting on data provided by these three sources can find the correct scheduled departure time. For *Flight 4*, however, these sources provide three different times, resulting in a tie. It is hard to break such a tie unless S1 is identified as a more accurate source than others.

Now consider in addition sources S4 and S5. Since the data provided by S3 are copied by S4 and S5, a voting strategy would consider them as the majority and decide wrong scheduled departure times for three flights. The correct times cannot be decided unless the copying relationships are identified and the values provided by S4 and S5 are ignored in voting.

## 4.2    ADDRESSING THE VERACITY CHALLENGE

As illustrated in Example 4.2, rule-based data fusion is often inadequate when data sources have different qualities and copying exists between sources. Recently, many advanced solutions have been proposed to address the *veracity* challenge of big data. They resolve conflicts and prune erroneous data by leveraging the collective wisdom from the sources, identifying trustworthy sources, and detecting copying between the sources. These techniques typically contain some or all of the following three components.

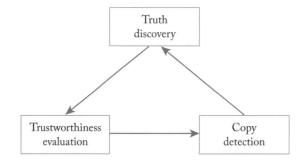

FIGURE 4.1:  Architecture of data fusion [Dong et al. 2009a].

**Truth discovery.**   Among conflicting values, discover the one that is true. Voting, which leverages agreements between sources, serves as a baseline approach. Essentially it considers that each value has one vote from each of its providing data sources, and the value with the highest vote count (i.e., the value provided by the largest number of sources) is taken as true.

**Trustworthiness evaluation.**   For each data source, evaluate its trustworthiness according to the correctness of its provided values. Accordingly, a higher vote count can be assigned to a more trustworthy source, and this can be used in voting.

**Copy detection.**   Detect copying between data sources, such that a discounted vote count can be assigned to a copied value in voting.

Note that evaluating source trustworthiness requires knowledge of value correctness from truth discovery, whereas the knowledge of source trustworthiness allows setting an appropriate vote count for each source to obtain better truth-discovery results. Thus, it is a chicken-and-egg problem. As shown later, copy detection requires knowledge of value correctness and source trustworthiness, whereas its results can benefit truth discovery; thus, it is also a chicken-and-egg problem. Because of such inter-dependence between these three components, they are often iteratively conducted until reaching convergence or after a certain number of iterations. The architecture is illustrated in Figure 4.1.

The majority of this section describes a solution for a core case that satisfies the following two conditions.

**Uniform false-value distribution.**   For each data item, there are multiple false values in the underlying domain and an independent source has the same probability of providing each of them.

**Categorical value.**   For each data item, values that do not match exactly are considered as completely different.

Section 4.2.5 discusses how to extend the basic approach to relax these conditions.

### 4.2.1    ACCURACY OF A SOURCE

The basic building block for advanced data fusion is to evaluate the trustworthiness of a source. There can be many different ways to measure source trustworthiness; we describe an approach that measures it as the fraction of true values provided by a source, called the *accuracy* of the source [Dong et al. 2009a]. The accuracy of source $S$ is denoted by $A(S)$. By its definition, the accuracy of $S$ can also be considered as the probability that a value provided by $S$ is the true value.

Since often times it is not known for sure which values are true, the accuracy of a source is computed as the average probability of its provided values being true (Section 4.2.2 describes how such probabilities are computed). Formally, let $\overline{V}(S)$ be the values provided by $S$. For each $v \in \overline{V}(S)$, $\Pr(v)$ denotes the probability that $v$ is true. Then, $A(S)$ is computed as follows:

$$A(S) = \text{Avg}_{v \in \overline{V}(S)} \Pr(v). \tag{4.1}$$

*Good* sources need to be distinguished from *bad* ones: a data source is considered to be good if for each data item it is more likely to provide the true value than any *particular* false value; otherwise, it is considered to be bad. Assume for each data item in $\mathcal{D}$ the number of false values in the domain is $n$. Then, the probability that $S$ provides a true value is $A(S)$ and that it provides a particular false value is $\frac{1-A(S)}{n}$ under the condition of *uniform false-value distribution*. So $S$ is good if $A(S) > \frac{1-A(S)}{n}$; that is, $A(S) > \frac{1}{1+n}$. The rest of this chapter focuses on good sources, which is important for the theorems to hold.

**Example 4.3**    Consider the five sources in Table 4.1. For source $S_1$, by definition its accuracy is $\frac{5}{5} = 1$. Suppose the probabilities of its five provided values are computed as 0.982, 0.991, 1, 0.910, and 0.991, respectively. Its accuracy can be computed by Eq. (4.1) as $\frac{0.982+0.991+1+0.910+0.991}{5} = 0.97$, which is very close to its real accuracy.

### 4.2.2    PROBABILITY OF A VALUE BEING TRUE

Now consider how to compute the probability that a value is true. For now it is assumed that the sources are independent and Section 4.2.3 considers copying between sources. Intuitively, the computation should consider both how many sources provide the value and the accuracy of those sources. Bayesian analysis can be applied for this purpose.

Consider a data item $D \in \mathcal{D}$. Let $\mathcal{V}(D)$ be the domain of $D$, including one true value and $n$ false values. Let $\overline{S_D}$ be the sources that provide information on $D$. For each $v \in \mathcal{V}(D)$, let $\overline{S_D}(v) \subseteq \overline{S_D}$ denote the set of sources that provide $v$ for $D$ ($\overline{S_D}(v)$ can be empty). Let $\Psi(D)$ denote the observation of which value each $S \in \overline{S_D}$ provides for $D$.

The probability $\Pr(v)$ for $v \in \mathcal{V}(D)$ can be computed as the *a posteriori* probability conditioned on $\Psi(D)$. Recall that among the values in $\mathcal{V}(D)$, there is one and only one true value; thus, their probabilities should sum up to 1. Assume the *a priori* belief of each value being true is the same, then according to the Bayes rule,

$$Pr(v) = Pr(v \text{ true}|\Psi(D)) \propto Pr(\Psi(D)|v \text{ true}). \tag{4.2}$$

Given the assumption of source independence for now, the probability $Pr(\Psi(D)|v \text{ true})$ can be computed as the product of the probabilities that each source in $\overline{S_D}(v)$ provides the true value and the probabilities that each source in $\overline{S_D} \setminus \overline{S_D}(v)$ provides an observed false value. The former, according to the definition of source accuracy, is $A(S)$; the latter, under the condition of *uniform false-value distribution*, is $\frac{1-A(S)}{n}$. Thus,

$$Pr(\Psi(D)|v \text{ true}) = \Pi_{S \in \overline{S_D}(v)} A(S) \cdot \Pi_{S \in \overline{S_D} \setminus \overline{S_D}(v)} \frac{1 - A(S)}{n}$$

$$= \Pi_{S \in \overline{S_D}(v)} \frac{nA(S)}{1 - A(S)} \cdot \Pi_{S \in \overline{S_D}} \frac{1 - A(S)}{n}. \tag{4.3}$$

In Eq. (4.3), $\Pi_{S \in \overline{S_D}} \frac{1-A(S)}{n}$ is the same for all values. In other words,

$$Pr(v) \propto \Pi_{S \in \overline{S_D}(v)} \frac{nA(S)}{1 - A(S)}. \tag{4.4}$$

Accordingly, the *vote count* of a data source $S$ is defined as

$$C(S) = \ln \frac{nA(S)}{1 - A(S)}. \tag{4.5}$$

The *vote count* of a value $v$, denoted by $C(v)$, can be computed as

$$C(v) = \sum_{S \in \overline{S_D}(v)} C(S). \tag{4.6}$$

Essentially, the vote count of a source is derived from its accuracy, and the vote count of a value is computed as the sum of the vote counts of its providers. A value with a higher vote count is more likely to be true. Combining Eqs. (4.2)–(4.6), the probability of each value can be computed as follows:

$$Pr(v) = \frac{\exp(C(v))}{\sum_{v_0 \in V(D)} \exp(C(v_0))}. \tag{4.7}$$

The following theorem shows three nice properties of Eq. (4.7). It states that a value provided by a larger number of data sources or by more accurate sources has a higher probability to be true.

**Theorem 4.1**   [Dong et al. 2009a] Equation (4.7) has the following properties.

1. If all data sources are good and have the same accuracy, when the size of $\overline{S_D}(v)$ increases, $\Pr(v)$ increases.

2. Fixing all sources in $\overline{S_D}(v)$ except $S$, when $A(S)$ increases for $S$, $\Pr(v)$ increases.

3. If there exists $S \in \overline{S_D}(v)$ such that $A(S) = 1$, and no $S' \in \overline{S_D}(v)$ such that $A(S') = 0$, then $\Pr(v) = 1$; if there exists $S \in \overline{S_D}(v)$ such that $A(S) = 0$, and no $S' \in \overline{S_D}(v)$ such that $A(S') = 1$, then $\Pr(v) = 0$.

*Proof.* The three properties can be proved as follows.

1. When all data sources have the same accuracy, they have the same vote count; when a source is good, it has a positive vote count. Let $c$ be that vote count and $|\overline{S_D}(v)|$ be the size of $\overline{S_D}(v)$. Then $C(v) = c \cdot |\overline{S_D}(v)|$ increases with $|\overline{S_D}(v)|$, and so does $\Pr(v)$, which is proportional to $\exp(C(v))$.

2. When $A(S)$ increases for a source $S$, $C(S)$ increases and so does $C(v)$ and $\Pr(v)$.

3. When $A(S) = 1$ for a source $S$, $C(S) = \infty$ and $C(v) = \infty$, so $\Pr(v) = 1$. When $A(S) = 0$ for a source $S$, $A'(S) = -\infty$ and $C(v) = -\infty$, so $\Pr(v) = 0$. ∎

Note that the first property is actually a justification for the voting strategy when all sources have the same accuracy. The third property shows that it is not recommended to assign very high or very low accuracy to a data source, which has been avoided by defining the accuracy of a source as the average probability of its provided values.

**Example 4.4** Consider S1, S2 and S3 in Table 4.1 and assume their accuracies are 0.97, 0.61, 0.4, respectively. Assuming there are 10 false values in the domain (i.e., $n = 10$), the vote count of each source can be computed as follows:

$$C(S1) = \ln \frac{10 * 0.97}{1 - 0.97} = 5.8; \quad C(S2) = \ln \frac{10 * 0.61}{1 - 0.61} = 2.7; \quad C(S3) = \log \frac{10 * 0.4}{1 - 0.4} = 1.9.$$

Now consider the three values provided for *Flight 4*. Value *21:40* is provided by S1 thus has vote count 5.8, *21:49* is provided by S2 thus has vote count 2.7, and *20:33* is provided by S3 thus has vote count 1.9. Among them, *21:40* has the highest vote count and so the highest probability to be true. Indeed, its probability is

$$\frac{\exp(5.8)}{\exp(5.8) + \exp(2.7) + \exp(1.9) + (10 - 2) * \exp(0)} = 0.914.$$

### 4.2.3    COPYING BETWEEN SOURCES

*Copying* exists between two data sources $S_1$ and $S_2$ if they derive the same part of their data directly or transitively from a common source (can be one of $S_1$ or $S_2$). Accordingly, there are two types of data sources: *independent sources* and *copiers*.

An *independent source* provides all values independently. It may provide some erroneous values because of incorrect knowledge of the real world, mis-typing, and so on.

A *copier* copies a part (or all) of data from other sources (independent sources or copiers). It can copy from multiple sources by union, intersection, and so on, and since a snapshot of data is considered, cyclic copying on a particular data item is impossible. In addition, a copier may revise some of the copied values or add additional values; though, such revised and added values are considered as independent contributions by the copier.

In many applications it is not known how each source obtains its data, so copying has to be discovered from a snapshot of data. We next describe how to detect copying between a pair of sources and how to apply this knowledge in truth discovery. For tractability, only *direct* copying is considered in copy detection and truth discovery. Section 4.2.5 briefly discusses how to distinguish transitive copying and co-copying from direct copying.

#### Copy Detection

Copy detection has been studied for text documents and software programs [Dong and Srivastava 2011], where reuse of sufficiently large text fragments is taken as evidence for copying. The problem is much harder for structured data. First, sharing common data does not in itself imply copying, since accurate sources can also share a lot of independently provided correct data; on the other hand, not sharing a lot of common data does not in itself imply no-copying, since a copier may copy only a small fraction of data from the original source. For the sources in Table 4.1, sources S3-S5 share 80–100% of their data and there is copying between them; however, S1 and S2 also share 60% of their data, but they are independent. Second, even when two sources are dependent, it is often not obvious which one is a copier. For the sources in Table 4.1, it is not clear among S3-S5, which one is the original source.

On structured data, copying is detected based on two important intuitions. First, copying is more likely between sources that share *uncommon* values, since sharing an uncommon value is typically a low-probability event when the sources are independent. Take correctness of data in consideration. Whereas there is a single true value for each data item, there are often multiple distinct false values; thus, a particular false value is often an uncommon value, and sharing a lot of false values indicates copying. In the motivating example (Table 4.1), with the knowledge of which values are true and which are false, one would suspect copying between S3-S5 because they provide the same false value for three data items. However, one would suspect copying between S1 and S2 much less, as they share only true values.

Second, typically a random subset of data from a source would have the same property (e.g., accuracy) as the full data set. However, if the source is a copier, the data it copies may have different properties from the data it provides independently. Thus, between two sources where copying is likely, the source whose own data differ significantly from the data shared with the other source has a higher likelihood to be a copier.

A Bayesian model is proposed to compute the probability of copying between a pair of data sources based on these two intuitions [Dong et al. 2009a]. The model makes the following three assumptions; Section 4.2.5 briefly discusses how extended techniques relax these assumptions.

**No mutual copying.**   There is no mutual copying between a pair of sources; that is, $S_1$ copying from $S_2$ and $S_2$ copying from $S_1$ do not happen at the same time.

**Item-wise independence.**   The data from a source on different data items are independent conditioned on being provided by the source.

**Independent copying.**   The copying between a pair of data sources is independent of the copying between any other pair of data sources.

Assume $\mathcal{S}$ consists of two types of data sources: good independent sources and copiers. Consider two sources $S_1, S_2 \in \mathcal{S}$. Under the assumption of *no mutual copying*, there are three possible relationships: $S_1$ and $S_2$ being independent, denoted by $S_1 \perp S_2$; $S_1$ copying from $S_2$, denoted by $S_1 \to S_2$; and $S_2$ copying from $S_1$, denoted by $S_2 \to S_1$. Bayesian analysis is applied to compute the probability of copying between $S_1$ and $S_2$ given observation of their data, denoted by $\Phi$.

$$\Pr(S_1 \perp S_2 | \Phi) = \frac{\alpha \, \Pr(\Phi | S_1 \perp S_2)}{\alpha \, \Pr(\Phi | S_1 \perp S_2) + \frac{1-\alpha}{2} \Pr(\Phi | S_1 \to S_2) + \frac{1-\alpha}{2} \Pr(\Phi | S_2 \to S_1)}. \quad (4.8)$$

Here, $\alpha = \Pr(S_1 \perp S_2)(0 < \alpha < 1)$ is the *a priori* probability that two data sources are independent. As there is no *a priori* preference for copy direction, the *a priori* probability for copying in each direction is set to $\frac{1-\alpha}{2}$.

Now consider how to compute the probability of the observed data, conditioned on independence of or copying between the sources. Consider the data items for which both $S_1$ and $S_2$ provide values, denoted by $\overline{D_{12}}$. With the assumption *item-wise independence*, one can compute $\Pr(\Phi | S_1 \perp S_2)$ (similar for $\Pr(\Phi | S_1 \to S_2)$ and $\Pr(\Phi | S_2 \to S_1)$) as the product of probabilities for the observation on each individual data item, denoted by $\Phi(D)$ for data item $D$.

$$\Pr(\Phi | S_1 \perp S_2) = \Pi_{D \in \overline{D_{12}}} (\Phi(D) | S_1 \perp S_2). \quad (4.9)$$

Such data items can be partitioned into three subsets: $\overline{D_t}$, denoting the set of data items on which $S_1$ and $S_2$ provide the same true value, $\overline{D_f}$, denoting the set of data items on which they provide the same false value, and $\overline{D_d}$, denoting the set of data items on which they provide different values ($\overline{D_t} \cup \overline{D_f} \cup \overline{D_d} = D_{12}$). The conditional probability of $\Phi(D)$ for each type of data items can be computed as follows.

First, consider the case where $S_1$ and $S_2$ are independent (i.e., $S_1 \perp S_2$). Since there is a single true value, the probability that $S_1$ and $S_2$ provide the same true value for data item $D$ is

$$\Pr(\Phi(D : D \in \overline{D_t})|S_1 \perp S_2) = A(S_1) \cdot A(S_2). \tag{4.10}$$

Under the *uniform-false-value-distribution* condition, the probability that source $S$ provides a particular false value for data item $D$ is $\frac{1-A(S)}{n}$. Thus, the probability that $S_1$ and $S_2$ provide the same false value for $D$ is

$$\Pr(\Phi(D : D \in \overline{D_f})|S_1 \perp S_2) = n \cdot \frac{1 - A(S_1)}{n} \cdot \frac{1 - A(S_2)}{n} = \frac{(1 - A(S_1))(1 - A(S_2))}{n}. \tag{4.11}$$

Then, the probability that $S_1$ and $S_2$ provide different values on a data item $D$, denoted by $P_d$ for convenience, is

$$\Pr(\Phi(D : D \in \overline{D_d})|S_1 \perp S_2) = 1 - A(S_1)A(S_2) - \frac{(1 - A(S_1))(1 - A(S_2))}{n} = P_d. \tag{4.12}$$

Next, consider the case when $S_2$ copies from $S_1$ (the equations when $S_1$ copies from $S_2$ are similar). Assume the copier $S_2$ copies on each data item with probability $c$ ($0 < c \leq 1$). There are two cases where $S_1$ and $S_2$ provide the same value $v$ for a data item $D$. First, with probability $c$, $S_2$ copies $v$ from $S_1$ and so $v$ is true with probability $A(S_1)$ and false with probability $1 - A(S_1)$. Second, with probability $1 - c$, the two sources provide $v$ independently and so its probability of being true or false is the same as in the case where $S_1$ and $S_2$ are independent. Thus,

$$\Pr(\Phi(D : D \in \overline{D_t})|S_2 \to S_1) = A(S_1) \cdot c + A(S_1) \cdot A(S_2) \cdot (1 - c), \tag{4.13}$$

$$\Pr(\Phi(D : D \in \overline{D_f})|S_2 \to S_1) = (1 - A(S_1)) \cdot c + \frac{(1 - A(S_1))(1 - A(S_2))}{n} \cdot (1 - c). \tag{4.14}$$

If $S_1$ and $S_2$ provide different values, $S_2$ must provide the value independently (with probability $1 - c$) and its provided value is different from $S_1$'s provided value (with probability $P_d$). Thus,

$$\Pr(\Phi(D : D \in \overline{D_d})|S_2 \to S_1) = P_d \cdot (1 - c). \tag{4.15}$$

Combining Eqs. (4.8)–(4.15), one can compute the probability of $S_1 \perp S_2$, $S_1 \rightarrow S_2$, $S_2 \rightarrow S_1$ accordingly. Note that Eqs. (4.13)–(4.14) are different for conditions $S_1 \rightarrow S_2$ and $S_2 \rightarrow S_1$; thus, different probabilities may be computed for different directions.

The resulting equations have several nice properties that conform to the intuitions discussed earlier in this section, formalized as follows.

**Theorem 4.2** [Dong et al. 2009a] Let $k_t$, $k_f$, $k_d$ be the size of $\overline{D_t}$, $\overline{D_f}$, $\overline{D_d}$, respectively. Let $\mathcal{S}$ be a set of good independent sources and copiers. Equation (4.8) has the following three properties on $\mathcal{S}$.

1. Fixing $k_t + k_f$ and $k_d$, when $k_f$ increases, the probability of copying (i.e., $\Pr(S_1 \rightarrow S_2|\Phi) + \Pr(S_2 \rightarrow S_1|\Phi)$) increases.

2. Fixing $k_t + k_f + k_d$, when $k_t + k_f$ increases and none of $k_t$ and $k_f$ decreases, the probability of copying increases.

3. Fixing $k_t$ and $k_f$, when $k_d$ decreases, the probability of copying increases.

*Proof.* The three properties are proved with the assumption that each source has accuracy $1 - \varepsilon$ ($\varepsilon$ can be considered as the error rate). The proof can be easily extended for the case where each source has a different accuracy.

1. Let $k_0 = k_t + k_f + k_d$. Then, $k_d = k_0 - k_t - k_f$.

$$\Pr(S_1 \perp S_2|\Phi) = 1 - \left(1 + (\frac{1-\alpha}{\alpha})(\frac{1-\varepsilon-c+c\varepsilon}{1-\varepsilon+c\varepsilon})^{k_t}(\frac{\varepsilon-c\varepsilon}{cn+\varepsilon-c\varepsilon})^{k_f}(\frac{1}{1-c})^{k_0}\right)^{-1}.$$

As $0 < c < 1$, it holds that $0 < \frac{1-\varepsilon-c+c\varepsilon}{1-c\varepsilon} < 1$ and $0 < \frac{\varepsilon-c\varepsilon}{cn+\varepsilon-c\varepsilon} < 1$. When $k_t$ or $k_f$ increases, $(\frac{1-\varepsilon-c+c\varepsilon}{1-c\varepsilon})^{k_t}$ or $(\frac{\varepsilon-c\varepsilon}{cn+\varepsilon-c\varepsilon})^{k_f}$ decreases. Thus, $\Pr(S_1 \perp S_2|\Phi)$ decreases.

2. Let $k_c = k_t + k_f$. Then, $k_t = k_c - k_f$.

$$\Pr(S_1 \perp S_2|\Phi) = 1 - \left(1 + (\frac{1-\alpha}{\alpha})(\frac{1-\varepsilon}{1-\varepsilon+c\varepsilon})^{k_c}(\frac{\varepsilon(1-\varepsilon+c\varepsilon)}{(1-\varepsilon)(cn+\varepsilon-c\varepsilon)})^{k_f}(\frac{1}{1-c})^{k}\right)^{-1}.$$

Because $\varepsilon < \frac{n}{n+1}$, $\varepsilon(1-\varepsilon+c\varepsilon) < (1-\varepsilon)(cn+\varepsilon-c\varepsilon)$. Thus, when $k_f$ increases, $(\frac{\varepsilon(1-c\varepsilon)}{(1-\varepsilon)(n-cn+c\varepsilon)})^{k_f}$ decreases and so $\Pr(S_1 \perp S_2|\Phi)$ decreases.

3. Because $k_d$ increases, $(\frac{1}{1-c})^{k_d}$ increases, and so $\Pr(S_1 \perp S_2|\Phi)$ increases. ∎

**Example 4.5** Continue with the motivating example. Consider the possible copying relationship between S1 and S2. They share no false values (all values they share are correct), so copying is unlikely. With $\alpha = 0.5$, $c = 0.8$, $A(S1) = 0.97$, $A(S2) = 0.61$, the Bayesian analysis goes as follows.

Start with computation of $\Pr(\Phi|S1 \bot S2)$. In case $D \in \overline{D_t}$, $\Pr(\Phi(D : D \in \overline{D_t})|S1 \bot S2) = 0.97 * 0.61 = 0.592$. There is no data item in $\overline{D_f}$. Let $P_d$ denote the probability $\Pr(\Phi(D : D \in \overline{D_d})|S1 \bot S2)$. Thus, $\Pr(\Phi|S1 \bot S2) = 0.592^3 * P_d^2 = 0.2P_d^2$.

Next consider $\Pr(\Phi|S1 \to S2)$. In case $D \in \overline{D_t}$, $\Pr(\Phi(D : D \in \overline{D_t})|S1 \to S2) = 0.8 * 0.61 + 0.2 * 0.592 = 0.61$. In case $D \in \overline{D_f}$, $\Pr(\Phi(D : D \in \overline{D_f})|S1 \to S2) = 0.2P_d$. Thus, $\Pr(\Phi|S1 \to S2) = 0.61^3 * (0.2P_d)^2 = 0.009P_d^2$. Similarly, $\Pr(\Phi|S2 \to S1) = 0.029P_d^2$.

According to Eq. (4.8), $\Pr(S1 \bot S2|\Phi) = \dfrac{0.5*0.2P_d^2}{0.5*0.2P_d^2 + 0.25*0.009P_d^2 + 0.25*0.029P_d^2} = 0.91$, so independence is very likely.

## Considering Copying in Truth Discovery

Previous subsections have described how to decide if two sources are dependent. However, even if a source copies from another, it is possible that it provides some of the values independently, so it would be inappropriate to completely ignore a copier. Instead, for each value $v$ on $D$ and its providers, denoted by $\overline{S_D}(v)$, the copiers should be identified and vote count $C(v)$ should be computed from only the independent providers. However, deciding which provider copies the value $v$ is at best probabilistic, because: (1) instead of deterministic decisions, only a probability is known for copying in each direction between a pair of sources; and (2) the copier may not copy every value. Ideally, one should enumerate all possible worlds of the copying relationships, compute the vote count of $v$ in each possible world, and take the weighted sum. But this takes exponential time and one can estimate the vote count in polynomial time.

Consider sources in $\overline{S_D}(v)$ one by one. For each source $S$, denote by $\overline{Pre}(S)$ the set of sources that have already been considered and by $\overline{Post}(S)$ the set of sources that have not been considered yet. The probability that $S$ provides $v$ independently of a source $S_0 \in \overline{Pre}(S)$ is $1 - c(\Pr(S_1 \to S_0|\Phi) + \Pr(S_0 \to S_1|\Phi))$. Accordingly, the probability that $S$ provides $v$ independently of any data source in $\overline{Pre}(S)$, denoted by $I(S, v)$, is

$$I(S, v) = \Pi_{S_0 \in \overline{Pre}(S)}(1 - c(\Pr(S_1 \to S_0|\Phi) + \Pr(S_0 \to S_1|\Phi))). \tag{4.16}$$

Note, however, that $I(S, v)$ is not precisely the probability that $S$ provides $v$ independently, because $S$ may copy from sources in $\overline{Post}(S)$. There are two possibilities. First, if none of those sources copies from any source in $\overline{Pre}(S)$, when examining each of them, the possibility of copying between it and $S$ would still be considered so the vote count would be discounted. However, the accuracy of the sources can be different, so the discounted vote count may be different. Second, if some of those sources copy from sources in $\overline{Pre}(S)$, $S$ actually transitively copies from sources in $\overline{Pre}(S)$, so its vote count is not discounted appropriately. Thus, it is important to order the sources to minimize such errors. Source ordering can proceed in a greedy fashion.

1.  If the probability of $S_1 \to S_2$ is much higher than that of $S_2 \to S_1$, consider $S_1$ as a copier of $S_2$ with probability $\Pr(S_1 \to S_2|\Phi) + \Pr(S_2 \to S_1|\Phi)$ (recall that it is assumed that there is no mutual-copying) and order $S_2$ before $S_1$. Otherwise, consider both directions as equally possible and there is no particular order between $S_1$ and $S_2$; consider such copying *undirectional*.

2.  For each subset of sources between which there is no particular ordering yet, sort them as follows: in the first round, select a data source that is associated with the undirectional copying of the highest probability $(\Pr(S_1 \to S_2|\Phi) + \Pr(S_2 \to S_1|\Phi))$; in later rounds, each time select a data source that has the copying with the maximum probability with one of the previously selected sources.

Finally, the vote count of value $v$ is adjusted by taking only the "independent fraction" of the original vote count (decided by source accuracy) from each source:

$$C(v) = \sum_{S \in \overline{S_D}(v)} C(S)I(S, v). \tag{4.17}$$

**Example 4.6**  Consider three data sources S1, S2, and S3 that provide the same value $v$ on a data item. Assume $c = 0.8$ and between each pair of sources the probability of copying is 0.4 (0.2 in each direction). Enumerating all possible worlds would compute 2.08 as the vote count of $v$.

Now estimate the vote count of $v$. As all copyings have the same probability, the data sources can be considered in any order. Consider the order of $S_1$, $S_2$, $S_3$. The vote count of $S_1$ is 1, that of $S_2$ is $1 - 0.4 * 0.8 = 0.68$, and that of $S_3$ is $0.68^2 = 0.46$. So the estimated vote count is $1 + 0.68 + 0.46 = 2.14$, very close to the real one, 2.08.

The following theorem has been proved to show the scalability and quality of the estimation.

**Theorem 4.3**  [Dong et al. 2009a] The vote-count estimation algorithm has the following two properties.

1.  Let $t_0$ be the vote count of a value computed by enumerating all possible worlds and $t$ be the estimated vote count. Then, $t_0 \le t \le 1.5 t_0$.

2.  Let $s$ be the number of sources that provide information on a data item. The vote count of all values of this data item can be estimated in time $O(s^2 \log s)$.

*Proof.*

1.  Consider $m$ data sources that vote for a value and assume they are ranked as $S_1, \ldots, S_m$. Let $\overline{D}$ be a subset of copying relationships. Let $G$ be a copying graph with copying in $\overline{D}$. If $G$ contains nodes $S_i$, $S_j$, $S_k$, $1 \le i < j < k \le m$, where $S_j$ depends on $S_k$, and $S_k$ depends on $S_i$,

the estimation will (incorrectly) count the vote by $S_j$; otherwise, the estimation computes the correct vote count for $G$. For any three nodes in $G$, the probability that the previously described case happens is at most $\frac{1}{3}$ (by Bayesian analysis). So the probability that the estimated vote count is more than the ideal vote count is at most $\frac{1}{3}$. Thus, the total estimated vote count is at most $\frac{1/3}{1-1/3} = 0.5$ more than the ideal vote count.

2. Let $d$ be the number of copying relationships between the sources; $d \leq \frac{s(s-1)}{2}$. The bottleneck of vote-count estimation is to order the sources, which can be done by iteratively finding the highest-probability copying between an already sorted source and an unsorted source. This can be done using heap sort in time $O(d \log d)$, so the time complexity is $O(s^2 \log s)$. ∎

### 4.2.4  THE END-TO-END SOLUTION

The end-to-end algorithm, AccuCopy, is described in Algorithm 4.1. The algorithm is consistent with the architecture shown in Figure 4.1.

Algorithm AccuCopy starts by setting the same accuracy for each source and the same probability for each value, then iteratively (1) computes probabilities of copying based on the probabilities of values computed in the previous round, (2) updates probabilities of values, and (3) updates accuracy of sources, and terminates when the accuracy of the sources becomes stable. Note that it is crucial to consider copying from the beginning. Otherwise, a data source that has been duplicated many times can dominate the vote results in the first round; later on the source is

---

**Algorithm 4.1: AccuCopy: Discover true values by considering accuracy of and copying between data sources**

**Input:** $S, D$.
**Output:** the true value for each data item in $D$.

1  Set default accuracy for each source
2  **while** accuracy of sources changes && no oscillation of decided true values **do**
3      Compute probability of copying between each pair of sources by Eqs. (4.8)–(4.15)
4      Sort sources according to the copyings
5      Compute probability of each value for each data item by Eqs. (4.2)–(4.7) and Eq. (4.17)
6      Compute accuracy of each source by Eq. (4.1)
7      **forall** $D \in D$ **do**
8          Among all values of $D$, select the one with the highest vote count as the true value
9      **endfor**
10  **endwhile**

---

considered to share only "true" values with other sources, and the copying can hardly be detected. However, in the first round it is not known which values are correct. Thus, Eq. (4.8) is applied to compute the probability conditioned on the value being true and the probability conditioned on the value being false, and the probability of copying is computed as the average weighted by the *a priori* belief of truthfulness of a value.

It is proved that if source accuracy is ignored (i.e., assuming all sources have the same accuracy), Algorithm AccuCopy converges.

**Theorem 4.4** [Dong et al. 2009a] Let $S$ be a set of good independent sources and copiers that provide information on data items in $\mathcal{D}$. Let $l$ be the number of data items in $\mathcal{D}$ and $n_0$ be the maximum number of values provided for a data item by $S$. The AccuVote algorithm converges in at most $2ln_0$ rounds on $S$ and $\mathcal{D}$ if it ignores source accuracy.

*Proof.* It can be proved that if the decision on the true value for data item $D$ changes back and forth between two values $v$ and $v'$, for each oscillation there needs to be decision changes on more of the other data items than in the previous oscillation. The number of data items in $\mathcal{D}$ is finite, so the algorithm converges.                                                                                  ∎

Once accuracy of sources is considered, AccuCopy may not converge: when different values are selected as the true values, the direction of the copying between two sources can change and in turn suggest different true values. One can stop the process after detecting oscillation of decided true values or after a certain number of rounds. The complexity of each round is $O(|\mathcal{D}||S|^2 \log |S|)$.

**Example 4.7** Revisit the motivating example. Figure 4.2 shows the probability of copying, Table 4.2 shows the computed accuracy of each data source, and Table 4.3 shows the probabilities of values computed for *Flight 4* and *Flight 5*.

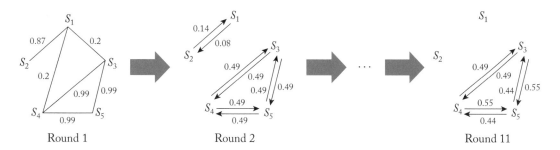

FIGURE 4.2:   Probabilities of copying computed by AccuCopy on the motivating example [Dong et al. 2009a]. An arrow from source $S$ to $S'$ indicates that $S$ copies from $S'$. Copyings are shown only when the sum of the probabilities in both directions is over 0.1.

TABLE 4.2: Accuracy of data sources computed by AccuCopy on the motivating example

|          | S1   | S2   | S3   | S4   | S5   |
|----------|------|------|------|------|------|
| Round 1  | 0.52 | 0.42 | 0.53 | 0.53 | 0.53 |
| Round 2  | 0.63 | 0.46 | 0.55 | 0.55 | 0.41 |
| Round 3  | 0.71 | 0.52 | 0.53 | 0.53 | 0.37 |
| Round 4  | 0.79 | 0.57 | 0.48 | 0.48 | 0.31 |
| ⋮        |      |      |      |      |      |
| Round 11 | 0.97 | 0.61 | 0.40 | 0.40 | 0.21 |

TABLE 4.3: Vote count computed for the scheduled departure time for *Flight 4* and *Flight 5* in the motivating example

|          | Flight 4 | | | Flight 5 | |
|----------|-------|-------|-------|-------|-------|
|          | *21:40* | *21:49* | *20:33* | *18:15* | *18:22* |
| Round 1  | 3.69  | 3.69  | 4.57  | 4.81  | 4.57  |
| Round 2  | 2.38  | 1.98  | 3.00  | 4.01  | 3.00  |
| Round 3  | 2.83  | 2.14  | 3.10  | 4.97  | 3.10  |
| Round 4  | 3.20  | 2.38  | 3.00  | 5.58  | 3.00  |
| ⋮        |       |       |       |       |       |
| Round 11 | 5.78  | 2.75  | 2.35  | 8.53  | 2.35  |

Initially, Line 1 of Algorithm AccuCopy sets the accuracy of each source to 0.8. Accordingly, Line 3 computes the probability of copying between sources as shown on the left of Figure 4.2. Taking the copying into consideration, Line 5 computes confidence of the values; for example, for *Flight 4* it computes 5.30 as the confidence of value *21:40* and *21:49*, and 6.57 as the confidence of value *20:33*. Then, Line 6 updates the accuracy of each source to 0.52, 0.42, 0.53, 0.53, 0.53, respectively, according to the computed value probabilities; the updated accuracy is used in the next round.

Starting from the second round, S1 is considered more accurate and has a higher vote count. In later rounds, AccuCopy gradually increases the accuracy of S1 and decreases that of S3-S5. At the fourth round, AccuCopy decides that *21:40* is the correct scheduled departure time for *Flight*

*4* and finds the right scheduled departure time for all flights. Finally, AccuCopy terminates at the eleventh round and the source accuracy it computes converges close to the expected ones (1, 0.6, 0.4, 0.4, 0.2, respectively).

### 4.2.5    EXTENSIONS AND ALTERNATIVES
#### Extensions for Truth Discovery
First, the two conditions described at the beginning of this section for the core case in truth discovery can be relaxed as follows.

**Non-uniform distribution of false values.** In reality, false values of a data item may not be uniformly distributed; for example, an out-of-date value or a value similar to the true value can occur more often than others. Dong et al. [2012] extend the basic model by considering the popularity of each value.

Let $Pop(v|v_t)$ denote the *popularity* of $v$ among all false values conditioned on $v_t$ being true. Then, the probability that source $S$ provides the correct value remains $A(S)$, but the probability that $S$ provides a particular incorrect value $v$ becomes $(1 - A(S))Pop(v|v_t)$. Deriving from the Bayesian analysis, the vote count of a source and that of a value $v$ can be computed as follows. Recall that $\overline{S_D}$ denotes the set of sources that provide data item $D$ and $\overline{S_D}(v)$ denotes the set of sources that provide value $v$ on $D$.

$$C(S) = \ln \frac{A(S)}{1 - A(S)}; \tag{4.18}$$

$$C(v) = \sum_{S \in \overline{S_D}(v)} C(S) - \rho(v); \tag{4.19}$$

$$\rho(v) = |\overline{S_D}(v)| \ln(|\overline{S_D}(v)|) + (|\overline{S_D}| - |\overline{S_D}(v)|) \ln(|\overline{S_D}| - |\overline{S_D}(v)|). \tag{4.20}$$

**Similarity of values.** Dong et al. [2009a] extend the basic model by considering similarity between values. Let $v$ and $v'$ be two values that are similar. Intuitively, the sources that vote for $v'$ also implicitly vote for $v$ and should be considered when counting votes for $v$. For example, a source that claims *21:49* as the departure time may actually mean *21:40* and should be considered as an implicit voter of *21:40*.

Formally, let $sim(v, v') \in [0, 1]$ denote the *similarity* between $v$ and $v'$, which can be computed based on edit distance of strings, difference between numerical values, etc. After computing the vote count of each value of data item $D$, the vote counts can be adjusted according to the similarities between them:

$$C^*(v) = C(v) + \sigma \cdot \sum_{v' \neq v} C(v') \cdot sim(v, v'), \tag{4.21}$$

where $\sigma \in [0, 1]$ is a parameter controlling the influence of similar values. The adjusted vote count is used in computation in later rounds.

## Other Methods of Measuring Source Trustworthiness
There have been many other ways proposed for measuring the trustworthiness of a source and they can be categorized into four classes.

**Web-link based methods** [Kleinberg 1999, Pasternack and Roth 2010, Pasternack and Roth 2011, Yin and Tan 2011] measure source trustworthiness and value correctness using PageRank [Brin and Page 1998]. A source providing a value induces a link between the source and the value. The PageRank of a source is computed as the sum of those from its provided values, whereas the PageRank of a value is computed as the sum of those from its provider sources.

**IR-based methods** [Galland et al. 2010] measure source trustworthiness as the *similarity* between the provided values and the true values. They use similarity metrics that are widely accepted in information retrieval, such as cosine similarity. The trustworthiness of a source is computed as the cosine similarity between its provided values and the inferred true values. Value correctness is decided by the accumulated source trustworthiness.

**Graphical-model methods** [Pasternack and Roth 2013, Zhao and Han 2012, Zhao et al. 2012] apply probabilistic graphical models to jointly reason about source trustworthiness and value correctness. As an example, LTM [Zhao and Han 2012] proposes a latent truth model that models the quality of sources, truthfulness of values, and observations of data as random variables.

**Precision/Recall-based methods** [Pochampally et al. 2014, Zhao et al. 2012] use *precision* and *recall* (or *specificity* and *sensitivity*) to measure source trustworthiness in case the value is a set or a list of atomic values. With such measures they can distinguish imprecise sources that provide incorrect atomic values and incomplete sources that miss some atomic values.

## Extensions for Copy Detection
Finally, there have been several extensions for copy detection, including how to relax the assumptions described in Section 4.2.3.

**Considering other aspects of data.**   In addition to value correctness, Dong et al. [2010] discuss obtaining evidence for copying from other aspects of data, such as coverage of the data and formatting of the data. Copying is considered likely if two sources share a lot of data items that are rarely provided by others, if they use common rare formats, and so on.

**Correlated copying.**   The basic model assumes *item-wise independence*, which seldom holds in reality. One can imagine that a copier often copies in one of two modes: (1) it copies data for a subset of entities on a subset of attributes, called *per-entity copying*; and (2) it copies on a subset of attributes for a set of entities that it provides independently or copies from other sources, called *per-attribute* copying. As an example, a third-party source may copy flight information including flight number, departure and arrival airport and time, from airline websites (per-entity copying); it then copies information about departure and arrival gate from corresponding airport websites (per-attribute copying). Blanco et al. [2010] and Dong et al. [2010] discuss how to distinguish these two modes in copy detection.

**Global copy detection.**   The previously described techniques consider only local copy detection where a pair of sources are considered each time. There can also be co-copying and transitive copying. For example, $S_2$ and $S_3$ may both copy from $S_1$ so they are co-copiers; $S_4$ may copy from $S_2$, so it transitively copies from $S_1$. Local copy detection may conclude that there is copying between every pair of sources in this case. Dong et al. [2010] discuss how to apply global copy detection, such that direct copying, co-copying, and transitive copying can be distinguished.

**Broader correlation between sources.**   In addition to direct copying between a pair of sources, a subset of sources may be correlated or anti-correlated. For example, a subset of data sources may apply similar semantics for some particular attributes such as flight departure time and arrival time, thus are correlated; in case they apply different semantics, they are anti-correlated. Pochampally et al. [2014] and Qi et al. [2013] discuss how to detect such broader correlation between a subset of sources.

## Main Results
Li et al. [2012] compare the algorithms proposed by Dong et al. [2009a, 2012], Galland et al. [2010], Pasternack and Roth [2010], and Yin et al. [2007] on the Stock and Flight data described in Section 1.2.4. The data sets are publicly available at http://lunadong.com/fusionDataSets.htm, and the main results are as follows.

1. On the Stock data set, where copying is rare and mainly happens between high-quality sources, the models that consider accuracy of sources typically out-perform naive voting. Among the different models, the one presented in Sections 4.2.1–4.2.2, combined with consideration of value similarity, obtains the highest precision, 0.93, 2.4% higher than that by naive voting.

2. On the Flight data set, where copying happens a lot between low-quality sources, most models that consider source accuracy obtain even lower precision than naive voting. AccuCopy, on the other hand, significantly improves the precision of the results over naive voting, by 9.1%.

3. As data sources are gradually added in decreasing order of their quality, on both domains the best results are not obtained after adding all sources, but after adding only sources with the highest quality. This motivates selecting the best sources for integration, as we describe in Section 5.2.

## 4.3    ADDRESSING THE VOLUME CHALLENGE

The fusion algorithms described in Section 4.2 assume that fusion would be conducted offline. This section describes two extensions to address the *volume* challenge of big data. First, Section 4.3.1 briefly describes a MapReduce-based algorithm that scales to billions of data items and data sources. Then, Section 4.3.2 describes how to conduct data fusion at query-answering time in an online fashion.

### 4.3.1    A MAPREDUCE-BASED FRAMEWORK FOR OFFLINE FUSION

Conducting each component of data fusion sequentially for billions of data items and billions of data sources can be prohibitively expensive. A natural thought is to parallelize the computation in a MapReduce-based framework. Recall that the complexity of truth discovery and of trustworthiness evaluation are both linear in the number of data items and in the number of data sources; the MapReduce-based framework is effective in scaling them up. On the other hand, the complexity of copy detection is quadratic in the number of data sources, since copying needs to be detected for every pair of sources. Li et al. [2015] study how to scale up copy detection; however, parallelization for pairs of billions of sources remains an open problem. The rest of this sub-section focuses on data fusion techniques that include only truth discovery and trustworthiness evaluation. Figure 4.3 shows the architecture of a MapReduce implementation of the algorithm.

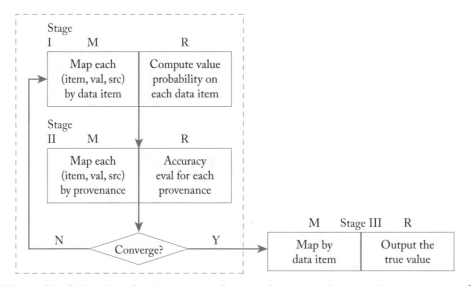

FIGURE 4.3:  MapReduce-based implementation for truth discovery and trustworthiness evaluation [Dong et al. 2014b].

There are three stages; each stage is a MapReduce process and so is performed in a parallel fashion. The algorithm takes as input the provided data, each being a (data item, value, source) triple.

I. The *Map* step partitions the triplet by the data item; the *Reduce* step applies Bayesian inference on all values provided for the same data item and computes the probability for each of them.

II. The *Map* step partitions the triplet by the source; the *Reduce* step computes the accuracy of each source from its value probabilities.

III. The first two stages iterate until convergence. The third stage outputs the results: the *Map* step partitions the triplet by the data item; the *Reduce* step selects the value with the highest probability as the fusion result for output.

## 4.3.2    ONLINE DATA FUSION

The algorithms described so far are targeted for an offline process. In many domains some part of the data are frequently changing over time, such as estimated arrival time of flights. Frequently performing offline fusion to keep up with the update of the data is infeasible given the sheer volume of the data, the large number of data sources, and the high frequency of the updates. Instead, it is desired to fuse data from different sources at query answering time. However, AccuCopy runs over all sources and all data items, and may take many iterations before convergence, thus can be quite time-consuming so inappropriate for online fusion.

Liu et al. [2011] propose an online data fusion technique to address this problem. It assumes that source accuracy and copying relationships have been evaluated in an offline process and would not change much over time. At query answering time it conducts truth discovery. Instead of waiting for truth discovery to complete and returning all answers in a batch, online data fusion starts with returning the answers from the first probed source, then refreshes the answers as it probes more sources. For each returned answer, it shows the likelihood that the answer is correct based on the retrieved data and knowledge of the source quality. When the system gains enough confidence that data from the unprocessed sources are unlikely to change the returned answers, it terminates without necessarily probing all sources. The next example illustrates how one can reduce the latency of truth discovery at query answering time.

**Example 4.8**    Consider answering "*When is the estimated arrival time for Flight 49?*" on 9 data sources shown in Figure 4.4. These sources provide three different answers, among which *21:45* is correct.

Table 4.4 shows how the online fusion system answers the query. The system starts with probing S9, returning *21:25* with probability .4 (how the sources are ordered and how the probabilities are computed are described shortly). It then probes S5, observing a different answer *21:45*; as a

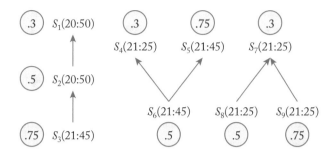

FIGURE 4.4: Nine sources that provide the estimated arrival time for *Flight 49*. For each source, the answer it provides is shown in parenthesis and its accuracy is shown in a circle. An arrow from $S$ to $S'$ means that $S$ copies some data from $S'$.

TABLE 4.4: Output at each time point in Example 4.8. The time is made up for illustration purposes

| | | Output | | |
|---|---|---|---|---|
| Time | Answer | Probability | Probability Range | Probed Source |
| Sec 1 | *21:25* | .4 | (0, 1) | S9 |
| Sec 2 | *21:25* | .22 | (0, 1) | S5 |
| Sec 3 | *21:45* | .94 | (0, 1) | S3 |
| Sec 4 | *21:45* | .84 | (0, 1) | S4 |
| Sec 5 | *21:45* | .92 | (0, 1) | S6 |
| Sec 6 | *21:45* | .97 | (.001, 1) | S2 |
| Sec 7 | *21:45* | .97 | (.014, 1) | S1 |
| Sec 8 | *21:45* | .98 | (.45, 1) | S7 |

result, it lowers the probability for answer *21:25*. Next, it probes S3 and observes *21:45* again, so it refreshes the answer to *21:45* with a probability .94. Probing sources S4, S6, S2, S1, and S7 does not change the answer, and the probability first decreases a little bit but then gradually increases to .98. At this point, the system is confident enough that the data from S8 are unlikely to change the answer and so terminates. Thus, the user starts to see the correct answer after 3 sources are probed rather than waiting till the system completes probing all 9 sources.

As shown in Figure 4.5, such an online fusion system has four major components: one component for offline preprocessing–*source ordering*, and three components for online query answering—

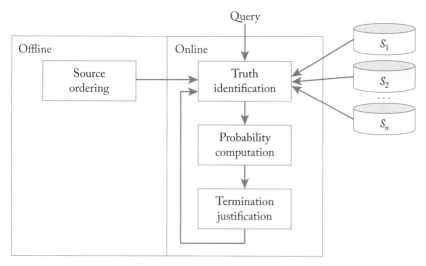

FIGURE 4.5:  Architecture of online data fusion [Liu et al. 2011].

*truth identification*, *probability computation*, and *termination justification*. They are next described in detail for truth discovery considering only source accuracy, assuming all sources are independent and provide all data items. Liu et al. [2011] present a complete solution that considers in addition source coverage and copying relationships.

### Truth Identification

Consider probing the sources in the pre-decided order. As a new source is probed, incrementally update the vote count for each already encountered answer. In case all sources are independent, incremental vote counting is straightforward: when a new source $S$ is probed, add its vote count, $C(S)$, to the vote count of the value it provides. The value with the highest vote count is returned.

For the example in Table 4.4, after querying S9, the vote count of *21:25* is updated to 3.4 so it will be returned as an answer. After querying S1, the vote count of *21:45* is updated to 3.4; so either *21:25* or *21:45* is returned.

### Probability Computation

When a value $v$ is returned as the answer, it is desired to return the expected probability and the range of the probability for this value to be true. Previous sections have described how one may compute the probability of a value according to the available data from a set $\overline{S}$ of sources, denoted by $\Pr(v|\overline{S})$. However, during query answering there are a lot of sources that are not probed yet and it is not known which values they may provide; when the expected probability and the range of the probability are returned, those sources should be taken in consideration. The problem is solved as follows.

Consider all possible worlds that describe the possible values provided by the unseen sources in $\mathcal{S} \setminus \overline{S}$, denoted by $\mathbf{W}(\mathcal{S} \setminus \overline{S})$. For each possible world $W \in \mathbf{W}(\mathcal{S} \setminus \overline{S})$, denote by $\Pr(W)$ its probability and by $\Pr(v|\overline{S}, W)$ the probability that $v$ is true based on data provided in the possible world. Then, the maximum probability of $v$ is the maximum probability computed among all possible worlds (similarly for minimum probability), and the expected probability of $v$ is the sum of these probabilities weighted by the probabilities of the possible worlds. They are formally defined as follows.

**Definition 4.2** (Expected/Maximum/Minimum Probability)   [Liu et al. 2011] Let $\mathcal{S}$ be a set of data sources and $\overline{S} \subseteq \mathcal{S}$ be the probed sources. Let $v$ be a value for a particular data item. The *expected probability* of $v$, denoted by $\mathrm{expPr}(v|\overline{S})$, is defined as

$$\mathrm{expPr}(v|\overline{S}) = \sum_{W \in \mathbf{W}(\mathcal{S} \setminus \overline{S})} \Pr(W) \Pr(v|\overline{S}, W). \tag{4.22}$$

The *maximum probability* of $v$, denoted by $\mathrm{maxPr}(v|\overline{S})$, is defined as (similarly for *minimum probability*)

$$\mathrm{maxPr}(v|\overline{S}) = \max_{W \in \mathbf{W}(\mathcal{S} \setminus \overline{S})} \Pr(v|\overline{S}, W). \tag{4.23}$$

As a new source is probed, the expected, maximum, and minimum probabilities need to be efficiently computed based on the counted votes. Enumerating all possible worlds takes exponential time so is not a feasible solution. In fact, it is proven that the expected probability for $v$ is exactly the same as $\Pr(v|\overline{S})$. The intuition is that the probability of an unseen source providing $v$ or any other value fully depends on the probability of $v$ being true, which is computed from data in $\overline{S}$; thus, the unseen sources do not add any new information and so cannot change the expected probability.

**Theorem 4.5**   [Liu et al. 2011] Let $\mathcal{S}$ be a set of independent sources, $\overline{S} \subseteq \mathcal{S}$ be the sources that have been probed, and $v$ be a value for a particular data item. Then, $\mathrm{expPr}(v|\overline{S}) = \Pr(v|\overline{S})$.

**Proof.**   One can compute the probability of each possible world according to the probabilities of the values being true, which are in turn computed based on observations on $\overline{S}$.

$$\Pr(W) = \sum_{v \in \mathcal{D}(D)} \Pr(W|v) \Pr(v|\overline{S}) = \Pr(W|\overline{S}).$$

Obviously, $W$ and $v$ are independent conditioned on $\overline{S}$. According to the definition of expected probability,

$$\exp\Pr(v|\overline{S}) = \sum_{W \in \mathbf{W}(\mathcal{S}-\overline{S})} \Pr(W) \Pr(v|\overline{S}, W)$$

$$= \sum_{W \in \mathbf{W}(\mathcal{S}-\overline{S})} \Pr(W|\overline{S}) \cdot \frac{\Pr(v, \overline{S}, W)}{\Pr(\overline{S}, W)}$$

$$= \sum_{W \in \mathbf{W}(\mathcal{S}-\overline{S})} \Pr(W|\overline{S}) \cdot \frac{\Pr(\overline{S}) \Pr(v|\overline{S}) \Pr(W|\overline{S})}{\Pr(\overline{S}) \Pr(W|\overline{S})}$$

$$= \sum_{W \in \mathbf{W}(\mathcal{S}-\overline{S})} \Pr(W|\overline{S}) \Pr(v|\overline{S}) = \Pr(v|\overline{S}).$$

$\blacksquare$

For the maximum probability of value $v$, obviously it is obtained when all unseen sources provide $v$.

**Theorem 4.6**  [Liu et al. 2011] Let $\mathcal{S}$ be a set of independent sources, $\overline{S} \subseteq \mathcal{S}$ be the sources that have been probed, and $v$ be a value for a data item $D$. Let $W$ be a possible world in which all sources in $\mathcal{S} \setminus \overline{S}$ provide value $v$ on $D$. Then, $\max\Pr(v|\overline{S}) = \Pr(v|\overline{S}, W)$.

Obtaining the minimum probability of value $v$ certainly requires that none of the unseen sources provides $v$. Among the rest of the values, it is proven that if all unseen sources provide the same value, and the value has the highest probability to be true according to the probed sources, $v$ has the minimum probability.

**Theorem 4.7**  [Liu et al. 2011] Let $\mathcal{S}$ be a set of independent sources, $\overline{S} \subseteq \mathcal{S}$ be the sources that have been probed, $v$ be a value for a data item $D$, and $v_{max} = \text{argmax}_{v' \in \mathcal{D}(D) - \{v\}} \Pr(v'|\overline{S})$. Let $W$ be a possible world in which all sources in $\mathcal{S} \setminus \overline{S}$ provide value $v_{max}$ on $D$. Then, $\min\Pr(v|\overline{S}) = \Pr(v|\overline{S}, W)$.

Consider the example in Table 4.4. Assume independence of the sources for illustrative purpose (so the numbers presented here can be different from those in Table 4.4). After querying S9 and S5, it is computed that $\exp\Pr(21{:}45) = \frac{\exp(3.4)}{\exp(3.4)+\exp(3.4)+\exp(0)*9} = .43$. If all other sources provide *21:45*, there are 8 providers for *21:45* and 1 provider for *21:25*; thus, $\max\Pr(21{:}45) = 1$. If all other sources provide *21:25*, there is 1 provider for *21:45* and 8 providers for *21:25*; thus, $\min\Pr(21{:}45) = 0$.

## Termination Justification

As the sources are probed, the results often converge before finishing probing all sources. In such situations, it is desired to terminate early. Thus, for each data item a termination condition is checked and data retrieval stops for it after the condition is satisfied.

To guarantee that probing more sources will not change the returned value $v$ for data item $D$, one should terminate only if for each $v' \in \mathcal{D}(D)$, $v' \neq v$, it holds that $\mathrm{minPr}(v) > \mathrm{maxPr}(v')$. However, this condition is very strict to be satisfied. It can be loosened in two ways: (1) for the value $v'$ with the second highest vote count, $\mathrm{minPr}(v) > \mathrm{expPr}(v')$; (2) for such $v'$, $\mathrm{expPr}(v) > \mathrm{maxPr}(v')$. Liu et al. [2011] show that these loose conditions lead to much faster termination, while sacrificing the quality of the results only a little, if at all.

For the example in Table 4.4, after querying S7, $\mathrm{minPr}(21{:}45) = .45$ but $\mathrm{expPr}(21{:}25) = .02$. Data retrieval can terminate without probing the remaining source S8.

## Source Ordering

The algorithm assumes an ordered list of sources as input and probes the sources in the given order. The sources should be ordered such that (1) the correct answers can be returned as early as possible and (2) data retrieval can terminate as soon as possible. To reduce the overhead at runtime, source ordering is conducted offline. Intuitively, when the sources are independent, the sources should be ordered in non-increasing order of their accuracy.

## Main Results

Liu et al. [2011] evaluate the online data fusion algorithm on a book data set that Yin et al. [2007] crawled from AbeBooks.com by searching computer-science books. The data set is publicly available at http://lunadong.com/fusionDataSets.htm, and the main results are as follows.

1. Liu et al. [2011] propose a query asking information about 100 books on 100 top coverage sources. Results for 90% books are returned after probing around 15 sources, get stable after probing 70 sources, and terminate after probing around 95 sources. The number of books with results (correspondingly, stable results, terminated results) climbs quickly at the beginning and then flattens out.

2. In terms of the number of *correctly* returned answers, it also increases quickly at the beginning, flattens out later, but decreases when probing the last 32 sources, among which some have very low accuracy. Considering copying performs better than considering only accuracy, which in turn performs better than naive voting.

3. Among various termination conditions, $\mathrm{minPr}(v) > \mathrm{Pr}(v')$ terminates faster while obtains the highest precision (note that $\mathrm{Pr}(v') = \mathrm{expPr}(v')$ when the sources are independent).

4. The proposed source ordering techniques are effective and out-perform random ordering or ordering by coverage.

# 4.4    ADDRESSING THE VELOCITY CHALLENGE

So far, static values are assumed for data fusion; that is, the truth does not change over time and the sources are static. The real world is dynamic; for example, scheduled departure and arrival time of the same flight may change over time, there may be new flights, and existing flights may be terminated. To capture such changes, data sources often update their data. When the sources fail to update their data in time, there can be stale data; that is, they are true for a past period of time but not up-to-date. This section very briefly discusses how to extend the fusion techniques designed for static sources to address the *velocity* challenge of big data.

Note that online data fusion in a sense also addresses the velocity challenge but it focuses on finding the currently true values. This section describes *temporal data fusion*, where the goal is to find all correct values and their valid periods in the history, when the true values evolve over time.

**Example 4.9**    Consider the sources S1–S3 in Table 4.5; they provide information for five flights. The scheduled departure time for the same flight may be changing over time. For example, *Flight 1* was scheduled to depart at *19:18* in January, and in March was rescheduled to depart at *19:02*. As another example, *Flight 4* is a new flight in March and was scheduled to depart at *20:33*; in September it was rescheduled to depart at *21:40*. The sources are updating their data accordingly. For example, S3 started to provide information about *Flight 1* in February and it provided the correct scheduled

TABLE 4.5: Three data sources updating information on the scheduled departure time of five flights. False values are in italic.

| History | S1 | S2 | S3 |
|---|---|---|---|
| 1.  (Jan, 19:18) | (Apr, 19:02) | (Jan, 19:18) | (Feb, 19:18) |
| (Mar, 19:02) | | | (Jul, 19:02) |
| 2.  (Jan, 17:50) | (Jan, 17:50) | (Jan, *17:00*) | (Feb, *17:00*) |
| (Sep, 17:43) | (Oct, 17:43) | (Feb, 17:50) | (Mar, 17:50) |
| | | (Sep, 17:43) | |
| 3.  (Jan, 9:20) | (Jan, 9:20) | (Jan, 9:20) | (Feb, 9:20) |
| 4.  (Mar, 20:33) | (Apr, 20:33) | (Sep, *21:49*) | (Jul, 20:33) |
| (Sep, 21:40) | (Oct, 21:40) | | |
| 5.  (Jan, 18:22) | (Jan, 18:22) | (Jan, *18:25*) | (Feb, *18:25*) |
| (Jun, 18:15) | (Aug, 18:15) | (Mar, 18:22) | (Jul, *18:22*) |
| | | (Jul, 18:15) | |

time *19:18*. After the rescheduling in March, it updated its provided time to *19:02* correctly, but not until July.

In such a dynamic setting erroneous data can be caused by several reasons. First, the sources may provide erroneous values; for example, S2 wrongly provided *21:49* for *Flight 4* in September. Second, the sources may fail to update their data; for example, after *Flight 1* was rescheduled, S2 did not update its data accordingly. Third, some sources may not update their data in time; for example, *Flight 1* was rescheduled in March, but S3 did not update its data until July.

It is desired to find not only the currently correct values, but also the correct values in the history and their valid period.

Formally, consider a set $\mathcal{D}$ of data items, each associated with a value at each particular time $t$ and can be associated with different values at different times; if $D$ does not exist at $t$, it is associated with a special value $\top$. The *life span* of $D$ is defined as a sequence of *transitions* $(tr_1, v_1), \ldots, (tr_l, v_l)$, where (1) $l$ is the number of periods in $D$'s life time; (2) the value of $D$ changes to $v_i$ at time $tr_i, i \in [1, l]$; (3) $v_1 \neq \top$, and $v_i \neq v_{i+1}$ for each $i \in [1, l-1]$; and (4) $tr_1 < tr_2 < \ldots < tr_l$. The life span of the scheduled departure time of the five flights are shown in the first column of Table 4.5.

Consider a set $\mathcal{S}$ of data sources, each providing values for data items in $\mathcal{D}$ and can change the data over time. Data provided by the sources are observed at different times; by comparing an observation with its previous observation, a series of *updates* can be inferred. Denote by $\mathbf{T} = \{t_0, \ldots, t_n\}$ the set of observation points and by $\overline{U}(S, t_i), i \in [0, n]$, the updates at time $t_i$; as a special case, $\overline{U}(S, t_0)$ contains values $S$ provided at the beginning observation point $t_0$. Note that an update in $\overline{U}(S, t_i), i \in [1, n]$, can happen at any time in $(t_{i-1}, t_i]$ and updates that are overwritten before the next observation may be missing; thus, frequent collection can often preserve more information. Table 4.5 shows the updates of sources S1–S3.

**Definition 4.3**  (Temporal data fusion)    Let $\mathcal{D}$ be a set of data items. Let $\mathcal{S}$ be a set of data sources, each providing values for a subset of data items in $\mathcal{D}$ over time, observed in a set $\mathbf{T}$ of observation time points. *Temporal data fusion* decides the true value for each data item in $\mathcal{D}$ at each time in $\mathbf{T}$.

The solution to this problem contains two major parts. First, the quality metrics of the data sources are defined for the dynamic setting. Second, Bayesian analysis is applied to decide the lifespan of each data item.

## Source Quality

Recall that for static data the quality of a source is captured by its accuracy. The metrics are much more complex for the dynamic case. Ideally, a high-quality source should provide a new value for a data item *if and only if*, and *right after*, the value becomes true. These three conditions are captured by three measures: the *coverage* of a source measures the percentage of all transitions of different

TABLE 4.6: CEF-measures for the data sources in Table 4.5

| Source | Coverage | Exactness | Freshness $F(0)$ | Freshness $F(1)$ |
|--------|----------|-----------|------------------|------------------|
| S1 | .92 | .99 | .27 | .4 |
| S2 | .64 | .8 | .25 | .42 |

data items that it captures (by updating to the correct value); the *exactness* is the complement of the percentage of transitions that the source mis-captures (by providing a wrong value); and *freshness* is a function of time $\Delta T$, measuring among the captured transitions, the percentage that are captured within time $\Delta T$. These three measures are orthogonal and collectively referred to as the *CEF-measure*.

Table 4.6 shows the CEF-measures computed for sources S1 and S2. It is observed that S1 has high coverage and exactness; for 27% transitions it captures in time $\Delta T = 0$ (i.e., within the same month), whereas for 40% transitions it captures in time $\Delta T = 1$ (i.e., within the next month). In comparison, S2 has lower coverage (e.g., it fails to capture the re-scheduling of *Flight 1*), and has much lower exactness (e.g., it provides wrong time at some points for *Flights 2, 4*, and *5*); however, its freshness is similar to that of S1.

## Lifespan Discovery

Consider a data item $D \in \mathcal{D}$. To discover its life span, both the time and the value of each transition need to be decided. This is done by Bayesian analysis based on the CEF-measures of its providers.

1. First, decide the value of $D$ at time $t_0$.

2. Then, find for $D$'s next transition the most likely time point in $\mathbf{T}$ and the most likely value, and repeat this process until it is decided that there is no more transition.

Finally, note that there can still be copying relationships between the sources and the copying relationships may even change over time. Dong et al. [2009b] describe how to apply an HMM model to find such evolving relationships.

## Main Results

Dong et al. [2009b] evaluate the dynamic data fusion algorithm on a restaurant data set including over 5K restaurants in Manhattan, crawled from 12 web sources weekly in a period of 8 weeks. The data set is publicly available at http://lunadong.com/fusionDataSets.htm, and the main results are as follows.

1. In this period 467 restaurants were marked by some source as being closed and among them 280 were indeed closed. The proposed method obtains a F-measure of 0.86 (precision = 0.86, recall = 0.87) in identifying these closed restaurants. In comparison, considering all these restaurants as closed has a low precision of 0.60, while considering restaurants marked by at least two data sources as closed has a low recall of 0.34.

2. Among the 66 pairs of data sources, Dong et al. [2009b] identified 12 pairs of sources with copying relationships.

3. An experiment on synthetic data shows that considering CEF-measures and copying both improve lifespan discovery.

## 4.5    ADDRESSING THE VARIETY CHALLENGE

All data fusion techniques presented so far assume that schema alignment and record linkage have been conducted and the data are well aligned. However, this assumption is too idealistic in the context of big data: oftentimes the input of data fusion may contain many errors resulting from schema alignment and record linkage. This section describes an initial step in addressing the *variety* challenge of big data.

The input of data fusion can be visualized as a two-dimensional data matrix shown in Figure 4.6: each row represents a data item, each column represents a data source, and each cell represents the value provided by the data source on the data item. However, because of the possible

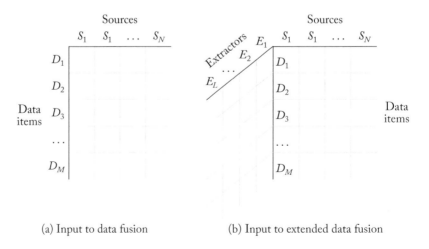

(a) Input to data fusion          (b) Input to extended data fusion

FIGURE 4.6: Input for data fusion is two-dimensional, whereas input for extended data fusion is three-dimensional [Dong et al. 2014b].

errors in schema alignment and record linkage, a (data item, value) pair obtained from a source may not be really what the source provides. Thus, a third dimension is introduced to represent *extractors*, which conduct schema alignment and record linkage, and extract (data item, value) pairs from sources. Different techniques may be applied for alignment and linkage; thus, there can be several extractors on the same source. In the three-dimension input matrix, each cell represents what the corresponding extractor extracts from the corresponding source on the corresponding data item. In other words, a (data item, value) pair is not necessarily what is provided by a source, but what is extracted by an extractor from the source. The definition of data fusion is extended to incorporate addressing possible mistakes from the extractors.

**Definition 4.4** (Extended data fusion)    Let $\mathcal{D}$ be a set of data items. Let $\mathcal{S}$ be a set of data sources, each providing values for a subset of data items in $\mathcal{D}$. Let $\mathcal{E}$ be a set of extractors, each extracting the values provided by $\mathcal{S}$ on $\mathcal{D}$. *Extended data fusion* decides the true value for each data item in $\mathcal{D}$.

To reduce the dimension of the input to extended data fusion, Dong et al. [2014b] consider each (extractor, source) pair as a whole, called a *provenance*. Having a large number of provenances indicates that the (data item, value) pair is either supported by many sources, or extracted by many different extractors; both presumably would increase the confidence in its correctness.

On the other hand, the effectiveness of this approach is limited by the correlation of the provenances, since an extractor may make a lot of common mistakes on different sources. A better approach would be to distinguish mistakes made by extractors and erroneous information provided by sources, which in turn would enable evaluating the quality of the sources and the quality of the extractors independently. Then, one could identify possible mistakes by the same extractor on many different sources, and avoid being biased by a false triple provided by only a couple of sources but extracted by many different extractors. This still remains as an open problem.

## Main Results

Dong et al. [2014b] experiment on the knowledge base described in Section 1.2.6 and evaluate how well the traditional data fusion techniques can solve the problem of extended data fusion. Their main results are as follows.

1. Treating (extractor, source) as a provenance obtains reasonably good results in solving the extended data fusion problem. When it computes a probability above 0.9 for a (data item, value) pair, the real accuracy is indeed high (0.94); when it computes a probability below 0.1 for a (data item, value) pair, the real accuracy is indeed low (0.2); and when it computes a medium probability in [0.4, 0.6] for a (data item, value) pair, the real accuracy also matches well (0.6).

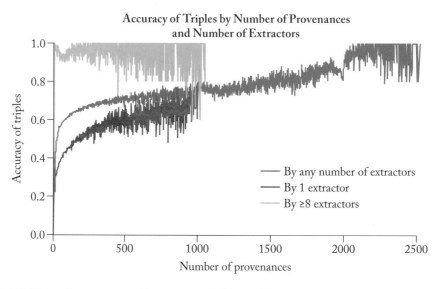

FIGURE 4.7: Fixing #provenances, (data item, value) pairs from more extractors are more likely to be true [Dong et al. 2014b].

2. On the other hand, taking the cross product of the source and the extractor as provenances *does* lose important signals. Figure 4.7 shows the accuracy of (data item, value) pairs by the number of provenances on the knowledge base. For triples with the same number of provenances, those being extracted by at least 8 extractors have a much higher accuracy (on average 70% higher) than those being extracted by a single extractor.

CHAPTER 5

# BDI: Emerging Topics

The previous chapters in this book have made it abundantly clear that big data integration offers both significant new challenges and new opportunities to derive value by integrating data available from a myriad of sources.

In this chapter, we describe some emerging topics and techniques that are expected to be critical to the success of BDI. In Section 5.1, we describe some recent work that takes advantage of the practice of crowdsourcing to seek human help to address challenges in data integration. Next, in Section 5.2, we present recent work that observes that data integration comes with a cost, which needs to be traded off with the potential benefit of integrating new sources to determine which sources are worth integrating. Finally, in Section 5.3, we present some work that can serve as the foundation for users to understand unfamiliar sources with data that are relevant to meet their needs.

## 5.1    ROLE OF CROWDSOURCING

Crowdsourcing systems seek help from a crowd of humans to effectively solve a variety of problems that are quite easy for humans, but much more difficult for computers to solve. They have become ubiquitous on the web in the last decade. Doan et al. [2011] provide an insightful survey of this emerging field, and define crowdsourcing systems as follows.

**Definition 5.1** (Crowdsourcing Systems)    A system is a *crowdsourcing system* if it enlists a crowd of humans to help solve a problem defined by the system owners, and if in doing so, it addresses the following four fundamental challenges: How to recruit and retain users? What contributions can users make? How to combine user contributions to solve the target problem? How to evaluate users and their contributions?

Given the challenging nature of data integration, it is only natural that a variety of crowdsourcing approaches have been proposed for various data integration tasks. An early work in this area was the MOBS project [McCann et al. 2003, McCann et al. 2008], which studies how to collaboratively build data integration systems, especially schema alignment between data sources. More recently, there has been a number of works that have focused on crowdsourcing for record linkage [Wang et al. 2012, Wang et al. 2013, Whang et al. 2013, Demartini et al. 2013, Gokhale et al. 2014, Vesdapunt et al. 2014].

In this section, we present a couple of prominent works in the area of crowdsourcing for record linkage. In Section 5.1.1, we present a hybrid human-computer approach which aims to crowdsource a small number of record pairs to label all candidate record pairs as matches or non-matches. In Section 5.1.2, we describe the first approach to crowdsource the end-to-end workflow of the record linkage task. Finally, we outline some directions for future work in this area.

## 5.1.1    LEVERAGING TRANSITIVE RELATIONS

Wang et al. [2012] observe that a naive approach to crowdsourcing record linkage would be to ask humans in the crowd to decide for each pair of records whether or not the two records refer to the same entity. For a table with $n$ records, this naive approach would result in $O(n^2)$ human intelligence tasks (HITs), which is not scalable. Instead, they propose a hybrid human-computer approach CROWDER that first uses computational techniques (e.g., the ones described in Chapter 3) to discard all pairs of records with a low likelihood of being matches, and only ask humans to label all the remaining candidate record pairs as matches or non-matches.

This approach, while clearly much better than a human-only approach, does not take advantage of the fact that record linkage satisfies the *transitive* relations [Wang et al. 2013].

**Positive Transitive Relation.**   If records $R_1$ and $R_2$ refer to the same entity, and records $R_2$ and $R_3$ refer to the same entity, then $R_1$ and $R_3$ must refer to the same entity too.

Note that the order in which these record pairs are considered for labeling by the crowd does not matter, if the labels by the crowd for different record pairs are consistent: any two pairs can be labeled as matches by the crowd, and the label of the third pair can be inferred to be a match by the system.

**Negative Transitive Relation.**   If records $R_1$ and $R_2$ refer to the same entity, but records $R_2$ and $R_3$ refer to different entities, then $R_1$ and $R_3$ must refer to different entities too.

Note that the order in which these record pairs are considered for labeling by the crowd *does* matter, even if the labels by the crowd for different record pairs are consistent. If record pairs $(R_1, R_2)$ and $(R_2, R_3)$ are labeled by the crowd as match and non-match, respectively, the label of the third pair $(R_1, R_3)$ can be inferred to be a non-match by the system. However, if the crowd labels the pairs $(R_1, R_3)$ and $(R_2, R_3)$ as non-matches, this does not allow the system to infer any label for the pair $(R_1, R_2)$.

Given a set of candidate record pairs with unknown labels, it is easy to see that considering the record pairs for labeling in different orders can lead to different numbers of record pairs being labeled by the crowd, and hence a different number of record pairs whose labels can be inferred.

| ID | Record | | ID | Record Pair | Likelihood |
|----|--------|---|----|-------------|------------|
| $R_1$ | iPhone 2nd generation | | $L_1$ | $(R_2, R_3)$ | 0.85 |
| $R_2$ | iPhone Two | | $L_2$ | $(R_1, R_2)$ | 0.75 |
| $R_3$ | iPhone 2 | | $L_3$ | $(R_1, R_6)$ | 0.72 |
| $R_4$ | iPad Two | | $L_4$ | $(R_1, R_3)$ | 0.65 |
| $R_5$ | iPad 2 | | $L_5$ | $(R_4, R_5)$ | 0.55 |
| $R_6$ | iPad 3rd generation | | $L_6$ | $(R_4, R_6)$ | 0.48 |
| | | | $L_7$ | $(R_2, R_4)$ | 0.45 |
| | | | $L_8$ | $(R_5, R_6)$ | 0.42 |

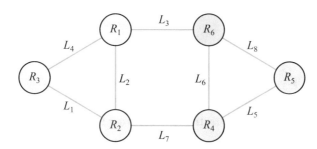

FIGURE 5.1:  Example to illustrate labeling by crowd for transitive relations [Wang et al. 2013].

Consider the example shown in Figure 5.1. It shows six records $\{R_1, \ldots, R_6\}$ and eight pairs of records $\{L_1, \ldots, L_8\}$ whose labels need to be determined. These are depicted using a graph, with records as nodes, and record pairs as edges: there are three entities, and the records corresponding to the same entity are in the same color. Edges connecting nodes of the same color are matches, while edges connecting nodes of different colors are non-matches. If the record pairs are considered in the order $L_1, L_2, L_3, L_4, L_8, L_7, L_6, L_5$, seven record pairs would need to be crowdsourced; only the label of $L_4$ can be inferred. However, if the record pairs are considered in the order $L_1, L_2, L_3, L_4, L_5, L_6, L_7, L_8$, only six record pairs would need to be crowdsourced; the labels of $L_4$ and $L_8$ can be inferred. In this example, the minimum number of crowdsourced labels needed is 6.

This raises the following problem: given a set of candidate record pairs with unknown labels, which strategy should be used to ensure that the *minimum* number of record pairs needs to be labeled by the crowd, such that for all other pairs, their labels can be inferred from the crowdsourced pairs based on transitive relations? Vesdapunt et al. [2014] showed that this problem is NP-hard. Wang et al. [2013] and Vesdapunt et al. [2014] present heuristics to solve this problem in practice. We describe the approach of Wang et al. [2013] in this section.

### Challenges

Identifying a good strategy for crowdsourcing the labels of record pairs faces two key challenges.

First, under the model of labeling record pairs sequentially, is it better to ask humans in the crowd to label record pairs that have a high likelihood of matching (i.e., a likely match), a low likelihood of matching (i.e., a likely non-match), or a medium likelihood of matching (i.e., it is unclear if it is a match or a non-match). It might seem intuitive to ask humans in the crowd to label those record pairs that have a medium likelihood of matching, where the information gain from the correct label is the highest. But is this intuition correct?

Second, in a real crowdsourcing system like Amazon Mechanical Turk (AMT), asking humans to label one record pair at a time can take too many iterations, and hence is infeasible. How much parallelism can be achieved while still ensuring that the number of record pairs labeled is the minimum possible?

### Key Contributions

Wang et al. [2013] address the challenges to identify good sequential and parallel strategies for crowdsourcing the labels of record pairs, and make many interesting contributions.

First, they show that a good sequential labeling order to take advantage of transitive relations is to label record pairs in the *decreasing* order of the match likelihood, assuming that the match likelihoods of the different record pairs are independent of each other. This is because conclusively establishing which record pairs match can be used to infer labels in both positive transitive relations and negative transitive relations.

This can be seen using the example shown in Figure 5.1. By labeling record pairs in the order $L_1, L_2, L_3, L_4, L_5, L_6, L_7, L_8$ (decreasing order of match likelihood), only six record pairs would need to be crowdsourced, which is optimal in this example.

Second, they show that it is feasible to have a high degree of parallelism, while ensuring that the number of record pairs labeled is the same as the sequential ordering. The key intuition here is to start with the sequential order described above, and sequentially identify those record pairs whose labels would need to be crowdsourced (i.e., not inferred), *independent* of the actual label of preceding record pairs in the sequential order. While trying all combinations of match/non-match labels of preceding record pairs to make this identification is exponential, an efficient algorithm can be obtained by checking if a record pair would need to be crowdsourced, assuming only that *all preceding record pairs had a match label*.

This approach can be illustrated using the example shown in Figure 5.1. Given the sequential order of $L_1, L_2, L_3, L_4, L_5, L_6, L_7, L_8$, the record pairs $L_1, L_2, L_3, L_5, L_6$ can be processed in parallel in the first iteration, since none of their labels can be inferred by knowing the actual label of the preceding record pairs in the sequential order. Once the labels of these record pairs are crowdsourced, the labels of $L_4$ and $L_8$ can be inferred, and only the label of $L_7$ needs to be crowdsourced. Again, only six labels are crowdsourced, using two iterations, instead of the six iterations taken by the sequential strategy.

## Main Results

Wang et al. [2013] experimentally evaluate their sequential and parallel strategies on two public real-world data sets, the Cora data set of research publications and the Abt-Buy product data set, with different characteristics in the number of matching record pairs, using both simulation and with AMT. Their main results are as follows.

1. Transitive relations are very effective to reduce the number of record pairs whose labels need crowdsourcing.

   On the Cora data set, which has many entities with a large number of matching records, using transitive relations reduces the number of crowdsourced record pairs by 95%. On the Abt-Buy data set, which has only a few entities with more than two matching records, using transitive relations is not as advantageous, but can still save about 20% crowdsourced record pairs. These results additionally assumed that all record pairs below a specified low likelihood threshold are indeed non-matches, which is quite reasonable in practice.

2. The number of record pairs whose labels need to be crowdsourced by the proposed sequential order can be over an order of magnitude better than the worst order (first labeling non-matching pairs, then the other matching pairs). Further, using a random order requires many more crowdsourced record pairs than the proposed order, but still much fewer than the worst order.

3. The parallel strategy reduced the number of iterations by up to two orders of magnitude over the sequential strategy.

   On the Cora data set, using a likelihood threshold of 0.3 for non-matches, the sequential strategy required 1237 iterations, while the parallel strategy reduced the number of iterations to 14.

4. The results on the actual crowdsourcing platform AMT are broadly consistent with the simulation results, and show that transitive relations can lead to significant cost savings with a little loss in result quality.

   For example, on the Cora data set, the transitive approach reduces the number of human intelligence tasks by 96.5%, and the time by 95% with about 5% loss in result quality. The reason for the loss of quality is that some pairs' labels are falsely inferred from incorrectly labeled record pairs based on transitive relations.

### 5.1.2   CROWDSOURCING THE END-TO-END WORKFLOW

Gokhale et al. [2014] observe that prior works on crowdsourcing record linkage are limited in that they crowdsource only parts of the end-to-end workflow of record matching (see Chapter 3), relying on expert software developers to program the remaining steps of the workflow. To address this issue, they propose to crowdsource the end-to-end workflow of the record linkage task, requiring very minimal input from a user who has a specific record linkage task to be performed. They characterize their approach as *hands-off crowdsourcing (HOC)*, and argue that it has the potential to enable wider use of crowdsourcing for record linkage.

### Challenges

HOC for record linkage clearly needs to address many challenges, as described below.

First, how can the blocking step of record linkage, which is essential to reduce the number of record pairs that need to undergo pairwise matching, be crowdsourced? Current approaches require a domain expert to carefully develop rules to ensure that blocking does not result in too many false negatives. How can the development of such rules be crowdsourced without requiring any effort from domain experts?

Second, the pairwise matching step of record linkage often uses learning-based approaches to predict matching and non-matching record pairs. How can the training step of such learning-based matchers use crowdsourcing in a cost-effective manner?

Third, how can the crowd be used to estimate the matching accuracy of the learning-based matcher? A key challenge here is that only a very small fraction of candidate record pairs are matches, thus the data is highly skewed. How can crowdsourcing be used to estimate precision and recall in a principled manner?

Fourth, when the matching accuracy of the learning-based matcher needs to be improved, iterative record linkage techniques focus on record pairs that earlier iterations fail to match correctly. How can crowdsourcing be used to make this iterative step rigorous?

### Key Contributions

Gokhale et al. [2014] address all the aforementioned challenges, making effective use of random forests [Breiman 2001] and active learning [Settles 2012]. They dub their proposed HOC approach as Corleone, named after the eponymous character from the Godfather movies. Corleone consists of four main modules: blocker, matcher, accuracy estimator, and difficult pairs locator, to address the above challenges, and requires only minimal input from a user who has a specific record linkage task to be performed: the two tables to be matched, a short textual instruction to the crowd about what it means for two records to match, two positive examples of record pairs that match, and two negative examples of record pairs that do not match. Corleone's key contributions are as follows.

First, given two tables $\overline{R}_1$ and $\overline{R}_2$ on which record linkage needs to be performed, Corleone's blocker identifies a main-memory sized sample of record pairs from $\overline{R}_1 \times \overline{R}_2$ (which includes the two positive and two negative examples of record pairs supplied by the user). Each record pair in this sample is then converted into a feature vector, using features from a standard library of similarity functions, like edit distance, Jaccard measure, and so on. Corleone then uses crowdsourced active learning on these feature vectors to learn a random forest $F$, using the four user supplied examples to build the initial forest, which is iteratively refined. Since a random forest is a set of decision trees, candidate blocking rules can be identified by extracting all negative rules (i.e., root-to-leaf decision tree paths that lead to a "no" leaf); such rules identify record pairs that *do not match* and hence can serve as blocking rules. Crowdsourcing is then used to evaluate a subset of high precision and high coverage candidate blocking rules, which are used to identify the subset of $\overline{R}_1 \times \overline{R}_2$ on which the matcher is applied.

Second, Corleone applies a standard strategy of training a random forest classifier using crowdsourced active learning on feature vectors of record pairs to build a matcher. The key challenge is to use crowdsourcing in a cost-effective manner, since excessive training both wastes money and can decrease the matcher's accuracy due to potential errors in crowdsourced results. This is done by identifying the "confidence" of the matcher using information theoretic tools, monitoring the confidence as the matcher trains, and stopping when the confidence has peaked.

Third, Corleone uses crowdsourcing to estimate the accuracy of the matcher. The challenge, as mentioned previously, is to deal with the highly skewed data, in which only a very small fraction of candidate record pairs are matches. This makes the use of a random sample of record pairs labeled using crowdsourcing to estimate accuracy inadequate, since it would find too few positive examples. The key idea proposed by Gokhale et al. [2014] is to use the negative rules extracted from the random forest of the matcher (which are different from the blocking rules) to eliminate negative examples systematically, thereby increasing the density of positive examples used to estimate accuracy.

Fourth, Corleone uses crowdsourcing to make the iterative step of iterative record linkage rigorous and cost-effective using crowdsourcing. The basic idea of iterative record linkage is to locate record pairs that are difficult to match, then build a new matcher specifically for those. The key idea proposed by Gokhale et al. [2014] is to identify highly precise positive and negative rules, eliminate record pairs that are covered by those rules, and treat the remaining examples as difficult to match.

Combining these four components, Corleone obtains a HOC solution to the end-to-end workflow of record linkage.

## Main Results

Gokhale et al. [2014] empirically evaluate Corleone on three real-world data sets, Restaurants, which matches restaurant descriptions, Citations, which matches citations between DBLP and Google

Scholar, and Products, which matches electronics products between Amazon and Walmart; these three data sets are quite diverse, with varying matching difficulties. They use AMT (paying 1 cent per question for Restaurants and Citations, and 2 cents per question for Products) to obtain the following results.

1. Overall, Corleone achieves a high matching accuracy, with an $F1$ score of 89.3–96.5% across the three data sets, at a reasonable crowdsourcing cost of only a few hundred dollars (for Products).

   The low cost is due to the fact that the number of labeled pairs is low compared to the total number of pairs, even after blocking. Further, Corleone achieves comparable or better accuracy than traditional solutions, while being totally hands-off.

2. The results on blocking demonstrate that crowdsourced blocking is quite effective, reducing the total number of pairs to be matched to be just 0.02–0.3% of the cross product, for Citations and Products, at a low cost of only a few tens of dollars (for Products) with a high precision (over 99.9%) and a high recall (over 92%).

3. Corleone needs only 1–2 iterations on the three data sets, and the estimated $F1$ score is quite accurate, typically within 5% of the true $F1$. This low error is despite the noisy labels from the crowd.

### 5.1.3   FUTURE WORK

The work on using crowdsourcing for data integration provides a good foundation for using crowdsourcing to address the challenges of BDI, but considerable work remains to be done. We outline a couple of promising directions of future work.

First, how does one leverage the algorithmic innovations that have been described in earlier chapters on schema alignment, record linkage and data fusion in BDI with advances in crowdsourcing to scale up to data sets with high volume, high velocity and high variety?

Second, crowdsourcing often produces noisy labels. When the data itself has low veracity, one needs to better understand the correlations between the quality of the data and the quality of crowdsourcing results, and its impact on BDI.

## 5.2   SOURCE SELECTION

The abundance of useful information available from a myriad of sources has been a boon to data integration systems to increase the utility of integrated data. With more sources, the coverage of the integrated data increases. Similarly, in the presence of inconsistency, the accuracy of the integrated data can be improved by leveraging the collective wisdom of the sources using the fusion techniques described in Chapter 4. However, data collection and integration come with a *cost*: many data

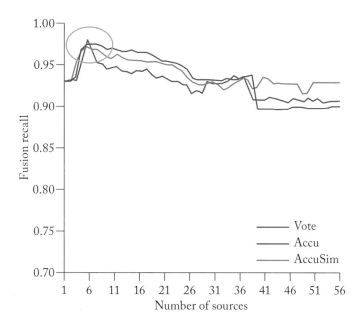

FIGURE 5.2:  Fusion result recall for the Stock domain [Li et al. 2012].

sources charge for their data, and even for sources that are free, integration costs (i.e., human and computational costs) can be substantial. Clearly, incurring these costs for a new source may not be worthwhile if the additional benefit of this source is limited.

Dong et al. [2012] show using several real-world data sets that it is not always worthwhile to integrate all available sources in a domain. For example, in the presence of redundancy among data sources in a domain, integrating new sources may not increase the coverage by much, if at all, while adding to the total cost. This can be observed in the *k*-coverage plots in Figure 1.2, especially for smaller *k* values. Even worse, some low-quality data sources can even hurt the accuracy of integrated data and bring a negative benefit, while still adding to the total cost. This can be observed in the plots of Figure 5.2, which show the recall of fusion results for the Stock domain in the study by Li et al. [2012]; the orange oval shows that peak benefit is attained well before integrating all the sources.

To address such concerns, Dong et al. [2012] identify the novel problem of *source selection*, which is performed before real integration to balance the cost and the benefit of integration. This can be important in many scenarios, ranging from web data providers that aggregate data from multiple sources, to enterprises that purchase data from third parties, and to individual information users who shop for data from data markets [Dong et al. 2012].

**Definition 5.2** (Source Selection)    Consider a set of data sources $\mathcal{S}$, and let $I$ denote an integration model. Let $cost_I(\overline{S})$ and $benefit_I(\overline{S})$ denote the cost and benefit of integrating sources $\overline{S} \subseteq \mathcal{S}$ by model $I$ respectively. Let $opt$ and $thresh$ denote two binary functions, and $\tau$ be a constant. The *source selection* problem finds a subset of sources $\overline{S} \subseteq \mathcal{S}$ that maximizes $opt(cost_I(\overline{S}), benefit_I(\overline{S}))$ under the constraint $thresh(cost_I(\overline{S}), benefit_I(\overline{S})) \leq \tau$.

Dong et al. [2012] study the problem of source selection for static sources and propose an approach inspired by the *marginalism* principle in economic theory [Marshall 1890]; this technique is described in Section 5.2.1. In follow-up work, Rekatsinas et al. [2014] study the problem of source selection for sources whose content changes over time, and propose techniques for characterizing and selecting fresh data sources; this is presented in Section 5.2.2. Finally, we outline some directions for future work in this area.

## 5.2.1    STATIC SOURCES
Source selection, based on the metrics of cost and benefit, falls in the category of resource optimization problems. There are two traditional ways to formulate the optimization problem.

- Find the subset of sources that maximizes the result benefit for a given maximum cost:

$$opt(cost_I(\overline{S}), benefit_I(\overline{S})) = benefit_I(\overline{S})$$

$$thresh(cost_I(\overline{S}), benefit_I(\overline{S})) = cost_I(\overline{S}).$$

- Find the subset of sources that minimizes the cost while having a minimal desired benefit:

$$opt(cost_I(\overline{S}), benefit_I(\overline{S})) = -cost_I(\overline{S})$$

$$thresh(cost_I(\overline{S}), benefit_I(\overline{S})) = -benefit_I(\overline{S}).$$

Dong et al. [2012] observe that neither of these formulations is ideal for source selection, and instead formulate a problem inspired by the marginalism principle in economic theory: assuming that cost and benefit are measured in the same unit (e.g., dollars), they propose to continue selecting sources until *the marginal benefit is less than the marginal cost*; equivalently, they propose to select the set of sources with the maximum *profit*, for a given maximum cost, defined as follows:

$$opt(cost_I(\overline{S}), benefit_I(\overline{S})) = benefit_I(\overline{S}) - cost_I(\overline{S})$$

$$thresh(cost_I(\overline{S}), benefit_I(\overline{S})) = cost_I(\overline{S}).$$

Dong et al. [2012] focus on the case where the integration model is a data fusion model, and benefit is a function of the accuracy of the fusion result.

## Challenges

Applying the marginalism principle to source selection for data integration faces many challenges [Dong et al. 2012].

First, the law of diminishing returns (i.e., continuing to add resources will gradually yield lower per-resource-unit returns) does not necessarily hold in data integration, so there can be multiple marginal points, with maximal profits. This suggests that a straightforward greedy approach may not be adequate to solve the problem.

Second, since data sources are not independent of each other, integrating sources in different orders can lead to different quality (or benefit) curves, and each curve has its own marginal points. This suggests that a solution would need to be able to compare multiple marginal points to choose the best one.

Third, since source selection needs to be performed before real integration, the actual benefits of integration in terms of result quality are not known. This suggests that the costs and benefits of integrating subsets of sources would need to be analytically or empirically estimated.

## Key Contributions

Dong et al. [2012] address the aforementioned challenges for source selection in the context of data fusion for offline data integration, that is, the case of *static sources*, and make several key contributions.

First, they show that source selection in the context of data fusion is NP-complete in general, and that a straightforward greedy algorithm can generate an arbitrarily bad solution.

Second, they propose an algorithm that applies the *greedy randomized adaptive search procedure (GRASP)* meta-heuristic [Festa and Resende 2011] to solve the marginalism problem. GRASP addresses the limitations of the greedy approach in two ways. First, instead of making a greedy decision in every step, in each step it randomly chooses from the top-$k$ candidates in terms of resulting profit as the initial solution, and chooses the best selection from $r$ repetitions as described next. Second, in each repetition, after generating the initial solution, it performs local search in a hill-climbing fashion. Both components are critical to avoid exploring the sources in a fixed order and so make it possible to reach a near-optimal selection. However, GRASP does not come with any approximation guarantees.

Third, they propose efficient (PTIME or pseudo-PTIME) dynamic-programming algorithms that estimate the accuracy (and hence the benefit) of data fusion results based purely on the accuracy of the input sources and the popularity of the most popular false value, assuming independence of the input sources.

## Main Results

Dong et al. [2012] experimentally evaluate their source selection algorithm and the algorithms to estimate the accuracy of data fusion results on a variety of data sets, including the Flight data used by Li et al. [2012]. Their main results are as follows.

1. GRASP is significantly better than Greedy in selecting the subset of sources with the highest profit, for a variety of benefit and cost functions and data fusion strategies.

   Increasing the number of candidates ($k$) from which the initial solution is chosen and the number of repetitions ($r$) improves the fraction of times for which GRASP obtains the highest profit, at the cost of a higher run-time. GRASP with $k = 10$, $r = 320$ often obtains the best source selection; even when the solution is not the best, the profit difference with the best selection is under 2.5%. Even higher values of $k$ can actually lower the result quality since it makes the initial solution close to random selection.

   Greedy rarely selects the best subset of sources, and the profit difference with the best selection can be as high as 19.7%.

2. The algorithms to estimate the accuracy of data fusion results are quite accurate for a variety of data fusion strategies, with a less than 10% absolute difference between the estimated and real fusion recalls, and a less than 12% relative difference.

   However, estimating accuracy for sophisticated data fusion strategies such as ACCU (see Chapter 4) takes much more time than for simpler strategies such as majority voting.

3. The subset of sources selected by GRASP is relatively insensitive to the choice of data fusion strategies, suggesting the use of simpler data fusion strategies during the source selection phase, and more sophisticated strategies during the actual fusion phase.

4. Finally, the source selection algorithms are quite scalable, taking less than 1 hour for synthetic data with up to a million sources of various accuracy distributions. This is quite acceptable since source selection is conducted offline and only once in a while.

### 5.2.2 DYNAMIC SOURCES

Rekatsinas et al. [2014] study the problem of source selection for dynamic sources, that is, sources whose content changes over time. One motivation for this problem comes from the scenario of *listing aggregation*, such as business, job or rental listings. Here, aggregators offer a search service to end users by integrating listings from multiple sources, and each source provides a set of listings and regular updates as new listings become available, or existing listings get updated or removed. A second motivation comes from the increasingly popular scenario of collective analysis of online news media for societal-event monitoring. Here, the analyst integrates events mentioned in a diverse set of news media sources and analyzes them collectively to detect patterns characterizing the domain of interest. For example, the global database of events, languages, and tone (GDELT) aggregates news articles from 15,275 sources in a single repository, and makes them available for analytic tasks.

### Challenges

Source selection for dynamic data sources raises several additional challenges over the same problem for static data sources.

First, a source with a high update frequency does not necessarily imply that the source has a high freshness (i.e., up-to-date values compared to the real world). This can be observed in the plot of average freshness versus average update frequency per day of 43 data sources providing records for US businesses over 23 months, shown in Figure 5.3. In particular, the red oval shows that even sources that are updated every day have a big range of possible average freshness values. The main reason for this is that sources that add to their content frequently may still be ineffective at deleting stale data or capturing value changes of older data items.

Second, the benefit of available sources may change over time and often the subset of sources that maximizes the integration benefit may also change over time. This can be observed in the evolution of coverage of the integration result for two sets of sources in the business listing sources discussed above, shown in Figure 5.4. Both sets contain the two largest sources. Moreover, the first set contains one other source while the second set contains three other sources, with comparable sizes to the source added in the first set.

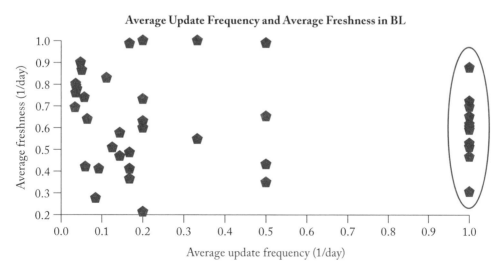

FIGURE 5.3:  Freshness versus update frequency for business listing sources [Rekatsinas et al. 2014].

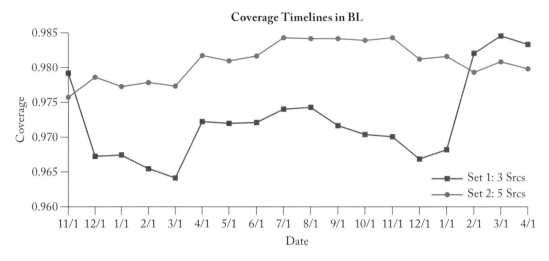

FIGURE 5.4: Evolution of coverage of the integration result for two subsets of the business listing sources [Rekatsinas et al. 2014].

## Key Contributions

Rekatsinas et al. [2014] study the problem of *time-aware source selection*, and use the same problem formulation as Dong et al. [2012], of reasoning about the *profit* of acquiring and integrating dynamic sources to select the optimal subset of sources to be integrated. Their key contributions are as follows.

First, they use time-dependent definitions of data quality metrics such as coverage, freshness, and accuracy to quantify the benefit of data integration.

Second, they introduce a theoretical framework that uses parametric statistical models to describe the evolution of the world, and uses an ensemble of empirical distributions to describe the complex update patterns and data quality changes of different data sources.

Third, they show that while the time-aware source selection problem is NP-complete, many of its instances (e.g., where the benefit is a function of time-dependent coverage, and the cost is linear) correspond to well-studied submodular optimization problems for which efficient local-search algorithms with constant factor approximations are known [Feige et al. 2011]. Further, in addition to selecting a subset of sources, these algorithms can also decide the optimal frequency to acquire data from each source. The submodular optimization algorithm is conceptually similar to GRASP, in that it starts by selecting the best source, explores the local neighborhood by adding and deleting sources, and finally returns the selected set or its complement.

## Main Results

Rekatsinas et al. [2014] experimentally evaluate (i) their source selection algorithms under different families of benefit and cost functions, and (ii) the accuracy of their proposed models to predict the data changes in the sources and the world, on a variety of real-world and synthetic data sets, including the business listing data and the GDELT data. Their main results are as follows.

1. The proposed models to predict data changes are quite accurate, with an average relative error of around 2% on the business listing data, and an error increase rate of 0.1% per time unit. On GDELT, the proposed models have a relative error of no more than 8%, which is quite small considering that the amount of training data spanned only 15 days.

2. As in the study on static data sources by Dong et al. [2012], GRASP selects the subset of dynamic sources with the highest profit most of the time, for a variety of benefit and cost functions.

    Interestingly, the solutions of the submodular optimization algorithm are mostly comparable to the best solutions, with an average quality loss of less than 2% and a worst-case quality loss of about 10% compared to the best solution. However, there are some cases where GRASP is significantly worse than submodular optimization, with an average quality loss of about 9% and a worst-case quality loss of over 50% compared to the solutions by submodular optimization. As before, Greedy is the worst strategy overall.

3. Finally, submodular optimization is about 1–2 orders of magnitude faster than GRASP (depending on the number of iterations used by GRASP), and scales better as the number of sources increases. Coupled with the robust quality of its solutions, the significantly faster run-times makes submodular optimization a viable alternative to GRASP, especially for large instances of source selection.

### 5.2.3    FUTURE WORK

The work on source selection is still in its infancy, and much work remains to be done. We outline two promising directions of future work.

First, existing research [Dong et al. 2012, Rekatsinas et al. 2014] assumes independence of data sources. Extending these works to take into account copying between data sources [Dong et al. 2009a] and arbitrary correlations between data sources [Pochampally et al. 2014] have the potential to further improve the quality of the sources selected.

Second, existing research has only considered integration benefit to be a function of fusion quality metrics such as coverage, freshness and accuracy. A more comprehensive treatment of integration benefit, taking into account schema alignment and record linkage, in addition to data fusion, would make source selection more widely applicable to a diversity of data sources.

## 5.3    SOURCE PROFILING

The number and variety of data sources available for integration and analysis have been a blessing for data scientists and analysts, as they increasingly seek high quality evidence to make data-driven discoveries. However, not all available sources are likely to be relevant to the task at hand, and many of the relevant sources may not provide the desired quality of evidence that the users need. Given the myriad of sources, a key challenge is for users to be able to discover sources that contain data that are relevant and are of sufficiently high quality to meet their needs.

When the structure, semantics, and contents of the data sources are very well-understood, source selection techniques (described in Section 5.2) can be used to reason about the benefits and costs of acquiring and integrating data to identify the subset of sources that are worth integrating. However, in many scenarios, users are unfamiliar with the data domains of the sources, unaware of the entities contained in the sources, and how the entity properties and relationships between the entities are structured in the sources. The goal of *source profiling* is to effectively address the challenging problem of helping users understand the source contents, before they even decide whether integration needs to be performed [Naumann 2013].

An important step to achieving this understanding is to be able to relate the source contents to the ontologies, entities, entity properties and relationships present in knowledge bases such as Freebase [Bollacker et al. 2008], the Google knowledge graph [Dong et al. 2014b], ProBase [Wu et al. 2012], and Yago [Weikum and Theobald 2010], which users already understand. A related step is to characterize the quality of the source contents, using the variety of data quality metrics that have been proposed in the literature [Batini and Scannapieco 2006], such as coverage, freshness, and accuracy. Source profiling can be formalized as follows.

**Definition 5.3** (Source Profiling)   Consider a set of data sources $\mathcal{S}$, with attributes $\mathcal{A}$. Let $KB$ refer to a knowledge base, and $DQ$ denote a set of data quality metrics. The *source profiling* problem identifies (a) a mapping $\kappa: \mathcal{S} \times 2^{\mathcal{A}} \rightarrow 2^{KB}$, which associates a subset of attributes in each source with concepts, entities, and relationships in the knowledge base, and (b) a mapping $\mu: \mathcal{S} \times 2^{KB} \times DQ \rightarrow range(DQ)$, which quantifies the data quality of different portions of the sources expressed in terms of the knowledge base.

Source profiling is clearly challenging, and while some strides have been made towards this goal, a lot remains to be done. Most of the research in this area has focused on relational sources, and we present a couple of representative works in this section. In Section 5.3.1, we describe an early, pioneering work on source profiling to collect statistical summaries about the structure and content of sources; these summaries can be used to automatically discover the structural relationships between source schema elements. In Section 5.3.2, we present an approach that can make use of the discovered structural relationships between source schema elements to summarize the contents of a relational source; this enables users to quickly identify the data domains of the source, and the main tables in which each type of information resides. Finally, we outline some directions for future work in this area.

### 5.3.1    THE BELLMAN SYSTEM

Dasu et al. [2002] propose the Bellman system to enable analysts to understand the contents and structure of complex, unfamiliar relational sources. This work is motivated by the observation that large relational databases degrade in quality over time, due to a variety of factors such as incorrect data (e.g., a provisioning group may promptly enter in the service/circuits they provision but might not delete them as diligently), use of the database to model unanticipated events and entities (e.g., new services or customer types), and so on.

As an aid to be able to use such degraded data for new projects, including data analysis and data integration, Bellman performs mining on the content and structure of the source to quickly identify attributes with potential data quality issues, determine which attributes have similar values, construct complex entities using join paths and so on. These mining results allow the analyst to make sense of the source content.

### Challenges

Mining complex databases to extract semantically meaningful information faces many challenges [Dasu et al. 2002].

First, such databases often have thousands of tables with tens of thousands of attributes. Discovering the database structure can be difficult because of the scale of the problem.

Second, constructing complex entities (e.g., a corporate customer) in a normalized database often requires many joins with long join paths, which are non-trivial to automatically discover, since foreign key dependencies are often not maintained, may degrade over time, and the schema documentation is usually out-of-date.

Third, tables may contain heterogeneous entities (e.g., individual customers and small business customers) that have different join paths in the database.

Fourth, the convention for recording data may be different in different tables, for example, customer names may be present in one attribute in one table, but in two or more attributes in another.

### Key Contributions

Dasu et al. [2002] address the aforementioned challenges in the case of structured databases, and make several key contributions.

First, Bellman addresses the scale challenge by building and making use of a variety of concise summaries of the values in *individual attributes*, instead of directly using the contents of the database. This includes min-hash signatures [Broder et al. 2000], multiset signatures that extend min-hash signatures by additionally keeping track of counts, $q$-gram min-hash signatures, and so on. These are constant size signatures, independent of the number of records in database tables.

Second, Bellman uses the concise attribute summaries to efficiently and accurately answer a variety of exploration queries, such as finding similar attributes, finding composite attributes, finding join paths, and finding heterogeneous tables. Some of these are illustrated below.

- What other attributes have sets of values that are similar to the set of values in a given attribute $A$?

    The resemblance $\rho(A_1, A_2)$ of two sets of attribute values $A_1$ and $A_2$ is defined as $|A_1 \cap A_2|/|A_1 \cup A_2|$. This value can be easily estimated using the min-hash signatures of each of the two attributes.

    The min-hash signature of attribute $A$ is $(s_1(A), \ldots, s_n(A))$, where $s_i(A) = \min_{a \in A}(h_i(a))$, $1 \leq i \leq n$, and $\{h_i : 1 \leq i \leq n\}$ is a collection of pairwise independent hash functions. Intuitively, each hash function maps elements in the domain of all attribute values uniformly and randomly to the space of natural numbers, and $s_i(A)$ is the smallest hash value for any of the values in attribute $A$ using hash function $h_i$.

    Given two attributes $A_1$ and $A_2$, it can be shown [Broder et al. 2000] that $\Pr[s_i(A_1) = s_i(A_2)] = \rho(A_1, A_2)$, $1 \leq i \leq n$. To tighten confidence bounds, the estimate of $\rho(A_1, A_2)$ uses all $n$ signature components as follows:

$$\hat{\rho}(A_1, A_2) = \Sigma_{i=1, \ldots, n} I[s_i(A_1) = s_i(A_2)]/n$$

where $I[s_i(A_1) = s_i(A_2)]$ is the indicator function, which takes value 1 if $s_i(A_1) = s_i(A_2)$ and 0 otherwise.

- What other attributes have sets of values that are textually similar to the set of values in a given attribute $A$?

    This exploration query is useful in the presence of typographical errors.

    Finding substring similarity between two sets of attributes values is computationally difficult, because of the large numbers of substrings that may need to be compared. This can be simplified by summarizing the substrings in an attribute using $q$-grams (the set of all $q$-character substrings of this attribute), and using $q$-gram signatures (i.e., the min-hash signatures of the set of $q$-grams in the attributes). Then, the $q$-gram resemblance between attributes $A_1$ and $A_2$ can be used to answer the exploration query.

- What compositions of attributes have sets of values that are textually similar to the set of values in a given attribute $A$?

    This exploration query is useful for attributes such as customer name, which may be present in one attribute in one table, but in two or more attributes in another.

It can be answered using $q$-gram signatures, identifying candidate attributes present in the same table, and evaluating combinations of two or more candidate attributes. For this latter task, it is worth noting that min-hash signatures are summable, and $s_i(A_1 \cup A_2) = \min(s_i(A_1), s_i(A_2))$, $1 \le i \le n$.

## Main Results

Dasu et al. [2002] experimentally evaluate their techniques to determine the utility and scalability of their approach on a large, complex database. Their main results are as follows.

1. Bellman is able to compute all the signatures and sketches (with 250 signature components and 3-grams) on 1078 attributes that contain at least 20 distinct values in less than 3 hours.

   This shows that the offline processing needed to compute profiles of large, complex databases can be performed efficiently.

2. Finding all attributes with a large resemblance to a particular attribute takes about 90 seconds using 250 signature components on 1078 profiled attributes, with high accuracy.

   It is possible to significantly decrease the run time by reducing the number of signature components to 50–100, without significantly degrading the accuracy of the result.

   Accurately estimating 3-gram resemblance is even easier since the universe of possible values is quite small (there are only 2,097,152 possible 7 bit ASCII 3-grams).

## 5.3.2    SUMMARIZING SOURCES

Yang et al. [2009] propose an innovative approach to summarize the contents of a relational source, so that users can quickly identify the data domains of the source, and the main tables in which each type of information resides. This work is motivated by the observation that complex databases often have thousands of inter-linked tables, and users who are unfamiliar with the data need to spend a considerable amount of time understanding the schema before they can extract useful information out of the database.

Consider, for illustrative purposes, the TPCE benchmark schema graph shown in Figure 5.5. It consists of 33 tables, preclassified in four categories: Broker, Customer, Market and Dimension. The database models a transaction system in which customers trade stocks. Various additional information is stored about customers, securities, brokers, and so on. This figure also illustrates the desired summary of the TPCE schema: By clustering the tables into a few labeled categories (and color-coding the graph), the result gives any user a rough idea about what the database represents. This classification was done manually by the designer of the benchmark; more importantly, the labeling was also decided by the designer. Yang et al. [2009] propose a statistical model that automatically classifies and labels schema tables, and produces a summary defined as follows.

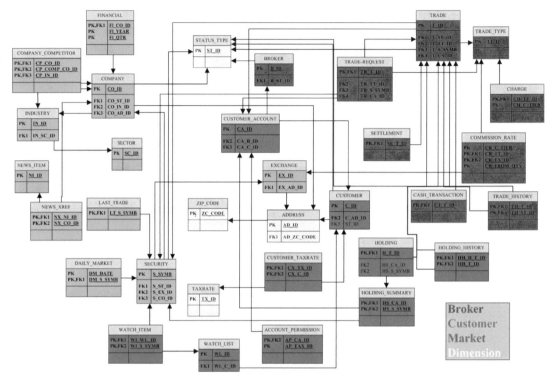

FIGURE 5.5:  TPCE schema graph [Yang et al. 2009].

**Definition 5.4** (Source Schema Summary)   [Yang et al. 2009] Given a schema graph $G$ for a relational source, a summary of $G$ of size $k$ is a $k$-clustering $\mathcal{C} = \{C_1, \ldots, C_k\}$ of the tables in the relational source, such that for each cluster $C_i$, a representative table $center(C_i) \in C_i$ is defined. The summary is represented as a set of labels $\{center(C_1), \ldots, center(C_k)\}$, and by a function that assigns each table in the relational source to a cluster.

### Challenges

Creating meaningful summaries of relational sources faces many challenges [Yang et al. 2009].

First, an automatic process for schema summarization needs to define a notion of table importance, based on its attributes, its records, and its join relationships. However, straightforward ways of defining table importance, such as being proportional to the number of records or the number of join relationships, are not always consistent with intuitions. For example, in the TPCE schema of Figure 5.5, table Trade_History is one of the largest tables with about $10^7$ records, but it contains only old transactions, which could be stale in a real-world system, hence not particularly important. In contrast, table Customer, which contains information on the people who initiate all the transactions in the system, is quite important even though it contains only about $10^3$ records. The key observation is that table Customer has 23 attributes, the most of any table, while Trade_History has only 2 attributes. As another example, table Status_Type has 6 join edges (the second most in the schema), yet it is arguably the least significant in the entire database. However, connectivity needs to play a role in the definition of table importance.

Second, in order to cluster tables one needs a definition of a metric space over database tables, so that the distance function is consistent with an intuitive notion of table similarity. In particular, notions of similarity assuming that all edges represent the same kind of relationship (e.g., number of phone calls between customers) are not appropriate, since different join edges in a schema graph represent different conceptual relationships.

## Key Contributions

Yang et al. [2009] address the aforementioned challenges in the case of relational sources, and make several key contributions.

First, table importance is defined in a principled fashion based on information theory and statistical models, and reflects the information content of a table, as well as how that content relates to the content of other tables. Since entropy is the well-known measure for information [Cover and Thomas 2006], the information content of a table is defined as the sum of its attribute entropies (including that of a key attribute). To take into account the join behavior of tables, join edges are viewed as vehicles for information transfer between tables, with weights depending on the entropies of their respective attributes. To identify the importance of a table, it is therefore natural to define a random walk process on the schema graph, whereby each table starts with its information content, and then repeatedly sends and receives information along its join edges, proportional to their weight. If the underlying schema graph is connected and non-bipartite, this process converges to a stable distribution. Yang et al. [2009] define the importance of a table as the value of this stable distribution for that table.

Second, Yang et al. [2009] define a novel similarity function between pairs of tables, which they refer to as *strength*. The strength of a join edge between two tables in the schema graph is (i) proportional to the fraction of values in each of its join attributes that have matching records in the other table, and (ii) inversely proportional to the average number of foreign key records that match a primary key record. The strength of a join edge is always in (0,1]. The strength of a join path is defined to be the product of the strengths of its join edges. Finally, the strength between any pair of tables in the schema graph is the maximum strength among all join paths that connect this pair of tables.

Third, Yang et al. [2009] propose using a weighted $k$-center algorithm for clustering the tables, where the weights are the table importance values, the distance between pairs of tables is defined as $1 - strength$, and $k$ is the desired number of clusters. Weighted $k$-center is NP-hard, so they employ a greedy approach. It starts by creating one cluster with the most important table as its cluster center. It then iteratively chooses the table whose weighted distance from its cluster center is largest, and creates a new cluster with that table as its cluster center; each table is then assigned to the cluster with the closest cluster center.

## Main Results

Yang et al. [2009] experimentally evaluate their approach to validate each of the three components of their method: the model for table importance, the distance function between tables, and the choice of weighted $k$-center as the appropriate clustering for source schema summarization. They conduct their study over multiple significantly different instances of the TPCE schema. Their main results are as follows.

1. The proposed entropy-based approach to defining table importance is both accurate and consistent, outperforming alternate approaches.

   In particular, the top-5 important tables in TPCE are determined to consist of one table from the Broker category, and two tables each from the Customer and Market categories in Figure 5.5. Further, the set of important tables remains quite consistent over the different instances of the TPCE schema.

2. The proposed distance measure between tables has high accuracy in determining that TPCE tables within each of the pre-classified categories have higher similarity to each other than to tables in different categories.

   In particular, the distance measure has an accuracy over 70% on the three main categories of Broker, Customer, and Market.

3. Weighted $k$-center is shown to have high accuracy and robustness in clustering tables, in conjunction with the proposed table importance and distance measures.

   More specifically, the proposed source schema summarization obtains about 70% accuracy on the three pre-classified categories, which is shown to be significantly higher than using alternate approaches.

### 5.3.3    FUTURE WORK

The work on source exploration is still in its early stages, and a huge amount of work remains to be done. We outline a couple of promising directions of future work.

First, current work focuses on profiling relational sources, where attributes and tables are well-defined schema elements. However, sources in BDI can be quite diverse, ranging from tables and RDF triples to DOM trees and free text. Extending current techniques to these kinds of data sources are critical for users to be able to discover the diversity of sources that contain data that are relevant to meet their needs.

Second, BDI sources are not static, and evolve over time. Developing techniques that can continually and incrementally profile sources to determine when they become relevant to a user's needs are important for the promise of BDI to enable data-driven discoveries to be fulfilled.

CHAPTER 6

# Conclusions

Addressing the BDI challenge is critical to realizing the promise of big data, of enabling us to make valuable, data-driven decisions to alter all aspects of society. This book explores the progress that has been made by the data integration community on the topics of schema alignment, record linkage and data fusion in addressing these novel challenges faced by big data integration. It also presents emerging topics that are expected to be critical to the success of BDI.

Chapter 1 describes the problem of data integration and the components of traditional data integration, before discussing the specific challenges that arise in BDI. It identifies the dimensions of volume, velocity, variety, and veracity along which BDI differs from traditional data integration. A number of recent case studies are then presented that empirically study the nature of data sources in BDI. BDI also offers opportunities that did not exist in traditional data integration, and some of these are highlighted as well.

Chapters 2–4 cover the core topics of schema alignment, record linkage, and data fusion in a systematic way. First, each chapter starts with a quick tour of the topic in the context of traditional data integration. Then, subsequent sections in the chapter present a detailed, example-driven exposition of recent innovative techniques that have been proposed to address the BDI challenges of volume, velocity, variety and veracity.

Finally, Chapter 5 presents a few works on the emerging topics of crowdsourcing, source selection and source profiling. These highlight novel challenges and opportunities that arise in BDI, outside the topics of schema alignment, record linkage, and data fusion.

The techniques presented in this book are not intended to be an exhaustive list of works relevant to BDI, nor can they be expected to be in such an important, fast-moving field of research. However, we do hope that this book serves as a starting point for interested readers to pursue additional work on these exciting topics, and fulfill the promise of big data.

# Bibliography

[1] Serge Abiteboul and Oliver M. Duschka. Complexity of answering queries using materialized views. In *Proc. 17th ACM SIGACT-SIGMOD-SIGART Symp. on Principles of Database Systems*, pages 254–263, 1998. DOI: 10.1145/275487.275516. 43

[2] Nikhil Bansal, Avrim Blum, and Shuchi Chawla. Correlation clustering. *Machine Learning*, 56 (1-3): 89–113, 2004. DOI: 10.1023/B:MACH.0000033116.57574.95. 68, 86, 88

[3] Carlo Batini and Monica Scannapieco. *Data Quality: Concepts, Methodologies and Techniques*. Springer, 2006. 154

[4] Richard A. Becker, Ramón Cáceres, Karrie Hanson, Sibren Isaacman, Ji Meng Loh, Margaret Martonosi, James Rowland, Simon Urbanek, Alexander Varshavsky, and Chris Volinsky. Human mobility characterization from cellular network data. *Commun. ACM*, 56 (1): 74–82, 2013. DOI: 10.1109/MPRV.2011.44. 1

[5] Zohra Bellahsene, Angela Bonifati, and Erhard Rahm, editors. *Schema Matching and Mapping*. Springer, 2011. 33

[6] Dina Bitton and David J. DeWitt. Duplicate record elimination in large data files. *ACM Trans. Database Syst.*, 8 (2): 255–265, 1983. DOI: 10.1145/319983.319987. 69

[7] Lorenzo Blanco, Valter Crescenzi, Paolo Merialdo, and Paolo Papotti. Probabilistic models to reconcile complex data from inaccurate data sources. In *Proc. 22nd Int. Conf. on Advanced Information Systems Eng.*, pages 83–97, 2010. DOI: 10.1007/978-3-642-34213-4_1. 125

[8] Jens Bleiholder and Felix Naumann. Data fusion. *ACM Comput. Surv.*, 41 (1), 2008. DOI: 10.1007/s13222-011-0043-9. 109

[9] Kurt D. Bollacker, Colin Evans, Praveen Paritosh, Tim Sturge, and Jamie Taylor. Freebase: a collaboratively created graph database for structuring human knowledge. In *Proc. ACM SIGMOD Int. Conf. on Management of Data*, pages 1247–1250, 2008. DOI: 10.1145/1376616.1376746. 1, 26, 59, 154

[10] Leo Breiman. Random forests. *Machine Learning*, 45 (1): 5–32, 2001. DOI: 10.1023/A:1010933404324. 144

[11] Sergey Brin and Lawrence Page. The anatomy of a large-scale hypertextual web search engine. *Comp. Netw.*, 30 (1-7): 107–117, 1998. DOI: 10.1.1.109.4049. 124

[12]  Andrei Z. Broder, Moses Charikar, Alan M. Frieze, and Michael Mitzenmacher. Min-wise independent permutations. *J. Comp. and System Sci.*, 60 (3): 630–659, 2000. DOI: 10.1.1.121 .8215. 155, 156

[13]  Michael J. Cafarella, Alon Y. Halevy, Daisy Zhe Wang, Eugene Wu, and Yang Zhang. Webtables: exploring the power of tables on the web. *Proc. VLDB Endowment*, 1 (1): 538–549, 2008a. 54, 55, 56, 57

[14]  Michael J. Cafarella, Alon Y. Halevy, Yang Zhang, Daisy Zhe Wang, and Eugene Wu. Uncovering the relational web. In *Proc. 11th Int. Workshop on the World Wide Web and Databases*, 2008b. 23, 24, 25

[15]  Michael J. Cafarella, Alon Y. Halevy, and Jayant Madhavan. Structured data on the web. *Commun. ACM*, 54 (2): 72–79, 2011. DOI: 10.1145/1897816.1897839. 49

[16]  Moses Charikar, Venkatesan Guruswami, and Anthony Wirth. Clustering with qualitative information. In *Proc. 44th Annual Symp. on Foundations of Computer Science*, pages 524–533, 2003. DOI: 10.1.1.90.3645. 68, 86

[17]  Yueh-Hsuan Chiang, AnHai Doan, and Jeffrey F. Naughton. Modeling entity evolution for temporal record matching. In *Proc. ACM SIGMOD Int. Conf. on Management of Data*, pages 1175–1186, 2014a. DOI: 10.1145/2588555.2588560. 94

[18]  Yueh-Hsuan Chiang, AnHai Doan, and Jeffrey F. Naughton. Tracking entities in the dynamic world: A fast algorithm for matching temporal records. *Proc. VLDB Endowment*, 7 (6): 469–480, 2014b. 94

[19]  Shui-Lung Chuang and Kevin Chen-Chuan Chang. Integrating web query results: holistic schema matching. In *Proc. 17th ACM Int. Conf. on Information and Knowledge Management*, pages 33–42, 2008. DOI: 10.1145/1458082.1458090. 50

[20]  Edith Cohen and Martin Strauss. Maintaining time-decaying stream aggregates. In *Proc. 22nd ACM SIGACT-SIGMOD-SIGART Symp. on Principles of Database Systems*, pages 223–233, 2003. DOI: 10.1.1.119.5236. 98

[21]  Eli Cortez and Altigran Soares da Silva. *Unsupervised Information Extraction by Text Segmentation*. Springer, 2013. DOI: 10.1007/978-3-319-02597-1. 89

[22]  Thomas M. Cover and Joy A. Thomas. *Elements of Information Theory* (2nd ed.). Wiley, 2006. 159

[23]  Nilesh N. Dalvi, Ashwin Machanavajjhala, and Bo Pang. An analysis of structured data on the web. *Proc. VLDB Endowment*, 5 (7): 680–691, 2012. 15, 17, 18, 19, 28

[24]  Anish Das Sarma, Xin Luna Dong, and Alon Y. Halevy. Bootstrapping pay-as-you-go data integration systems. In *Proc. ACM SIGMOD Int. Conf. on Management of Data*, pages 861–874, 2008. 36, 38, 40, 41, 46

[25]  Anish Das Sarma, Lujun Fang, Nitin Gupta, Alon Y. Halevy, Hongrae Lee, Fei Wu, Reynold Xin, and Cong Yu. Finding related tables. In *Proc. ACM SIGMOD Int. Conf. on Management of Data*, pages 817–828, 2012. DOI: 10.1145/1376616.1376702. 55, 57, 59, 60

[26]  Tamraparni Dasu, Theodore Johnson, S. Muthukrishnan, and Vladislav Shkapenyuk. Mining database structure; or, how to build a data quality browser. In *Proc. ACM SIGMOD Int. Conf. on Management of Data*, pages 240–251, 2002. DOI: 10.1.1.89.4225. 155, 157

[27]  David L. Davies and Donald W. Bouldin. A cluster separation measure. *IEEE Trans. Pattern Analy. Machine Intell.*, PAMI-1 (2): 224—227, 1979. DOI: 10.1109/TPAMI.1979.4766909. 105

[28]  Jeffrey Dean and Sanjay Ghemawat. Mapreduce: Simplified data processing on large clusters. In *Proc. 6th USENIX Symp. on Operating System Design and Implementation*, pages 137–150, 2004. DOI: 10.1.1.163.5292. 71

[29]  Gianluca Demartini, Djellel Eddine Difallah, and Philippe Cudré-Mauroux. Large-scale linked data integration using probabilistic reasoning and crowdsourcing. *VLDB J.*, 22 (5): 665–687, 2013. DOI: 10.1007/s00778-013-0324-z. 140

[30]  AnHai Doan, Raghu Ramakrishnan, and Alon Y. Halevy. Crowdsourcing systems on the world-wide web. *Commun. ACM*, 54 (4): 86–96, 2011. DOI: 10.1145/1924421.1924442. 139

[31]  AnHai Doan, Alon Y. Halevy, and Zachary G. Ives. *Principles of Data Integration*. Morgan Kaufmann, 2012. 2

[32]  Xin Luna Dong and Divesh Srivastava. Large-scale copy detection. In *Proc. ACM SIGMOD Int. Conf. on Management of Data*, pages 1205–1208, 2011. DOI: 10.1145/1989323.1989454. 114

[33]  Xin Luna Dong, Laure Berti-Equille, and Divesh Srivastava. Integrating conflicting data: The role of source dependence. *Proc. VLDB Endowment*, 2 (1): 550–561, 2009a. DOI: 10.1.1.151.4068. 110, 111, 112, 115, 117, 119, 121, 123, 125, 153

[34]  Xin Luna Dong, Laure Berti-Equille, and Divesh Srivastava. Truth discovery and copying detection in a dynamic world. *Proc. VLDB Endowment*, 2 (1): 562–573, 2009b. DOI: 10.1.1.151 .5867. 135, 136

[35]  Xin Luna Dong, Alon Y. Halevy, and Cong Yu. Data integration with uncertainty. *VLDB J.*, 18 (2): 469–500, 2009c. DOI: 10.1007/s00778-008-0119-9. 36, 40, 44, 45

[36]  Xin Luna Dong, Laure Berti-Equille, Yifan Hu, and Divesh Srivastava. Global detection of complex copying relationships between sources. *Proc. VLDB Endowment*, 3 (1): 1358–1369, 2010. 124, 125

[37]  Xin Luna Dong, Barna Saha, and Divesh Srivastava. Less is more: Selecting sources wisely for integration. *Proc. VLDB Endowment*, 6 (2): 37–48, 2012. 123, 125, 147, 148, 149, 150, 152, 153

[38]  Xin Luna Dong, Evgeniy Gabrilovich, Geremy Heitz, Wilko Horn, Ni Lao, Kevin Murphy, Thomas Strohmann, Shaohua Sun, and Wei Zhang. Knowledge vault: a web-scale approach to

probabilistic knowledge fusion. In *Proc. 20th ACM SIGKDD Int. Conf. on Knowledge Discovery and Data Mining*, pages 601–610, 2014a. 1

[39]   Xin Luna Dong, Evgeniy Gabrilovich, Geremy Heitz, Wilko Horn, Kevin Murphy, Shaohua Sun, and Wei Zhang. From data fusion to knowledge fusion. *Proc. VLDB Endowment*, 7 (10): 881–892, 2014b. 26, 27, 126, 136, 137, 138, 154

[40]   Ahmed K. Elmagarmid, Panagiotis G. Ipeirotis, and Vassilios S. Verykios. Duplicate record detection: A survey. *IEEE Trans. Knowl. and Data Eng.*, 19 (1): 1–16, 2007. DOI: 10.1.1.147 .3975. 66

[41]   Hazem Elmeleegy, Jayant Madhavan, and Alon Y. Halevy. Harvesting relational tables from lists on the web. *VLDB J.*, 20 (2): 209–226, 2011. DOI: 10.1007/s00778-011-0223-0. 55

[42]   Ronald Fagin, Laura M. Haas, Mauricio A. Hernández, Renée J. Miller, Lucian Popa, and Yannis Velegrakis. Clio: Schema mapping creation and data exchange. In *Conceptual Modeling: Foundations and Applications—Essays in Honor of John Mylopoulos*, pages 198–236, 2009. DOI: 10.1007/978-3-642-02463-4_12. 31, 34

[43]   Wenfei Fan, Xibei Jia, Jianzhong Li, and Shuai Ma. Reasoning about record matching rules. *Proc. VLDB Endowment*, 2 (1): 407–418, 2009. DOI: 10.14778/1687627.1687674. 65

[44]   Uriel Feige, Vahab S. Mirrokni, and Jan Vondrák. Maximizing non-monotone submodular functions. *SIAM J. on Comput.*, 40 (4): 1133–1153, 2011. DOI: 10.1137/090779346. 152

[45]   Ivan Fellegi and Alan Sunter. A theory for record linkage. *J. American Statistical Association*, 64 (328): 1183–1210, 1969. DOI: 10.1080/01621459.1969.10501049. 66

[46]   Paola Festa and Mauricio G. C. Resende. GRASP: basic components and enhancements. *Telecommun. Syst.*, 46 (3): 253–271, 2011. DOI: 10.1007/s11235-010-9289-z. 149

[47]   Michael J. Franklin, Alon Y. Halevy, and David Maier. From databases to dataspaces: a new abstraction for information management. *ACM SIGMOD Rec.*, 34 (4): 27–33, 2005. DOI: 10.1145/1107499.1107502. 35

[48]   Alban Galland, Serge Abiteboul, Amélie Marian, and Pierre Senellart. Corroborating information from disagreeing views. In *Proc. 3rd ACM Int. Conf. Web Search and Data Mining*, pages 131–140, 2010. DOI: 10.1145/1718487.1718504. 124, 125

[49]   Chaitanya Gokhale, Sanjib Das, AnHai Doan, Jeffrey F. Naughton, Narasimhan Rampalli, Jude W. Shavlik, and Xiaojin Zhu. Corleone: hands-off crowdsourcing for entity matching. In *Proc. ACM SIGMOD Int. Conf. on Management of Data*, pages 601–612, 2014. DOI: 10.1145/ 2588555.2588576. 140, 144, 145

[50]   Luis Gravano, Panagiotis G. Ipeirotis, H. V. Jagadish, Nick Koudas, S. Muthukrishnan, and Divesh Srivastava. Approximate string joins in a database (almost) for free. In *Proc. 27th Int. Conf. on Very Large Data Bases*, pages 491–500, 2001. DOI: 10.1.1.20.7673. 70

[51] Anja Gruenheid, Xin Luna Dong, and Divesh Srivastava. Incremental record linkage. *Proc. VLDB Endowment*, 7 (9): 697–708, 2014. 82, 84, 86, 87, 88

[52] Songtao Guo, Xin Luna Dong, Divesh Srivastava, and Remi Zajac. Record linkage with uniqueness constraints and erroneous values. *Proc. VLDB Endowment*, 3 (1): 417–428, 2010. DOI: 10.14778/1920841.1920897. 100, 102, 105

[53] Rahul Gupta and Sunita Sarawagi. Answering table augmentation queries from unstructured lists on the web. *Proc. VLDB Endowment*, 2 (1): 289–300, 2009. 55

[54] Marios Hadjieleftheriou and Divesh Srivastava. Approximate string processing. *Foundations and Trends in Databases*, 2 (4): 267–402, 2011. DOI: 10.1561/1900000010. 9

[55] Alon Y. Halevy. Answering queries using views: A survey. *VLDB J.*, 10 (4): 270–294, 2001. DOI: 10.1007/s007780100054. 34

[56] Oktie Hassanzadeh, Fei Chiang, Renée J. Miller, and Hyun Chul Lee. Framework for evaluating clustering algorithms in duplicate detection. *Proc. VLDB Endowment*, 2 (1): 1282–1293, 2009. 68

[57] Bin He, Mitesh Patel, Zhen Zhang, and Kevin Chen-Chuan Chang. Accessing the deep web. *Commun. ACM*, 50 (5): 94–101, 2007. DOI: 10.1145/1230819.1241670. 13, 14, 15, 16, 20

[58] Mauricio A. Hernández and Salvatore J. Stolfo. Real-world data is dirty: Data cleansing and the merge/purge problem. *Data Mining and Knowledge Discovery*, 2 (1): 9–37, 1998. DOI: 10.1023/A:1009761603038. 65, 68, 69

[59] Shawn R. Jeffery, Michael J. Franklin, and Alon Y. Halevy. Pay-as-you-go user feedback for dataspace systems. In *Proc. ACM SIGMOD Int. Conf. on Management of Data*, pages 847–860, 2008. DOI: 10.1145/1376616.1376701. 47, 49

[60] Anitha Kannan, Inmar E. Givoni, Rakesh Agrawal, and Ariel Fuxman. Matching unstructured product offers to structured product specifications. In *Proc. 17th ACM SIGKDD Int. Conf. on Knowledge Discovery and Data Mining*, pages 404–412, 2011. DOI: 10.1145/2020408.2020474. 89, 90, 92, 93

[61] Jon M. Kleinberg. Authoritative sources in a hyperlinked environment. *J. ACM*, 46 (5): 604–632, 1999. DOI: 10.1145/324133.324140. 124

[62] Lars Kolb, Andreas Thor, and Erhard Rahm. Load balancing for mapreduce-based entity resolution. In *Proc. 28th Int. Conf. on Data Engineering*, pages 618–629, 2012. DOI: 10.1109/ICDE.2012.22. 71, 72, 75, 76

[63] Hanna Köpcke, Andreas Thor, and Erhard Rahm. Evaluation of entity resolution approaches on real-world match problems. *Proc. VLDB Endowment*, 3 (1): 484–493, 2010. 71

[64] Harold W. Kuhn. The hungarian method for the assignment problem. In Michael Jünger, Thomas M. Liebling, Denis Naddef, George L. Nemhauser, William R. Pulleyblank, Gerhard

Reinelt, Giovanni Rinaldi, and Laurence A. Wolsey, editors, *50 Years of Integer Programming 1958–2008—From the Early Years to the State-of-the-Art*, pages 29–47. Springer, 2010. DOI: 10.1007/978-3-540-68279-0_2. 105

[65] Larissa R. Lautert, Marcelo M. Scheidt, and Carina F. Dorneles. Web table taxonomy and formalization. *ACM SIGMOD Rec.*, 42 (3): 28–33, 2013. DOI: 10.1145/2536669.2536674. 23, 24, 25

[66] Feng Li, Beng Chin Ooi, M. Tamer Özsu, and Sai Wu. Distributed data management using mapreduce. *ACM Comput. Surv.*, 46 (3): 31, 2014. DOI: 10.1145/2503009. 71

[67] Pei Li, Xin Luna Dong, Andrea Maurino, and Divesh Srivastava. Linking temporal records. *Proc. VLDB Endowment*, 4 (11): 956–967, 2011. DOI: 10.1007/s11704-012-2002-5. 94, 97, 98, 99, 100

[68] Xian Li, Xin Luna Dong, Kenneth Lyons, Weiyi Meng, and Divesh Srivastava. Truth finding on the deep web: Is the problem solved? *Proc. VLDB Endowment*, 6 (2): 97–108, 2012. 20, 21, 22, 23, 28, 125, 147, 150

[69] Xian Li, Xin Luna Dong, Kenneth Lyons, Weiyi Meng, and Divesh Srivastava. Scaling up copy detection. In *Proc. 31st Int. Conf. on Data Engineering*, 2015. 126

[70] Girija Limaye, Sunita Sarawagi, and Soumen Chakrabarti. Annotating and searching web tables using entities, types and relationships. *Proc. VLDB Endowment*, 3 (1): 1338–1347, 2010. 55, 60, 61

[71] Xuan Liu, Xin Luna Dong, Beng Chin Ooi, and Divesh Srivastava. Online data fusion. *Proc. VLDB Endowment*, 4 (11): 932–943, 2011. 127, 129, 130, 131, 132

[72] Jayant Madhavan, Shirley Cohen, Xin Luna Dong, Alon Y. Halevy, Shawn R. Jeffery, David Ko, and Cong Yu. Web-scale data integration: You can afford to pay as you go. In *Proc. 3rd Biennial Conf. on Innovative Data Systems Research*, pages 342–350, 2007. 13, 14, 15, 20

[73] Jayant Madhavan, David Ko, Lucja Kot, Vignesh Ganapathy, Alex Rasmussen, and Alon Y. Halevy. Google's deep web crawl. *Proc. VLDB Endowment*, 1 (2): 1241–1252, 2008. 50, 51, 52, 53

[74] Alfred Marshall. *Principles of Economics*. Macmillan and Co., 1890. 148

[75] Andrew McCallum, Kamal Nigam, and Lyle H. Ungar. Efficient clustering of high-dimensional data sets with application to reference matching. In *Proc. 6th ACM SIGKDD Int. Conf. on Knowledge Discovery and Data Mining*, pages 169–178, 2000. DOI: 10.1145/347090.347123. 70

[76] Robert McCann, AnHai Doan, Vanitha Varadarajan, Alexander Kramnik, and ChengXiang Zhai. Building data integration systems: A mass collaboration approach. In *Proc. 6th Int. Workshop on the World Wide Web and Databases*, pages 25–30, 2003. 139

[77]  Robert McCann, Warren Shen, and AnHai Doan. Matching schemas in online communities: A web 2.0 approach. In *Proc. 24th Int. Conf. on Data Engineering*, pages 110–119, 2008. DOI: 10.1109/ICDE.2008.4497419. 139

[78]  Felix Naumann. Data profiling revisited. *ACM SIGMOD Rec.*, 42 (4): 40–49, 2013. DOI: 10.1145/2590989.2590995. 154

[79]  George Papadakis, Georgia Koutrika, Themis Palpanas, and Wolfgang Nejdl. Meta-blocking: Taking entity resolutionto the next level. *IEEE Trans. Knowl. and Data Eng.*, 26 (8): 1946–1960, 2014. DOI: 10.1109/TKDE.2013.54. 71, 77, 79, 80, 81

[80]  Jeff Pasternack and Dan Roth. Knowing what to believe (when you already know something). In *Proc. 23rd Int. Conf. on Computational Linguistics*, pages 877–885, 2010. 124, 125

[81]  Jeff Pasternack and Dan Roth. Making better informed trust decisions with generalized fact-finding. In *Proc. 22nd Int. Joint Conf. on AI*, pages 2324–2329, 2011. 124

[82]  Jeff Pasternack and Dan Roth. Latent credibility analysis. In *Proc. 21st Int. World Wide Web Conf.*, pages 1009–1020, 2013. 124

[83]  Rakesh Pimplikar and Sunita Sarawagi. Answering table queries on the web using column keywords. *Proc. VLDB Endowment*, 5 (10): 908–919, 2012. DOI: 10.14778/2336664.2336665. 55

[84]  Ravali Pochampally, Anish Das Sarma, Xin Luna Dong, Alexandra Meliou, and Divesh Srivastava. Fusing data with correlations. In *Proc. ACM SIGMOD Int. Conf. on Management of Data*, pages 433–444, 2014. DOI: 10.1145/2588555.2593674. 124, 125, 153

[85]  Guo-Jun Qi, Charu C. Aggarwal, Jiawei Han, and Thomas S. Huang. Mining collective intelligence in diverse groups. In *Proc. 21st Int. World Wide Web Conf.*, pages 1041–1052, 2013. 125

[86]  Erhard Rahm and Philip A. Bernstein. A survey of approaches to automatic schema matching. *VLDB J.*, 10 (4): 334–350, 2001. DOI: 10.1007/s007780100057. 33

[87]  Theodoros Rekatsinas, Xin Luna Dong, and Divesh Srivastava. Characterizing and selecting fresh data sources. In *Proc. ACM SIGMOD Int. Conf. on Management of Data*, pages 919–930, 2014. DOI: 10.1145/2588555.2610504. 148, 150, 151, 152, 153

[88]  Stuart J. Russell and Peter Norvig. *Artificial Intelligence—A Modern Approach* (3rd internat. ed.). Pearson Education, 2010. 47

[89]  Sunita Sarawagi and Anuradha Bhamidipaty. Interactive deduplication using active learning. In *Proc. 8th ACM SIGKDD Int. Conf. on Knowledge Discovery and Data Mining*, pages 269–278, 2002. DOI: 10.1145/775047.775087. 66

[90]  Burr Settles. *Active Learning*. Morgan & Claypool Publishers, 2012. 144

[91]  Fabian M. Suchanek, Gjergji Kasneci, and Gerhard Weikum. Yago: a core of semantic knowledge. In *Proc. 16th Int. World Wide Web Conf.*, pages 697–706, 2007. DOI: 10.1145/1242572.1242667. 61

[92]  Fabian M. Suchanek, Serge Abiteboul, and Pierre Senellart. PARIS: probabilistic alignment of relations, instances, and schema. *Proc. VLDB Endowment*, 5 (3): 157–168, 2011. 55, 60

[93]  Peter D. Turney. Mining the web for synonyms: PMI-IR versus LSA on TOEFL. In *Proc. 12th European Conf. on Machine Learning*, pages 491–502, 2001. DOI: 10.1007/3-540-44795-4_42. 56

[94]  Petros Venetis, Alon Y. Halevy, Jayant Madhavan, Marius Pasca, Warren Shen, Fei Wu, Gengxin Miao, and Chung Wu. Recovering semantics of tables on the web. *Proc. VLDB Endowment*, 4 (9): 528–538, 2011. 55, 60

[95]  Norases Vesdapunt, Kedar Bellare, and Nilesh N. Dalvi. Crowdsourcing algorithms for entity resolution. *Proc. VLDB Endowment*, 7 (12): 1071–1082, 2014. 140, 141

[96]  Jiannan Wang, Tim Kraska, Michael J. Franklin, and Jianhua Feng. Crowder: Crowdsourcing entity resolution. *Proc. VLDB Endowment*, 5 (11): 1483–1494, 2012. 140

[97]  Jiannan Wang, Guoliang Li, Tim Kraska, Michael J. Franklin, and Jianhua Feng. Leveraging transitive relations for crowdsourced joins. In *Proc. ACM SIGMOD Int. Conf. on Management of Data*, pages 229–240, 2013. DOI: 10.1145/2463676.2465280. 140, 141, 142, 143

[98]  Gerhard Weikum and Martin Theobald. From information to knowledge: harvesting entities and relationships from web sources. In *Proc. 29th ACM SIGACT-SIGMOD-SIGART Symp. on Principles of Database Systems*, pages 65–76, 2010. DOI: 10.1145/1807085.1807097. 1, 154

[99]  Steven Euijong Whang and Hector Garcia-Molina. Entity resolution with evolving rules. *Proc. VLDB Endowment*, 3 (1): 1326–1337, 2010. 82

[100]  Steven Euijong Whang and Hector Garcia-Molina. Incremental entity resolution on rules and data. *VLDB J.*, 23 (1): 77–102, 2014. DOI: 10.1007/s00778-013-0315-0. 82, 84

[101]  Steven Euijong Whang, Peter Lofgren, and Hector Garcia-Molina. Question selection for crowd entity resolution. *Proc. VLDB Endowment*, 6 (6): 349–360, 2013. 140

[102]  Wentao Wu, Hongsong Li, Haixun Wang, and Kenny Qili Zhu. Probase: a probabilistic taxonomy for text understanding. In *Proc. ACM SIGMOD Int. Conf. on Management of Data*, pages 481–492, 2012. DOI: 10.1145/2213836.2213891. 1, 154

[103]  Xiaoyan Yang, Cecilia M. Procopiuc, and Divesh Srivastava. Summarizing relational databases. *Proc. VLDB Endowment*, 2 (1): 634–645, 2009. DOI: 10.14778/1687627.1687699. 157, 158, 159, 160

[104]  Xiaoxin Yin and Wenzhao Tan. Semi-supervised truth discovery. In *Proc. 20th Int. World Wide Web Conf.*, pages 217–226, 2011. DOI: 10.1145/1963405.1963439. 124

[105]  Xiaoxin Yin, Jiawei Han, and Philip S. Yu. Truth discovery with multiple conflicting information providers on the web. In *Proc. 13th ACM SIGKDD Int. Conf. on Knowledge Discovery and Data Mining*, pages 1048–1052, 2007. DOI: 10.1145/1281192.1281309. 125, 132

[106]  Meihui Zhang and Kaushik Chakrabarti. Infogather+: semantic matching and annotation of numeric and time-varying attributes in web tables. In *Proc. ACM SIGMOD Int. Conf. on Management of Data*, pages 145–156, 2013. DOI: 10.1145/2463676.2465276. 55, 60

[107]  Bo Zhao and Jiawei Han. A probabilistic model for estimating real-valued truth from conflicting sources. In *Proc. of the Int. Workshop on Quality in Databases*, 2012. 124

[108]  Bo Zhao, Benjamin I. P. Rubinstein, Jim Gemmell, and Jiawei Han. A bayesian approach to discovering truth from conflicting sources for data integration. *Proc. VLDB Endowment*, 5 (6): 550–561, 2012. DOI: 10.14778/2168651.2168656 124

# Authors' Biographies

## XIN LUNA DONG

**Xin Luna Dong** is a senior research scientist at Google Inc. Prior to joining Google, she worked for AT&T Labs-Research. She received her Ph.D. from University of Washington, received a Master's Degree from Peking University in China, and a Bachelor's Degree from Nankai University in China. Her research interests include databases, information retrieval, and machine learning, with an emphasis on data integration, data cleaning, knowledge bases, and personal information management. She has published more than 50 papers in top conferences and journals in the field of data integration, and got the Best Demo award (one of top-3) in Sigmod 2005. She is the PC co-chair for WAIM 2015 and has served as an area chair for Sigmod 2015, ICDE 2013, and CIKM 2011.

## DIVESH SRIVASTAVA

**Divesh Srivastava** is the head of Database Research at AT&T Labs-Research. He is a fellow of the Association for Computing Machinery (ACM), on the board of trustees of the VLDB Endowment, the managing editor of the *Proceedings of the VLDB Endowment* (*PVLDB*), and an associate editor of the *ACM Transactions on Database Systems*. He received his Ph.D. from the University of Wisconsin, Madison, and his Bachelor of Technology from the Indian Institute of Technology, Bombay, India. His research interests and publications span a variety of topics in data management. He has published over 250 papers in top conferences and journals. He has served as PC Chair or Co-chair of many international conferences including ICDE 2015 (Industrial) and VLDB 2007.

# Index

Printed in the United States
by Baker & Taylor Publisher Services